ENGLAND AND THE ITALIA

Sir John Hale is a Fellow of the British ~~~~~~~~~~~~~~~ Emeritus
Professor of Italian History at University College, London, where
he was head of the Italian Department from 1970 until his retire-
ment in 1988. He started his career as Fellow and Tutor in Modern
History at Jesus College, Oxford from 1949 until 1964, and has
taught at a number of American universities including Cornell
and the University of California. He has been Chairman of the
Trustees of the National Gallery and of the British Society for
Renaissance Studies and has also served as a trustee of the Victoria
and Albert Museum, British Museum and Museums and Galleries
Commission. He is the author of many books including *Italian
Renaissance Painting, Renaissance Europe 1480–1520, Florence and the
Medici: the Pattern of Control,* and *A Concise Encyclopaedia of the
Italian Renaissance.* His most recent book, *The Civilization of Europe
in the Renaissance,* won the 1993 Time-Life Silver Pen Award for
the best non-fiction book of the year, and the 1994 Royal Society
of Literature Heinemann Prize.

ENGLAND AND THE ITALIAN RENAISSANCE

THE GROWTH OF INTEREST IN ITS HISTORY AND ART

JOHN HALE

FontanaPress
An Imprint of HarperCollins*Publishers*

Fontana Press
An Imprint of HarperCollinsPublishers
77–85 Fulham Palace Road,
Hammersmith, London W6 8JB

Published by Fontana Press 1996
1 3 5 7 9 8 6 4 2

First published in Great Britain by
Faber and Faber Ltd 1954
Revised paperback edition by Grey Arrow 1963

ISBN 0 00 686347 7

Set in Bembo

**Printed and bound in Great Britain by
Caledonian International Book Manufacturing Ltd, Glasgow**

CONTENTS

PREFACE TO THE 1996 EDITION

England and the Italian Renaissance was first published in 1954. A new edition, nearly forty years later, needs no defence, for the book has long been established as a classic, is hard to find second-hand and is missing (presumed stolen) from many libraries. It is not impossible to imagine a young academic of today who would have courage and learning enough to survey much the same material, but he or she would be unlikely to review the field from so great an altitude, with such assurance, and then descend to details with such apparent ease, to achieve Hale's lightness of touch (untainted by condescension) and his humour (which is never flippant or facetious), and to ensure that the apparatus of scholarship was both carefully constructed and unostentatious. Hale's book is written neither to impress other academics nor to appeal to a mass public. The reader is pleased to be treated as an equal.

Perhaps the most elegant and suggestive feature of *England and the Italian Renaissance* is the way it ends where it does without any overt explanation. I suppose (without any special authority) that Hale perceived that we have inherited an attitude to the Renaissance and to Italy which has changed surprisingly little since the time of John Addington Symonds – at least if we think of the revolutions in historiography which he charts in the previous centuries. Since the book is consistently distinguished by a feeling for the way in which any understanding of the past is coloured by the conditions of the author's own day, it is interesting to speculate on what has changed since it was published – changed in our attitudes to

Italy as well as in our understanding of our ancestors. We need to speculate, because, paradoxically, it is difficult to focus on something that is so close to us.

In his last chapter Hale notes, 'Travel was cheap and easy. There were guide books and guided tours. From industrialized England lovers of quiet and beauty came, many of them to settle permanently in Italy, where life had such grace and was so inexpensive . . . Socially secure, and delighting in the sun, a host of intelligent Englishmen and women dipped their pens in a haze of aesthetic goodwill, and began, with scant historical equipment, to chronicle the towns, the men and the manners of the Renaissance.' That was written with reference to the 1870s, but, to a remarkable extent, it describes a situation which prevailed (with interruptions, of course, occasioned by war) until at least the 1970s, when the great-granddaughter of the author of *Strolls in Old Siena* was writing a paperback on Umbrian cookery, working in the archives on fifteenth-century Tuscan confraternities, or guiding the 'Friends' of this or that museum to Piero della Francesca's less accessible frescos.

But things have begun to change. Italy has become expensive. For this reason it is less of a magnet for students or a haven for their grandparents. It is much less quiet. It is also less beautiful. Of course the most famous sites retain their magic, but the charm has vanished from the plains and foot-hills in the north, where motorways, ugly light industry, and acres of agricultural polythene besiege the historic towns and villas. Italy is now noted more for elegance than for grace, for its high fashion and high technology rather than the charm of ancient and local traditions, and the fax machine and portable phone were adopted there with far greater alacrity than elsewhere in Europe. Italian cuisine, which enjoys in England a prestige, or at least a popularity, beyond French, may be marketed as that of a simple rural people but it is distinguished by a love of machine-driven metamorphosis – typified not only by ice cream and grissini, but by potatoes turned into gnocchi, meat folded into envelopes, milk whipped into froth, coffee expressed under great pressure, wheat paste extruded as telephone wires, bow-ties, and (recently) mini-skirts.

Curiously Italy may be in the process of reverting to what it was for the Elizabethans, as is so well evoked in the opening of Hale's book – an exciting place to go shopping, more sophisticated than England in its trading, transport, and manufacturing, where materialism (and crime) are distinguished by style.

What seems certain is that Italy is losing much of the pastoral character which was so important to the discovery (and invention) of the Renaissance in the last century. The subtle, complex and still-underestimated writer Walter Pater (towards whom Hale, probably wisely, only glances) discerned in Botticelli's virgins a subcurrent of pagan feeling and a kinship with the nimble urchins who 'hold out long brown arms to beg of you' on weekdays in Apennine villages but on Sunday appear in church as choirboys with 'crisp white linen on their sunburnt throats'. The sense that Italy may contain survivors, even unwitting carriers, of a classical past, and the idea that looking at charming youth might help one to understand the 'childhood of art' must be rare now. This is not to deny that there are still sun-tanned urchins (and sensitive bachelor tourists) in many parts of Italy; it is still a place where the educated Northern European, following Goethe or Forster, goes to improve the mind, only to be surprised and seduced by the body; and it is certainly true that Botticelli remains the famous artist that Pater first made him.

It is true too that 'guide books and guided tours' flourish. And it is hard to believe that Florence, Venice and Rome will cease to be among the objectives of modern mass tourism. But this conceals much significant change. It is often claimed that Italian art enjoys a 'hegemony' in the teaching of art history. In fact, despite the unrivalled fame of Raphael, Titian and Michelangelo – and, for the last century, Botticelli – fewer courses on these artists are taught in the universities of Britain than was the case twenty years ago, and it is possible to take a degree in art history without studying Italian paintings at all. To the careful observer there has also been a significant change in the National Gallery: many of the secondary masters of the Italian Renaissance who were esteemed in the second half of the nineteenth century – Gaudenzio Ferrari, Girolamo dai Libri, Buonconsiglio – attract little notice and are indeed on the lower floor, largely unvisited. The queues at the Uffizi may grow longer and longer but there are few travellers seeking out the masterpieces of Morando in the churches of Verona.

Meanwhile, however, Italy in the Renaissance, or in the 'late medieval' or 'early modern' era, continues to attract a large share of the historian's attention. It does so partly on account of its remarkable archives which, for example, supply so much more primary evidence about Venice or Florence than we can discover about Bruges or Cologne. But Italy will also always fascinate because of the very idea of the birth and rebirth of civilization. Whether we consider art or learning, systems of banking or enterprise in trade, something did awaken in Italy, and it did so amid the ruins of a great civilization. And what had reawakened spread elsewhere.

A disturbing thought occurs more than once to Hale's reader. Do the historians who study a foreign country find it more comfortable to do so if they can feel superior to its present occupants (whether decadent old nobility or suntanned urchins)? For most of the authors who are examined by Hale the idea of modern Italian genius was an impossibility.

It is this fact that makes the case of Canova so interesting.

No other artist has ever enjoyed greater or more universal esteem in his lifetime. And he did so despite a general predisposition to deny the possibility of a true resurrection in Italy of the fine arts. Hale describes briefly the fashion of Italian literature in England in the early nineteenth century when Foscolo was lionized at Holland House (and smart couples, we learn from Jane Austen, adapted Italian terms of endearment). One supposes a distaste for the France of Napoleon was a precondition for this vogue. It helps to explain the cult of Canova, but that cult is not a part of the story he tells. And indeed no writer in English investigated this question of modern Italian genius with the intelligence of Stendhal (although Byron did begin to address it). Stendhal of course was interested in music as well as sculpture, and in music, too, modern Italian genius could not be denied.

Foscolo, it is worth noting, wanted to make of Santa Croce a Westminster Abbey – that is, a national pantheon. Canova wished to retrieve the antiquities appropriated by Napoleon for Italy, not merely for Tuscany or the Vatican. Nationalist and republican aspirations soon infiltrated the history of Italy, as Hale notes. But neither Garibaldi nor Mazzini features in his index. And the intertwining of interest in the birth of modern Italy and in the Italy of the Renaissance is a subject for another book. Indeed, it is easy to discern the turnings which Hale did not take, and one almost always commends his judgement in not taking them.

A fuller account of the collecting and reassessment of early Italian art has since been supplied, above all by Francis Haskell in *Rediscoveries in Art* (1976). Symonds has been the subject of a major monograph by Phyllis Grosskurth (1964) as has Sir Charles Eastlake and the Victorian Art world (the title of David Robertson's monograph published in 1978). But the information Hale supplies, and the interpretations and judgements he makes, are seldom in need of revision or even of minor qualification.

Since 1954 much has been written about the Grand Tour which depicts this exercise as an implausibly high-minded venture. It was no more so than most foreign travel today and Hale is surely right to discern how insular prejudices were systematically confirmed by superficial cosmopolitanism. The comments on Italy by Francis Burney who was, significantly, a student and lover of music, were, it seems, unknown to Hale (his journal of 1770 was published in 1969) but Burney's curiosity and sympathy are very hard to match. Hale's severe judgement is fair. Nevertheless, we should not be too inclined to censor. In Edward Wright's travel book, Hale discovers, 'No mention of paintings in Sta. Croce or of the Benozzos in the Medici chapel. Nor did he record a visit to S. Marco.' No, indeed, but we all neglect something – the most zealous student of Donatello today does not bestow more than the briefest glance on Italian sculpture of the nineteenth century, even on Giuseppe Grandi's great monument to the *Cinque Giornate* in Milan, which merits the fame enjoyed by Verdi's greatest music.

The history of the writing of history has certainly its own rewards but an additional interest of this book is its relationship to the author's own subsequent work, most of it, of course, on the Italian Renaissance. In 1993 Sir John Hale (as J. R. Hale has become) published *The Civilization of Europe in the Renaissance*. The title adapts that of Burckhardt's masterpiece of 1860, and it is, for all its differences, a work of formidable but accessible scholarship written in Burckhardt's mode – for the great models for twentieth-century historians, as also for twentieth-century novelists, were created in the last century. The opening pages startle the reader by explaining that the idea of Europe, indeed the language for describing it, was once a novelty. Hale's earlier book traces the origin of the idea of the Renaissance itself.

It is an idea we cannot dispense with, but one with which we cannot feel comfortable. And the book also tells us why – deftly, engagingly and with great learning.

Nicholas Penny
September 1995

PREFACE

This book was first published in 1954, but the impulse to write it came some years before, soon after my first visit to Italy. The impact of this visit was violent and, as I was to discover, highly conventional. After a night in the crowded and filthy corridor of a post-war train I watched the sullen Swiss dawn open into a radiant Italian morning and exclaimed aloud. For the next three months I was constantly exclaiming aloud, in front of pictures, churches and sulphate-stained vineyard walls. I must have made a most objectionable companion. Indeed, on the second day in Florence I parted in a huff from one friend because he insisted that the baptistery was garish, and cancelled plans to return in a leisurely way through France with another because I was determined to bring my Italian impressions home intact.

The aftermath of this somewhat priggish love affair produced a number of questions. Just why had I been so affected by Italy? Just why had I so particularly liked the paintings, the sculpture and the architecture of the fourteenth and fifteenth centuries – when it was clear that travellers a century or so before had felt equally militant in their advocacy of the sixteenth and seventeenth? As I asked myself why I, and indeed nearly all my contemporaries, preferred this city to that, this painter to that, it became clear that our taste was not simply our own, it was conditioned by what others had thought about these cities and painters in the past. It was both chilling and exhilarating to realize that one's pleasures as well as so much else were to some extent inherited; if a delight in Domenico Veneziano became less personal, it became historically

more meaningful. And an essential preliminary to understanding my own appreciation of works of art was an
acquaintance with the history of taste.

This realization came at the same time as a determination
to concentrate, as a historian, on the Renaissance – or, as I
might have put it then, on the period known as the Renaissance – or, again, as I was even more likely to have put
it, on the 'period' misleadingly alleged to have witnessed a
so-called 'Renaissance'; for the late 'forties and early 'fifties
were very self-conscious about historical periodization in general and about the meaning and significance of the Renaissance in particular. However, after a year or so of juggling
with elaborately 'accurate' formulations like 'from the middle
or lateish fourteenth to the second decade of the sixteenth
century' to describe the life span of some phenomenon, I
decided that this was needlessly involved; the Renaissance was
a term that from the middle of the nineteenth century had
meant something fairly definite to a large number of intelligent
people, and so long as we were clear what they had meant, it
was needlessly sensitive to wash our hands of it.

This second realization fitted neatly with the consequences
of the first. The Renaissance, as far as Italy was concerned,
had come by the middle of the nineteenth century to mean
the period from Cimabue to Michelangelo, from independence and communes to foreign rule and principates. An
account of the way in which these years had come to be
considered the most significant part of Italy's history would
involve an account of successive generations' taste for Italian
art as well as their estimate of what was crucial about the
country's political and constitutional development. In even
the best of the books I read on Italian history and culture a
freshness and accuracy of vision was combined with a set of
inherited attitudes; they could only be used as guides if this
subjective element were understood and seen, indeed, as of
historiographical importance in its own right.

This book was intended, then, as a necessary preliminary to writing about the Renaissance itself in Italy. I wanted to be able to distinguish between what was inherited and what was original in the work of men who, from the sixteenth to the end of the nineteenth century, had written about the history and the arts of Italy. The book in consequence is not a comprehensive work on Anglo-Italian cultural relations. It is an introduction to such a study or, perhaps, it should be looked on as an extended and respectful footnote to the general work by W. K. Ferguson, *The Renaissance in Historical Thought* (1948). My excuse for publishing what was essentially a working tool was that in the first place it seemed of general interest to demonstrate from a single period that the history of taste and of historiography can greatly enhance our enjoyment of a painting or a history book. And on this score I think I have been justified. It is no longer unusual to assume that in looking at a picture the understanding of previous estimates of it is a bonus on the pleasure to be gained from an appreciation of its formal and intellectual content. It is no longer thought needless or, indeed, impertinent to wish to see how the character and preconceptions of a historian affect the tone and reliability of his work. In the second place, just as the wastepaper basket of a great *salonnière* is more likely to be worth rifling than that of a suburban housewife, so the by-products of an interest in Renaissance Italy have some special claim to salvage, for it is a period that has long exerted a seductive power over Englishmen. They had been told by writers on her history and art that it had been in her presence that humanity first drew a recognizably modern breath, first outgrew superstition, learned to love beauty for its own sake. Hallowed by classical association, made respectable by the names of great men, sensational by the éclat of great crimes and universal by the standard of great art – the symbol 'Italian Renaissance' was, and is, irresistible.

Two chapters here call perhaps for comment, the first and

the last. I have dealt somewhat fully with the period 1550–1650 because although men of this age were too close to the Renaissance to see it in perspective, their attitude to Italy and Italians was absorbed into that of later generations who could. As this is true of taste as well, I have sketched its history – as far as painting from 1250–1550 is concerned – for two and a half centuries, although it was only late in the eighteenth century that the historian, or the collector, was much interested in the social background of the arts. An understanding of Ruskin's taste, for instance, is incomplete without a knowledge of Evelyn's, just as John Addington Symonds is better understood if we know what drove the crazy Charles, second Lord Stanhope, to scribble this insult to Sir Walter Raleigh in the margin of a book:

> The originall of ye rude rauly
> it is too base to tell
> From Italy it came to us
> to Italy from Hell.[1]

Ruskin used the term Renaissance as a vessel for his likes and loathings. The historian Symonds, the subject of the last chapter, exploited it still further to stabilize a neurotic temperament. And since his writings still underlie much present understanding of the word and long influenced most popular English writing about the Renaissance, it is important to see this process in action, in spite of the risks involved in trying to 'explain' the psychological state of a dead man. Symonds's was a complicated personality,[2] and the portrait that emerges from an attempt to explain his historical work in terms of

---

[1] G. P. V. Akrigg, 'The Curious Marginalia of Charles, Second Lord Stanhope' in *Joseph Quincey Adams. Memorial Studies*, Washington, 1948, 797–8.

[2] 'Er vereinigte in sich englischen Liberalismus, französischen Rationalismus und Positivismus mit englischer Romantik und deutschen Idealismus' for instance. E. M. Bräm, *Die Italienische Renaissance in dem englischen Geistesleben des 19. Jahrhunderts*, Zürich, 1932, 70.

his character must be one-sided, must stress the dark at the expense of the light, for it was his writing, the release he found there, that enabled the brighter side of his nature to exist at all. In the year before he died, he told Arthur Symons (who noted 'the morbid, disquieting, nervous, contorted, painful expression of his face: the abnormal, almost terrible fixity of the eyes' – those of a man troubled in mind and body) that he had chosen to write the history of the Renaissance 'rather than the impossible one of writing the history of his own soul'.[1] But this was not the whole truth; there is much of his soul in his book. And the same is true of many subsequent books about the Renaissance: they conform to the contours shaped by the deposits of three centuries of opinion, to their authors' special interests, and, most misleading quality of all – this is the lesson of Symonds's work – to the special needs of their personalities.[2]

ACKNOWLEDGMENTS

I have to thank Mr John Murray for permission to quote from letters in his possession from Ruskin and Sir Francis Palgrave.

In preparing this new edition I have had the benefit of a good deal of printed criticism and, when I agreed with it, I have used it to amend the text. I am particularly indebted in this way to Professor Roberto Weiss, to Professor E. K. Waterhouse, and to the author of a helpful but, alas, anonymous review in the *Times Literary Supplement*. The evidence of a continued interest in the book, moreover, gives me the assurance, which I lacked before, to say that if the last chapter

---

[1] *Fortnightly Review*, February 1924, 229 and 231.
[2] These two paragraphs are from the original edition.

reads rather better than any other part of the book, this is because it benefited from the generous interest and criticism of Mr John Sparrow.

Several books dealing with aspects of this subject have appeared since I wrote. The more important of them will be found in a bibliographic note on page 220.

CHAPTER ONE

The Beginnings of Interest: mid–Sixteenth to mid–Seventeenth Centuries

During the sixteenth century Englishmen's interest in foreign countries and their awareness of the differences between them increased enormously. The shifting alliances of the Italian wars at the beginning of the century and the use of powerful armies had helped the political divisions of the continent to be seen more distinctly. Definition was helped by the rapid growth of formal diplomacy and, for England, by the reflection of prosperity at home in a revived aggressiveness abroad. The Reformation emphasized political divisions still further, and at the same time made it necessary that England should understand and take advantage of them. The stresses caused by internal change at home roused an interest in foreign institutions.

There was also more travel, but this alone did little to help the Englishman see Europe in terms of its component nations; the traveller went from town to town rather than from country to country. The revival of interest in classical learning quickened the attractiveness of foreign universities, especially those of Italy, but there had always been traffic of this sort, and of merchants and pilgrims; it was the political, not the cultural changes of the period that caused a real interest in foreign countries to replace a knowledge merely of the facts needed for dynastic diplomacy. And it was the political complexity of Italy that prevented writers from seeing her culture as a whole till the middle of the next century.

An interest in the history of foreign countries once aroused, Italian models were there, in the writings of Machiavelli and Guicciardini, to show how it could be expressed, and it was with a history of Italy that the new attitude showed itself in print, with William Thomas's *Historie of Italie*.

By 1549, when it was published, Italian influences were already affecting English learning and customs. But this had led to very little interest in modern Italy. The English humanists looked on Italy as a tutor with no private life. A hundred years of interest in Italian learning had only led to one work concerned with contemporary Italy, a Latin poem describing the Papal Court at the end of the fifteenth century.

Certainly the disinterest had been mutual, and it was with a desire to tell Italians something about England that Thomas made his first essay as a historian. His concern with Italy was not at first a voluntary one. While a member of the household of Sir Anthony Browne, Master of the Horse to Henry VIII, he had gambled too heavily, and embezzled some of his employer's funds to flee the country. He reached Venice to find word had gone before; he was arrested and imprisoned. On his release he thought it wiser to remain for a while in Italy, travelling and teaching. In the course of these wanderings he was so struck with the ignorance of life in England and the course of the Reformation there that he wrote for his Italian friends a short life of Henry VIII, defending him with some eloquence and courage from Catholic reproach. He then went on to write *The Historie of Italie, a boke excedyng profitable to be redde: Because it intreateth of the astate of many and divers common weales, how thei have ben, & now be governed.*

The states were so 'divers' that the term 'Italy' was only just becoming a definite one. A scorn of foreigners, *barbari*, did not make Italian a definite term even to the Italians themselves, and in spite of Machiavelli's plea that they should sink their differences in the face of foreign invaders, it is doubtful if his mental map of Italy included Venice, rich beyond others and constitutionally unique, or Naples, so long subject to Spanish interests.

In Thomas's time, Naples and Lombardy were governed by Spain, Genoa had only just broken free from France, and the other states had no interest in common action. The situation was reflected in a guide to Europe written before 1542 by Andrew Borde. It was intended, in a very small compass, to give the reader an idea of the situation, customs, language and coinage of each country, partly in doggerel, partly in prose, and partly in dialogue. Borde does not treat 'Italy' as a whole but has different chapters for *Sycel & of Calabry, Naples, Italy and of Rome, Venys, Lombardy,* and *Iene*. For Borde, then, 'Italy' means Rome and its environs. He goes on to point the disparities of the states by saying, for instance, that '*the napulians do use great marchandise & Naples is ioyned to Italy wherfore they do use* γ^e *fashios and maner of Italyons & Romayns*', and one of the notable characteristics of the Venetians is that they speak a tongue like that of the Romans.

He further emphasizes the difference between state and state by character sketches, a device which in the form of proverbial descriptions was to emphasize political differences for a century by running them into neat literary moulds. Borde's Lombard announces:

> I am a Lombart and subtyl crafft I have
> To decyve a gentylman a yemen or a knave
> I werke by poplyse *(policy)* subtylyte and craught
> The which other whyle doth bryng me to nought
> I am the next neyghbour to the Italion,

an assertion of the difference between Lombard and Roman that is the stronger because Borde seems to be talking about Rome's northern neighbour, Tuscany, and using the word Lombard in its vague sense of merchant from north Italy.

Thomas similarly had separate chapters for Rome, Venice,

Naples, Florence, Genoa, Milan, Mantua, Ferrara, Piacenza and Parma, and Urbino – the last still memorable for its usurpation by Leo X but soon to be largely unvisited and unrecorded until the nineteenth century. Rome, with the prestige of its past and the pomp and scandal of its present, 'the onelie iewell, myrrour, maistres, and beautie of this worlde' stood alone, and the isolation of the natural head of the peninsula emphasized its divisions. And though Thomas mentions the outstanding monuments of the states he deals with he is not interested in the common cultural achievement they represented; only religion, therefore, helped the historian to think of Italy as a whole.

From this, in fact, Thomas was expressly delivered by his motive in writing. He believed, conventionally, that history should teach, that it should encourage the good and show 'how naughtie doaynges have moste commonly naughtie endyng'. More specifically it should show how division and lawlessness can shatter a commonwealth, and more than any other country did disunited Italy provide examples of tyranny and revolution upsetting the accepted order of things. He had chosen Italy to show to what dangers the equilibrium of the Tudor state might be exposed. And he was establishing by this a persistent barrier to the efficient treatment of Italian history, the point of view that saw it as a storehouse of examples, often dreadful ones, with a history more suited to an anthology for the use of politician and moralist than to a simple, objective narrative.

To this end he wrote his chapter on the history of Florence in terms of two periods, both of which showed that the *status quo* in England must be preserved. The effect of the Guelf-Ghibelline factions of the fourteenth century was to degrade the nobility; this led to the decay of manners. The effect of the absolute rule of the Medici in the fifteenth was to restore them, to show that liberty that has been lost by a multitude can be restored by one man. And when Thomas returned to England in 1549, it was to apply to politics the lessons he had learned from Italian history. Machiavelli was to be his guide in the former as he had been in the latter science.

He found his enemies dead and his friends in positions of power. He was made a clerk of the Privy Council and quickly gained the ear of the young King Edward. For him he wrote a work that recalled Machiavelli's *Principe* in method and message: the *Disquisitions on Affairs Of State*. They discussed 'Wheather It Be Expedient To Varie With Tyme', concluding that men should change their opinions to suit events; 'What Princes Amitie Is Best', deciding that though natural amity is best men are so wicked nowadays that Princes have to think in terms of artificial, or politic amity; and 'Wheather It Be Better For A Common Wealth That The Power Be In The Nobilitie Or In The Commonaltie' where Thomas repeats the lessons of Florentine history to show that though aristocracy is better than commonalty, monarchy is best of all. Unfortunately, times changed too swiftly for Thomas himself; as a Protestant he was suspect when Mary came to the throne and in 1554 he was hung, drawn and quartered for treason, the *Historie* being suppressed and burnt by the common hangman.

There was to be a gap of 200 years before another history of all Italy was attempted. For a while interest in Italy was expressed through a study of her language and literature rather than the history of her states. And here, too, Thomas was a pioneer. In the year before he left Italy he wrote the first Italian grammar to be printed in English and added to it a dictionary that was unsuperseded for fifty years. He foresaw a time when Italian would be as widely read as Latin and Greek for its ease and for the wealth of literary and scientific work already written in it. The use of Latin as an international tongue was decreasing. It was already less widely known in the south than north of the Alps, and different pronunciations hampered its usefulness. By the end of the century Thomas's prophecy had come true.

His own grammar had been written at the request of a nobleman who wanted to make the most of his Italian travels. Similarly Sir Thomas Hoby, translator of Castiglione's *Courtier*, made up a grammar for Sir Henry Sidney, but before long language teaching passed into the hands of professionals. Henry Grantham translated a grammar from Latin to help his pupils Mary and Francys Berkeley in 1575, and in the same year Claudius Hollyband dedicated *The Italian School-Maister* to his pupil John Smith, who was led through a series of 'Familiar Talkes' with English and Italian in parallel columns, to a full romance, the 'fine Tuscan historie called Arnalt and Lucenda'. After this he was considered ready for Italian literature in general.

In 1578 the audience was widened when the most famous of Elizabethan Italian grammars, *Florio, His firste Fruites*, was dedicated to the Earl of Leicester for the benefit of all Englishmen who took pleasure in the Italian language.

John Florio's father, Michael Angelo, a religious refugee from the Roman inquisition, had settled in London under Edward VI as preacher to a church of Italian protestants. When he was turned out for fornication he took up language teaching, writing, as the custom was, grammars for his pupils among whom were Henry Herbert, Earl of Pembroke, and Lady Jane Grey. This was still a time when Italian influences on England were doctrinal as well as literary, but when John began to teach, the Church had been settled, and Italians were welcomed enthusiastically as literary advisers. Of this he took such advantage that he affected not only the fortunes of Italian in England but of English style itself, for Euphuism owed much to his model dialogues and discussions. His grammars are alive with his prejudices and enthusiasms. In a dedication he clamours for protection from his detractors, in a preface he rails against rivals, in a dialogue he scolds the English for their indifference to languages, for their social climbing, for their gluttony. In parallel columns he simultaneously praises the Queen, as becomes an alien, and works off a vocabulary:

'She may rather be called celestiall, than terrestrial: Shee is learned, wyse, gentle, courteous, noble, prudent, liberal, fayre, lovyng, vertuous: shee is gallant, mercyfull: shee is not hautie, proude, covetous, cruell, eger, furious, unnoble, but as I have told you before, shee is woorthye for to enioye any great thing: shee is the last refuge, defense, and bulwarke of al banished vertues.'

Sometimes he is practical, as when he helps the reader to decline a verb as well as 'To speake with a damsel':

> Fayre maybe, wyll you that I love you:
> I cannot hold you that you love not, if you wyl love.
> I have loved you, I love you, & wil love you.
> I have hated you, I hate you, & wil hate you . . .
> I will brake my fast with you.
> We wil have a pair of sasages,

and sometimes he is kind as well:

> Nowe let us come to the *Articles*.
> I pray you doo so sir, if you be not weery.
> To tel you the truth, I am almost weery, but
> neverthelesse we wyl follow.

But usually, both here and in his *Second Fruites* (1591), he makes little allowance for the beginner. The bulk of the works are taken up with opulently convoluted discussions on stock themes; the role of Fortune, the praise of books, and love – most of all about women and love. On this theme the long euphuistic passages, loaded with comparisons and proverbs, even break into verse, and far more is written for the gentleman seeking aid in elegant expression than for the man who wants simply a practical guide to the language for business or travel. So far from pointing out the easiness of Italian, Florio glories in its complexity. How can an Englishman, he asks in his dictionary, hope to master it when it differs so much between one dialect and another, between its use by Dante and its use by Boccaccio, when it consists not of a vocabulary like William Thomas's but of *A World of Wordes* (1598)? Even Benvenuto's *The Passenger* (1612), a work intended to appeal to middle-class readers, revolves in a rarefied literary atmosphere. Practical dialogues turn into matches of wit, and seem written for the stage rather than for business men abroad:

> Ho, within?
> Who knocks at the doore?
> Friends.
> Friends walke not in the night.
> Thou slovenly lubberd, and toyish fellow,
> what idle toyes goest thou fantasticating.

Long-winded and mouthing, Benvenuto is less concerned with being useful than with aping a courtesy book for the benefit of the aristocracy. 'In my opinion,' says one of his characters, 'wee have said more of the Courtier succinctly, than *Castilio* hath at large.'

It was only with the work of another *émigré* language teacher, Giovanni Torriano, that the needs of the middle-class traveller were met. Of two books published in 1640 one was dedicated to the Company of Turkey Merchants and the other contained dialogues a great deal more practical than anything that had yet appeared. One is 'Concerning buying and selling', and though there is another 'Concerning a Courtship', the aspirant is roundly told: 'You'd goe take upon you an imployment that you have no skill in; this is a burden for otherguess (*altri*) shoulders than yours.' By this time the first impact of Italian literature on England had relaxed and with greater numbers travelling and trading in Italy and the Levant the need was more to speak than to read the language. In 1659 Torriano recognized this when he issued the first English-Italian dictionary, and in the last dialogue of the last book he wrote, he sadly noted the end of the first great age of Italian teaching: 'We speak Italian,' says his Englishman with homely regret, 'but in this we are like hens, which lay eggs without the cocks tread, which bring not forth: we have never an Italian to correct us when we commit any error.'

The interest taken in Italian literature between Thomas's grammar and Torriano's dictionary is remarkable enough, and well known enough, only to touch on. Apart from scraps of Italian dialogue in authors like Ford and Marston, derived from language teaching at the universities, or the use of proverbs like Holofernes's *Venezia, Venezia, chi non ti vede non ti prezzia,* taken it may be from Florio, the plots of one-third of the extant plays show Italian influence. During the same time over four hundred separate titles were translated from the Italian, representing the work of some two hundred and twenty-five authors, and others, of course, were read in the original. Gabriel Harvey celebrated the favourite poets of the time: 'Sweet Petrarch, divine Aretine, worthie Ariosto, & excellent Tasso', and had read besides Bibiena, Boccaccio, della Casa, Castiglione, Guazzo, Guicciardini, and Paulo Giovio, Machiavelli and Strozzi. Dante was almost unknown owing to the obscurity of his language and imagery. The courtesy books were among the most influential as through their discussions the reader saw the scene, as well as the standards, of Italian social life, and despite occasional bawdiness they had a high moral tone that gained them access to households that barred admission to Boccaccio and the novelists. They were taken very seriously. Thomas grumbled when Urbino did not come up to the picture Castiglione had painted of it, and Lord Herbert of Cherbury in giving precepts for the education of the young broke off to refer them simply to Guazzo and della Casa.

Some Englishmen, like Henry Percy, 9th Earl of Northumberland, appear to have owned more Italian books than English ones, and Italian personal names had become so familiar that they were charged with meaning however vaguely used, as is shown by this passage from the Argument of the short tragedy, *Mulleasses the Turke* (1610):

'*Timoclea* finding the *Turke* enamoured on *Amada* kills her own daughter: *Borgias* after many cunning tragicall changes, strangles his wife in her owne haire, stabs *Ferrara*, being in the shape of an Eunuch. In the end *Mulleasses* and *Borgias* kill one another, & the Duke of *Venice* surviving all their blacke and trecherous plots, marries Iulia.'

Italian-printed books and English translations were supplemented by Italian books published in London. These were not only classics and works otherwise difficult to obtain after 1559 because of the censorship, like those of Aretino and Machiavelli; Stella's *Columbeid*, a panegyric on Columbus and his discoveries, was published in London at the instance probably of Hakluyt, to draw attention to Raleigh's plans for the Virginian venture.

Yet for all this familiarity with the literature and language of Italy, there was little sympathetic feeling for the country itself. In spite of all the references in plays and books there was not a single original poem on an Italian theme. Strong prejudices, economic, moral and religious, put the Italians as it were on a stage where action, however enthralling, was watched at a distance. There had been anger at the success of the Italian luxury trade since the early fifteenth century, at the wasting of money by bluff Englishmen on ephemeral kick-shaws. By the end of the sixteenth, enforced by geographers' opinions of the effect of climate on character, the idea that the quick, crafty Meridional peoples were milking the slower stolid Septentrials had become a plaintive obses-

sion. Machiavelli was judged by an age that expected to find
subtlety and cunning in the hot south. And it became a fixed
idea, in spite of travellers' accounts of the general sobriety of
Italian costume, that the Italians did not even turn the money
they cozened out of the northerners to good use, but squandered it on fantastic dress and curious vice.

The cross-gartered Puritan was a symbol of what might
happen to a god-fearing Englishman when such forces were
abroad; he was not only a figure of fun but a portent of
national decline. The *Inglese Italianato* mocked God in foreign-
bought ribbon that led straight from the tailor to the bawdy
house and the Pit. The traveller who had mastered the arts
of dressing and making a bow would probably bring back
as well the arts of atheism, epicurizing, whoring, poisoning
and sodomy; such, at least, was the opinion of Thomas
Nashe, and he was a lover of Italy as the home of poetry.
The insecurity of the English Reformation added fuel to this
sort of denunciation. Climatic volatility was bad, so was the
reputation of the early sixteenth century papacy, but when
the Elizabethan Church settlement was under blockade the
propaganda became more and more sweeping. A great part
of Ascham's *The Scholemaster* (1570) was given up to warning
youth against Italy; unless he went with a cautious tutor he
would fall into popery and filthy living; 'Some *Circes* shall
make him, of a plaine English man, a right Italian. And at
length to hell, or to some hellish place, is he likelie to go.'
Although Italian was the language Ascham loved next to
Greek and Latin, he would have his readers learn it at home,
and even then the tutor should be on the alert, for every shop
in London was selling translations of Italian books as part of
a papist plot to convert the English – 'Mo Papists be made,
by your merry bookes of Italie, than by your earnest bookes
of Lovain.' Only one book can advisedly be read, the *Courtier*
of Castiglione. It was to meet this sort of objection that
the Elizabethans often moralized the Italian tales they were

translating, interpolating corrective asides even into serious works. Fenton's translation of Guicciardini's *Storia d'Italia* (1579) does this and shows how a translator could make his author's characters seem as wicked as contemporaries expected them to be by choosing the less favourable of two possible renderings of words like 'astuto', and by elaborations like 'they [the Borgias] had recourse to their suttleties and wel experienced craftes' for 'si aiutano con le loro arti'.

Even when the Italians ceased to be a danger, the habit of thinking the worse of them persisted. Travellers still listened uncritically to tales of the 40,000 whores supported by the clergy in Rome, and of the 30,000 that died in one year of plague in Venice. In Webster's two plays, Italians poison their victims in four distinct ways: by the leaves of a book, the lips of a picture, the pommel of a saddle and an anointed helmet. Time after time poison and passion got in the way of observation. A Scottish Protestant visiting Rome starts his account of the place by describing the antiquities. Then he enters St Peter's, and we hope for more description. But the first thing he sees is the bronze statue of St Peter and worshippers kissing its toe. From that point, there is nothing but a furious denunciation of idolatry. Thomas Palmer, writing in 1606 an *Essay of the Meanes how to make our Travailes, into Forraine Countries, the more profitable and honourable*, points out that as far as Italy is concerned it is safest not to travel at all.

Interest in Italian literature did not attract attention to the times that gave it birth. Not till the latter half of the eighteenth century did interest in an author lead to work on his historical background. Nor did the numerous travel books dealing with Italy draw the attention of historians much more. Thomas's *Historie* was a sport. But when histories of the Italian states began to be written again in the middle of the seventeenth century their audience had been made familiar not only with the names of important Italians but with the geography of the peninsula.

That the travellers did no more is due to their point of view. All through the reigns of Elizabeth and James Englishmen saw Italy from the outside. From an atmosphere of prejudice at home they sailed abroad for some fixed purpose, to spy, to trade, to learn the language, and having got what they wanted, returned, hardly having mixed with the Italians themselves or having been tempted into a wider interest than the one they went to gratify. Apart from exceptions like Anthony Munday, who went to Rome for adventure, travel was commonly vocational.

The political activity of the Tudors on the Continent led them to seek men with experience of foreign parts and languages for diplomatic posts. Hoby, whose brother was resident Ambassador at Augsburg, went to Italy in 1548 to learn the language as an aid to his own career. And every traveller could be of use to his country. In 1535 Thomas Cromwell employed Borde to sound foreign opinions of Henry VIII, and as discussion as to the advantages and drawbacks of foreign travel increased, it became clear that one motive was to be of service to one's prince, to glean information that would later be of use and could not be come by in any other way.

Borde had found no one residing abroad for pleasure, only merchants, brokers and students. The educational value of foreign travel, especially to Italy, had been endorsed by the travels of English Humanists like Grocyn, Colet, Tunstall, Linacre and Lily – the names of the last two appearing with that of Warham, later Archbishop, in a list of admissions to the English Hospice of the Confraternity of the Most Holy Trinity and St Thomas of Canterbury in Rome for a single year, 1490. The Italian universities offered learning that was not only sound but fashionable and in visiting them the student could pick up the knowledge of men and affairs essential to a well-rounded education; the attractive power of Italy as the intellectual centre of Europe survived for a while the decline of its claims to be so. As the century wore on, however, fewer travellers went to take advantage of its universities than to look at its antiquities. And as educational ideals in England became less strenuous at the beginning of the next century, Italy came to be less visited for the qualities of a university than for those of a finishing school.

This only led to its being more frequented by Englishmen than ever, but they learned to fence and ride the great horse with as little interest in the affairs and history of Italy as had been shown by the more serious student. They admired certain modern monuments: St Peter's, the new Medici Chapel at S. Lorenzo in Florence, and certain mediæval ones, like the Cathedral at Siena, or S. Mark's at Venice, but did not speculate about their builders. Diplomatist, merchant and student came back with what he had gone to fetch and no more.

Part of this, of course, is explained by political circumstances. For much of the period, bringing back anything from Italy was like stealing information from the camp of a sleeping enemy, the mind alert but narrowly concentrated on its objective. While at war with Spain an Englishman was not safe in Sicily, Naples or Milan, or in Rome, Spain's ally. And when peace came, the Inquisition remained with its prisons to keep the country unsafe for Protestants. Although Cardinal Allen used to secure a few days' grace in the Pontificate of Sixtus V (1585–90) for Englishmen to see the antiquities of Rome, Anthony Munday found it wise to pose as a Catholic while he was there. Clement VIII (1592–1605) was less severe, but even so Fynes Moryson spent a good deal of time in disguise, in Rome and elsewhere, now dressed in Dutch, now in Italian or French costume. This did not ensure him complete freedom of movement. The convoys necessary to scare bandits often contained Englishmen by whom he feared recognition, and at Easter, when everyone who did not take the sacrament was questioned, he had to keep on the move to avoid interrogation. In 1588 Edward Webbe, newly ransomed from the Turkish galleys, made his way home across Italy. In Padua and again in Rome he was imprisoned as a suspected heretic, and he escaped from the Inquisition only to be imprisoned again in Naples. He was given the strappado three times, 'and then constrained to drinke salte water and quick-lime, and then fine Lawne or Callico thrust downe my throate and pluckt up again ready to pluck my heart out of my belly, al to make me confesse that I was an English spie'.

The tendency for the traveller to go straight to his goal and back again was fostered by the general insecurity of travel. South of Rome a large escort of soldiers was necessary, and this danger from bandits, coupled with the lack of food and shelter offered by a very thinly populated countryside, made travellers keep to the main routes. Formalities, too, were a reason for keeping to the beaten track. In order to leave England at all, a permit had to be obtained. When the danger from continental Catholicism was at its height, these warrants forbade the holder to visit Rome or St Omer. In 1614 news that Lord and Lady Arundel were looking at antiquities in Rome greatly perturbed the Embassy in Venice: 'The common recourse of his Maties subjects to Rome notwithstanding their direct inhibitions on their licenses for trauaile, to the contrarie, is continued with th^t freedom th^t both the Earle of Arundel and his Lady have spent many days in th^t place.' Once in Italy certain cities would not allow the traveller more than one night without a permit, and inns had to make returns of visitors at regular intervals.

The traveller's hand was continually in his pocket. The poorer states relied on customs dues which were exacted with pertinacity even on books. Then there were regulations about firearms to comply with, and from fear of plague a *Bolletino della sanità* had to be renewed in each town. All these aggravations were smoothest along beaten tracks.

To help travellers along these tracks, guide books were written, and these too did their bit to stereotype the routes, the routes that before the middle of the seventeenth century had assumed the pattern of the Grand Tour. A hundred years before this Borde had written a much fuller guide than his *Introduction of Knowledge*, with the distances between one town and another and the objects of interest within them. This book, which would have been the first of its kind, he lent to Thomas Cromwell, who lost it. Printed or not printed, however, the literature of travel, practical and moralizing, boomed. The late Elizabethan tourist had at his disposal books giving charts of distances, books telling him how, if necessary, to calculate his latitude and longitude, even books telling him how to write home. The number of works dealing with the technique of travel – where to go, where to eat, how to dress, what money would be required, was not matched again until the expansion of the tourist industry in the nineteenth century. But there was an important difference; instead of saying: Identify yourself as much as possible with the life of the country you visit, the Elizabethan and seventeenth-century work urged the visitor to return unspoiled, not to be off his guard for an instant. There was to be no relaxing, no browsing and, as a result, very little independent vision.

A work of 1610 gave advice as to inns, how to bribe the customs officers, points of interest and when to tip guides. The visitor was carefully nursed through the monuments of Venice: look left, now right, now up at the ceiling. And soon the Italian example of prescribing daily itineraries as the best way of getting through the sights was copied, so that everything in Rome could be seen in a few days. The market was becoming glutted by 1648 when the traveller John Raymond laid down his pen on reaching Rome. Already there was 'one volume of the Antiquities; another of the Pallaces; a third of the Churches; a fourth of the Gardens; a fifth of the Statues; a sixth of the Fountaines; a seventh of the Villas; in a word, the Presse is burdened with nothing more than descriptions of Rome.'

The routes were standardized early in the seventeenth century, a tour being in the form of a circuit, entering via the Mt. Cenis pass and leading from Milan and Florence to Rome and returning up the eastern side of the peninsula to Venice and, when political conditions allowed, the Brenner – or vice versa. The circuit could be completed by the link Milan–Mantua–Padua–Venice. Though most travellers wished to visit Rome, those with less time could find plenty of classical interest in the shorter route, Brenner–Venice–Padua–Verona–Mantua–Milan–Turin–Mt. Cenis.

The clockwise circuit led from the Alps to Padua, whose university, still strong in the sciences, was the most frequented in Europe, and by river to Venice, visited even more for the fame of its constitution and the notoriety of its festivities than for its beauty. The states of the Church lay south of the Po, and no frontier on the Continent divided two policies more different. It was from such juxtapositions as these that much of the political interest of the tour was derived. The first city to be visited in the papal dominions was Ferrara, held as a fief by the Este and attractive for its wide streets and fine gardens. Bologna, the scene of Greene's *Morando: The Tritameron of Love* (1597), was a prosperous commercial city and was visited too for the civil law of its university. It stood in the states of the Church as did the coastal towns Ravenna, Rimini and Ancona. Ravenna at this time had little to offer; travellers were not interested in Byzantine architecture. Rimini had a few classical remains, and Ancona, in spite of an important fair, was used mostly as a base for visiting Loreto and scoffing at the superstitious devotions squandered there. Thence to Rome the route was notable only for its discomfort, as the road south from Rome to Naples was fearful from bandits. Celebrated for its excellent climate and the amorousness of its inhabitants, Naples, with its 'oranges and lemons', became the site of many of the more scabrous stories about Italy; Italian and Spanish blood mixing to the worst possible effect. On the classical side the programme was severe; a visit to the tomb of Virgil at Pausilipo, to Puteoli and Baiae, Avernus and Acheron and the Elysian fields; the ascent of Vesuvius and the suffocation of a dog in Charon's cave to verify the poisonous effect of its vapours were other routine excursions.

The traveller usually returned from Naples to Rome. To the south, English merchants touched at the ports of Calabria and Apulia for cattle and oils; Hoby, it is true, in order to improve his Italian, had gone as far as Sicily to get away from the English, but with few exceptions, the wildness of the south ensured that the exploration of Magna Graecia, for all its classical echoes, was postponed till the late eighteenth century.

The way north through Tuscany offered the best opportunity for learning Italian at its purest. Siena, with its quietly pleasant social life, and Florence, suspect as the home of Machiavelli but proverbially the fairest of Italian cities, might both be visited for this purpose before moving north to Milan. As the capital of the Spanish province that contained some of the wealthiest and most strategically crucial land in Italy, Milan was of constant interest to statesmen and of growing concern to craftsmen in search of training and gentlemen in need of finishing. Thence the choice lay between leaving Italy via Turin or returning to Padua and Venice through the Veneto. From Bergamo, more visited then than now, the latter choice would lead the traveller to Mantua, a hereditary principality with a mild court life of its own, and into Venetian territory again at Verona, famous for its antiquities, especially its arena; then through Vicenza to Padua.

These places provided some or all of the following, the criteria of attraction: political interest, classical associations, religious notoriety, engineering feats (ancient, like the Colosseum, or modern, like the harbour at Genoa), academies of dancing, fencing or riding, special festivities like Ascension time at Venice or the Easter carnivals at Rome, universities, outstanding curiosities whether on the scale of the Leaning Tower of Pisa or the Venetian breviary which blew up when opened at a certain page, outstanding modern works of art. No town was visited exclusively for its mediæval buildings. Viterbo, which lay on the main road north of Rome, was largely ignored, and little or no attempt was made to reach towns like Perugia, Assisi, Orvieto, San Miniato, Urbino or Arezzo, which were off the main roads and had nothing but their mediæval past to offer; in the mere way of life of an Italian community there was no interest at all. Nor was a beautiful landscape an attraction. It is well known how late was a taste for mountain scenery, and even the lakes were passed by. Evelyn paused at the lake of Garda at the express wish of Lord Arundel, but found it no more than 'surprising'.

Taste on the whole was vulgar, admiring a work in terms of its materials, exclaiming at a profusion of gold leaf, pricing rare marbles, and exclaiming at ingenuity. While Michelangelo's tombs were passed by, the new Medici Chapel was the wonder of the age, 'so glorious, that whosoever enters, will even imagine himselfe in some place above terrestiall', as one tourist put it. There was the same uncritical spirit in the gullible acceptance of what the traveller read or was told by his guide – that the bronze doors of the Florentine Baptistery were brought from Jerusalem, or that the Elysian fields lay outside Rome. It was reflected in what he wrote – John Raymond passed for publication an engraving of the Amphitheatre at Verona which showed it as being taller than it was long; all he needed, in fact, was a hieroglyph, evidence that a famous object had been seen rather than an attempt to convey what it was like. The Elizabethan travellers had looked out what was most remarkable and their successors were content to follow their lead, relying more and more on the vision and opinions of others, becoming less and less capable of extending their interest to a new aspect of the country.

This was in spite of a considerable change that had come over the nature of travel. The slackening of religious antagonism under James, and the growing fashionableness of the tour led to contact with the Italian nobility. This might have meant that their country was seen less from the outside, but the English nobleman already treated his Italian confrères *de haut en bas*, an attitude that lasted till the mid-nineteenth century, when Italy became politically respectable again and when industrial nations began to idealize her culture and the southern way of life. An Italy of inferiors gained hardly more sympathetic understanding than an Italy of enemies.

Formulæ were increasingly relied on to describe what was seen. The literary vogue of the proverb, probably Italian in origin and certainly a copious feature of the Elizabethan grammars, helped the traveller to encapsulate his impressions without more difficulty. By the 1570s the cities had been labelled: 'Venice the richest, Milane the greatest, Genoa the proudest, Florents the fynest, Bolonia the fruitfullest, Ravenna the oldest, Neapolis the noblest,' and before long the difference between the nature of their inhabitants had been elaborately worked out. When it came to choosing a wife, according to Moryson, 'The Milanese are said to be little ielous and to hate fat women. The Mantuans to love women that can dance. The Florentines to love a modest woman, and one that loves home. The Neapolitanes to love a stately high-minded woman. Those of *Lucca* are said to love constantly, the Venetians contrarily, and to desire fat women with great dugs,' and so on, a catchphrase for each city's habits in eating, fighting and trading, each set emphasizing the divisions of the country and making it hard to think even of each state and its history as a whole. There were clichés to the effect that the Italians were more learned than the rest of Europe, and more skilful in the arts, but there was no suggestion apart from this that she had recently passed through a great age. The travellers said nothing to cause historians to see Italian culture between 1450 and 1550 as a phenomenon worth writing about.

To approach the English historians of Italy at this time is to be dazzled by the lustre of Venice. The main constituent of the modern Renaissance concept is Florence; the Italian Renaissance is seen largely in terms of Florentine civilization in the fifteenth century. But then Italy was seen in terms of Venice, and her greatest century was thought to be the sixteenth, when Titian, Veronese and Tintoretto were painting and her political reputation was at its height.

Her richness and her position on the pilgrim route to Jerusalem were the earliest factors to attract attention, but already by 1517 she was famed for political stability. Sir Richard Torkington, rector of Mulberton in Norfolk, wrote in the course of a pilgrimage to the holy land in that year that 'the richesse, the sumptuous buylding, the religius howses and the stabelyssng of ther Iustyces and Councylles with all other thinges that makyth a Cite glorius Surmownteth in Venys above all places that ever I sawe'. And the bulk of writing about Venice was to be in praise of her constitution; to understand it, by the end of the sixteenth century, was one of the motives for going to Italy.

The reasons for this admiration were derived in part from Italian authors. Guicciardini's history of Italy, for instance, which was translated in 1579, shows clearly that even while the other states of Italy feared and hated Venice her constitution was taken as a model of stability, and other writers supported this by comparing it favourably with those of

Sparta and Rome and claiming that it had remained unchanged since the original foundation of the city. It was true
that Venice had found greater tranquillity in the past than
the other states of Italy and had been the only one to resist
despotism, and if by now her fortunes were waning, this was
scarcely noticed; an age that saw government as an art was
loath to find flaws in the perfect example of it. Besides, as
guardian of Europe from the Turk, Venice, politically, was
invested with a sort of sanctity. Her famous arsenal, which,
together with St Mark's, was the biggest attraction to
sightseers, was the armoury not of herself alone but of
Christendom.

The first translation of a work devoted only to Venice was
made in 1599 by Samuel Lewkenor. It was Contarini's *The
Commonwealth and Government of Venice*, the work Jonson's
Sir Politic Would-be took with him when he set up house in
Venice. Contarini held up Venice as the model of mixed
governments, and where he praised, Lewkenor hyperbolized.
Not only did this constitution perfectly combine the elements
of monarchy, aristocracy and democracy, not only was it
ideally suited for the framing and execution of laws and for
the election of officers, but 'there are sundry other so marvel-
lous and miraculous considerations, and in their owne exceeding singularitie, beyond all resemblance or comparison
with any other Commonwealth so unspeakably strange, that
their wonderful rareness being verified, maketh the straung-
est impossibilities not seem altogether incredible'. One of
Contarini's considerations was that Venice surpassed the constitution of Rome and this suggested a link that was a congenial one to Englishmen who saw Venice as preserving the
continuity between antiquity and the present.

One result of this reverence for its constitution was that
Venice became popularly as celebrated for its justice as for
its courtezans. It was the state in which Shakespeare believed
a private suit would obtain a fair hearing in the middle of an

emergency council of war, and in *Volpone* Jonson contrasted the shoddy morality of his characters with the impartiality of the courts whose decision provided his *dénouement*. Coryate, too, in his *Crudities* (1611), dwells on both aspects without finding them contradictory. Because 'the name of a Cortezan of Venice is famoused over all Christendome', he gives an engraving of one with himself by her side endeavouring, he notes, to convert her. And because of the republic's 2,212-year long stability he gives a description of its government. He celebrates, too, its beauty, which was a rather later element in Venice's fame than her wealth and power.

There was a more practical reason for English concern with Venice. She was the first Italian state to which a resident Ambassador was sent, and from 1604 till 1630, when English concern with Italian politics slackened, the Embassy household became a focus of hospitality and advice. Especially was this true after 1606, when Venice showed itself through the opinions of Fra Paolo Sarpi and its action in resisting interdict to be akin to Protestants at least in opposing the papacy. To this friendly enclave on the enemies' border, then, the traveller came for hospitality and protection. But though the chorus of praise rang on, implying that even the wars of Venice had been for the good of other countries, England was content to learn about her history through translations. The first original work was a by-product of the Civil War.

For Protestant opponents of Stuart claims to dispense with Parliament, Venice offered some convenient arguments. Here was a state strong enough to resist papal interference and whose ruler, the Doge, though at the peak of the constitution, was unable to dictate to it. Venice had not gone uncriticized. Wotton, as Ambassador, had seen the seamy side of oligarchic power and that the complexity of her institutions caused decisions sometimes to be made too late. But as yet there was no general mistrust. The imagination of story-tellers had not been awakened by fear of the powerful and secret council of ten to make Venice the scene of horrid crime and more frightful punishment. Members of Parliament went so far in 1644 as to ask the Venetian Ambassador for an account of his country's constitution, and it was to point out the pertinence of certain features in it that James Howell wrote in 1651 his *S.P.Q.V. A Survey of the Signorie of Venice, Of Her admired policy, and method of Government* and dedicated it to Parliament.

Apart from a glowing description of her constitution Howell commended Venice to the notice of Englishmen in other ways. He pointed out that as maritime and Christian powers they had common interests dating from the Crusades, and his history of the doges conveniently omits their commercial agreements with the Turks and customs barriers to English goods. He explained away 'the large conscience She hath under the Navill' as an infection from her neighbours, the Greeks and Turks. And in a later book he went so far as to claim for the Venetians that they alone in all Europe retained their public spirit and patriotism. This enthusiasm made Howell responsible, in part at least, for the content as well as the form of a book more famous than any of his own – Harrington's *Oceana* (1656) dedicated (the Long Parliament being demised) to Cromwell.

True to his precept that no man can be a politician unless he is first a historian or a traveller, Harrington went to Italy and read its history. In the first three pages of *Oceana*, the perfect state, he refers to the perfection of Venice and to Machiavelli as 'the onely Politician of later Ages'. Some of the features of the ideal commonwealth he describes, the ballot, indirect election and the separation of deliberating and assenting chambers, are Venetian, and the work was, in fact, criticized for copying a state 'where Popery ruleth and whoredom abounds'.

Florence aroused no interest that could compare with this

and inspired no history as full as Howell's of Venice. Something was known of her past through the popularity of Boccaccio, and Greene's *Farewell to Folly* (1591) was set in Florence when 'the state of Italie was pestered with the mutinous factions of the Guelphes and Ghibellines'. She was known too, as the home of Guicciardini and of Machiavelli, whose *Florentine History* was the first history of a single Italian state to be translated (1595). She even had her partisans. At the turn of the century when one writer, after assuming that his readers would be familiar with Venice, takes pains to tell them whereabouts Florence is on the map, another was exalting her as leading the world in policy, usually a claim reserved exclusively for Venice.

The Medici, too, drew attention to Florence by their patronage of the learned. And as it was culture rather than statecraft that enabled Italy to be seen as a unit and underlay the later conception of a specific Italian civilization at the dawn of modern times, the early mentions of the Medici have a particular interest. Cosimo and Lorenzo had been noticed by William Thomas, though primarily for their political virtue, and his account was expanded in a book designed for the stay-at-home reader, Samuel Lewkenor's *A Discourse Not Altogether Unprofitable, Nor Unpleasant for such as are desirous to know the situation and customes of forraine Cities without travelling to see them* (1600). He is chiefly concerned with university cities and Cosimo receives a glowing tribute for his beautifying Florence with churches and villas, and establishing the university by sending for Argyropoulos to teach Greek. Lorenzo was similarly praised for his consorting with philosophers and as a 'noble Mecænas and Patrone of the Muses'. The political life of both men is represented as blameless; by their sole rule they rescued Florence from the faults of an aristocracy.

The same judgment was passed by Robert Dallington, whose *Survey of The Great Dukes State of Tuscany. In the yeare of our Lord 1596* contained the fullest sketch of Florentine history. Following Guicciardini (as Lewkenor had followed Machiavelli and Thomas – in turn based on Machiavelli) he celebrates the glorious position of Florence after the lives of Cosimo and Lorenzo and contrasts it with the misuse of authority by the present Duke. Florentine liberty, itself so distrusted by those jealous of hard-won order, like Ascham, had gone, the Florentines degraded by its loss, and the punning moral was now *Qui sub Medici vivit, misere vivit.* Dallington's book had no successor, but for Rome there was not even a Dallington. William Thomas's list of Roman bishops remained the handiest guide. He had mentioned the Medici pope, Leo X, with only the barest hint of his services to learning; it was again Lewkenor, as the historian of universities, who emphasized his interest in ancient literature and his patronage of scholars, and he mentioned, too, the earlier humanist pope, Nicholas V, before whom 'never were letters held in so great veneration nor learned men so much honoured and esteemed'. All these various references to cultural activity in Italy were slow in being converted into a wider picture of intellectual life.

Distrust of the Italian character, fear of Italy's Church and contempt for her political disintegration prevented the Englishman from seeing how great a debt his culture owed to her. While it is difficult to think of a department of social and intellectual life that was uninfluenced by Italian example, it is still harder to find an acknowledgment of it. In the same spirit that Hoby described himself and his friends in Rome – when they 'had throwghlie searched owt such antiquities as were here to be seene from place to place . . . we thowght it but losse of time to make anie longer abode here', Philemon Holland, in his translation of Livy (1600) expected his reader to look back to the glories of Italy's past without a glance at her present civilization. Many, he warned, have been moved by reading this history to visit themselves the monuments of

Rome. 'The journie they have found, for way long and tedious; for expense of money heavie and chargable; for hazard of religion, conscience and good manners, exceeding dangerous: so farre degenerate are the inhabitants now from that auncient people, so devoute, so vertuous and uncorrupt, in old time.' And he printed, as an appendix, a topographical account of ancient Rome, to save his readers the pain and risk of leaving home.

The same note was sounded in Bishop Hall's *Quo Vadis? A Iust Censure of Travell* (1617). There are only three just causes of going abroad, for health, for commerce and for matters of state. But otherwise, why leave home? 'Here is that sweet peace which the rest of the world admires and envies: Here is that gracious and well-tempered government, which no Nation under heaven may dare offer to parallel: Here all liberall Arts raigne and triumph' – what good do we owe to others, and on the other hand 'what mischiefe have we amongst us that we have not borrowed?' This was the national self-complacence that enabled the Englishman to say with the old Antick in Ford's *Love's Sacrifice*:

O, Giacopo, Petrarch was a dunce, Dante a jig-maker,
Sannazzar a goose, and Ariosto a puck-fist, to me!

The first change towards the modern position was to come in a freak work by James Howell, lexicographer, poet, writer of *belles-lettres*, and Historiographer Royal to Charles II.

Howell was also a much-travelled man and perhaps the first to make a livelihood out of his reminiscences. He went to Italy in 1618 as steward of a London glass factory whose owner coveted the methods of Venice. Having hired workmen there, Howell continued on a familiar route: Padua–Bologna–Rome–Naples and back via Florence–Milan–Turin. In this way he accumulated the impressions that were to appear in one guise or another in work after work, for as he was in prison as a Royalist spy from 1642 to 1650 and stayed in England after that, most of his work was done behind bars at a distance from his favourite subject matter: the different characteristics of the European nations. His style, with its short sharp sentences, has caused him to be hailed as the father of modern prose, but his thought, his power of observation, is bound by the proverbial clichés he made his special study; if energy saves his prose from tedium it is with a margin too narrow to save his historical work from neglect.

Besides the work on Venice he attracted attention to Naples, translating an account of Masaniello's revolt and editing a general history of the kingdom. His *Instructions for Forreine Travell* (1642) covered Italy as well as France, Spain and Germany and was widely read. But his most interesting treatment of Italy was in a number of Philosophical Discourses, one of which, *A German Diet: Or, The Ballance of Europe* (1653), shows more originality than the others.

The plan of the book is simple. At a convention of German princes a topic is proposed for debate: which is the preeminent country in Europe; is it Germany or France, Spain, England, Poland, Hungary, or is it '*Italy*, the Popedom, Repub: of *Venice* &c.'? Each country is represented by two orators, one to exalt and one to denigrate. The advocate of Italy is the Lord Laurence von Wensin and his main theme is her cultural leadership. To defend this he marshals facts that had not before been brought together in a connected narrative; the darkness of barbarism which followed the decline of Rome being pierced for the first time by Urban IV who called Aquinas to teach; Clement V urging on the study of Hebrew, Chaldaic and Arabic; Nicholas V by whom 'choice Agents were sent all *Europe* over to fish for old Authors, to which end he gave them golden hooks, and large allowance'; Cosimo and Lorenzo de' Medici and the Florentine academy; the revival of civil law; the wakening of literature under Dante, Petrarch and Boccaccio; lastly, the wide patronage of Leo X. 'From his time it is incredible how all kinds of Sciences did reflourish in *Italy*, and consequently in all Countries else; for Italy may be call'd the *Source* or great *Cestern* whence all kinds of Vertues flow to the Europæan World.' His opponent, the Lord George Roelderer von Hoch, could retaliate only by saying that Italy had fallen from her former glories, and now taught nothing so well as vice; from Empress of Europe, she had fallen to being the Queen of Pleasures.

Criticism on these lines would continue, culled sometimes from Howell's own works which were not sparing in criticism of the modern Italian character. But Italy had at last been seen as the country where the arts and sciences reflourished after the middle age of darkness, and this process had been roughly tabulated. Future historians would argue about the relative importance of the different ages in this long period of recovery, reaching from the thirteenth to the sixteenth centuries, but in doing so, they would henceforward be thinking in terms of Italian civilization as a whole.

CHAPTER TWO

From Description to Speculation: mid–Seventeenth to Late Eighteenth Centuries

For a hundred years interest in Italian history remained uncritical, spasmodic and sensational. It dealt with dramatic events, real or legendary, relied to a great extent still on translations and reflected little on what it read. But quietly two revolutions were taking place; the Englishman's preoccupation with Venice yielded to an affection for Florence, and the idea grew that there had been a Great Age at the beginning of modern times. In contrast, the second half of the eighteenth century devoted itself to speculation; what constitutes a Great Age? what causes it? how does it affect the present? and when did it really happen?

The prejudices of the age of persecution continued with increased violence. Italians still poisoned with the smoke of a candle or with perfumed gloves; still popular among the sights of San Giovanni in Laterano was the porphyry commode through which each new pope since Joan underwent a final scrutiny; the subtlety of Italians, the compensation for their weakness, was still supreme; more ingenious were they than ever in the lusts of the flesh. A tone formerly reserved for scurrilous pamphlets pervaded the whole of Ferrand Spence's *The Secret History of the House of Medici* (1686), which he translated, apparently in good faith, from a French charlatan who nevertheless quoted a good deal of chapter and verse. Varillas, the author of the original, put a bibliography at the end of each chapter and protested in his preface that he had been at pains to discount the evidence of those who might have been partial, spiteful, or scandalous. This moderation was not carried into the text, or even the Contents. Here, for instance, is the synopsis of the Sixth Book:

'*Erasmus* the Astrologer, and *Ficino* the Philosopher, prognosticate that Cardinal *Medici* should be Pope, tho' not any appearance of it then. He is carried to *Rome* in a litter by reason of an Imposthume he had in a place that modesty forbids mentioning. He enters the Conclave. The Imposthume breaks and exhales such a stink, that th' old Cardinals fancy'd, upon the Relation of a brib'd Physician, that he will suddenly dye, and so leave off crossing his Election. A Dream of his Mother, which he remembers of himself, makes him take the name of Leo. He repairs his cousin *Giulio*'s defect of Birth, and gives him his Cap. *Massimiliano Sforza* falls distracted, and puts it into *Leo's* head, to make his brother *Giuliano* Duke of *Milan*; but is deluded by *Fregossa*, who accommodates himself with the *French*. *Giuliano* dies, young *Lorenzo* succeeds him, and does not resemble him. The French pass the Alpes. The Pope's afraid, and sends them an Agent, who falls into the hands of the *Spaniards*, and makes 'em jealous. The Pope stops the progress of the Conquerours, by his interview with *Francis* the First at Bologna, where he paulmes upon the sincerity of that Prince. He despoils the Duke of *Urbin*, who recovers his State. The pope debauches that Duke's principal Officers, he prevents them, and causes their Souldiers to punish them. *Leo*, tho' indebted for the Popedom to Cardinal *Petrucci*, drives his House out of *Sienna*. The Cardinal conspires against him, is discover'd and strangled in a Dungeon, by an Æthiopian. A strange Conference of Cardinal *Cornetan* with a Magician, who tells him nothing but the Truth, and yet deludes him. The Sacred Colledge is animated against the Pope, who, out of spight, creates one and thirty Cardinals in one day; but the greatest Enemy of his House happens to be of the number. He frames a

League against the *French*, and, beyond all Hope, drives them out of *Italy*, but in the very moment he receives the Tydings, *Malespina* poysons him with Pills. The Rats eat off his Nose the Night following, by having but one servant left with him, who falls asleep.'

The even more promising domestic material of the Borgias was not long in being exploited. Already in 1669 Aglionby had warned readers of his *History of the Popes Nephews* that it was the sort of thing they should read in private and even greater scandalous promise was held out by Alexander Gordon's *Lives of Pope Alexander VI and his son Caesar Borgia* (1729). This folio volume, with an appendix of extracts from sources amounting to some hundred pages, was the first large-scale biography of an Italian by an Englishman. His authorities were the standard ones, Guicciardini, Burchard, Platina, Machiavelli and Bembo, and he pointed out that lest he should be accused of anti-Catholic bias, he had described the Court of Rome exclusively in the words of Catholic writers. But to this show of scholarship is added an approach that was to become drearily familiar, that of the missionary muck-raker. It is the duty of the historian, he feels, to show the evil of the past so that it can be avoided by the present. ' 'Tis on this Account that in the following sheets I am, with the utmost Fidelity and Truth, to present the Publick with a View of such Things as may make the World blush at the Pravity of Human Nature, and tremble, when they'll see such horrid impieties had ever possessed the Heart of Man.' Inside his *cabinet noir*, he warns, there lies 'the abominable Fruit of Murder, Rapine, Incest'. There is Lucretia, 'as famous for Lewdness, as the Roman Lucretia for Chastity', and Cesare, 'notorious for duplicated Fratricide and Incest with his own Sister'. Some passages will be too horrible to hear – so they will be left in Latin, a language familiar to most of his readers. It is a combination of things serious and salacious, high thought and low intent that long continued to mark a certain class of writing about the Renaissance, and that soon lost the excuse of real danger and useful warning.

For a while to write or translate a work dealing with the history of an Italian state other than Venice required an excuse, usually a parallel with English politics. James Crauford wrote a history of the house of Este to flatter the Duchess of Albany, Mary of Este, and to draw the moral that a race cannot flourish without patronage.

The learned court of Ferrara, basking in the patronage of its enlightened dukes, was contrasted with Scotland unfriended, languishing in virtue, her muses barren. Albany's Scotland, it was hinted, could flourish like Borso d'Este's Ferrara, if the lead were given. An account of Luigi Fiesco's unsuccessful revolt against the doge of Genoa was translated because it resembled the Glorious Revolution. It was dedicated to Queen Mary as an illustration of the truth 'that Providence seldom (I might say, never) fails even at the last Critical Instant to rescue an Established and well Administered Government from the Tyrannical Yoke of a Foreign Invader, or a Rebellious Subject' – references to the French invasion recently broken at La Hague and to the assumed treachery of Marlborough. And in 1729 an account of the Neapolitan Masaniello's bloody rising against excessive taxation was used to support the thesis that Heaven sees that avaricious ministers get the punishment they deserve.

The serious study of Italian literature, too, was in decline. The language was still learned for the purposes of the Grand Tour, and the introduction of the Italian opera from 1674 gave it an added, if frivolous, popularity. But the spate of publications was over; it was difficult even to find workmen who could set up Italian print, and the growing cult of correctness in the arts led to the neglect of incorrect authors like Petrarch and confirmed the neglect of Dante. This neglect, dating from the middle of the seventeenth century, was not to be countered until a taste for our own incorrect poets,

Chaucer and Spenser, revived in the second half of the eighteenth century along with the discovery of Italian influence in their work. And though more poetry was written about Italy than previously, it was of poor quality, concerned with ruins, melancholy and glories of the classical past, and all was vague, nothing was seen intensely. In fact, one period of discovery had passed, the next not yet arrived. Italy had fascinated and was again to inspire, but for a hundred years she was taken for granted.

Interest in Venice remained high for some time after the Restoration. Between 1668 and 1672 no fewer than ten books were published which were concerned in some way with her constitution. Travellers continued to mention its outstanding features, like the ballot box and the tortuously careful method of electing the doge, and in the most popular travel book of its day, Richard Lassels's *The Voyage of Italy* (1670), Venice is the only state whose government is described at all. Sarpi's reputation grew until he was hailed as the greatest genius of his age, or since antiquity – so Temple went so far as to suggest. As late as 1738 Johnson was recommending Sarpi's history of the Council of Trent as a work 'in which the Reader finds *Liberty without Licentiousness, Piety without Hypocrisy, Freedom of Speech without Neglect of Decency, Severity without Rigour, and extensive Learning without Ostentation*', and he was on the point of translating it when he discovered that, by a bizarre coincidence, another Samuel Johnson, librarian of St Martin-in-the-Fields, had the same intent. In the altercation that followed this discovery, their common project died. Even stronger was the influence of Venice across the Atlantic, where the constitutional plans for Pennsylvania, Carolina and New Jersey incorporated features that William Penn had admired either in the Venetian government itself or in Harrington's version of it.

These successes conceal the change that had taken place. By the end of the seventeenth century Englishmen had either lost interest in a state whose prosperity was so obviously declining, or were reading, not the optimistic works of the previous century, but the hostile descriptions that followed Venice's brush with the Papacy. It was the tyranny, the interference with personal liberty that was stressed now, the secrecy and guile. A handbook of unscrupulous political maxims was published under the name, not of Machiavelli, but of Sarpi. Whereas Jonson had portrayed a vicious society subject to upright justice, Otway, basing his *Venice Preserved* (1682) on an anti-Venetian account of the conspiracy he describes, shows a society vicious from top to bottom, where liberty and impartial justice alike are unattainable. The impassioned praise of earlier travellers who addressed the inviolable virgin of the sea as something alive became a quieter tribute to the beauties of something dying. Picturesque, an emporium of pleasures, she remained, but so swiftly was her history and its examples forgotten that a mid-eighteenth-century writer could comment that 'not a syllable of the history of the republic is to be met with in the language of this country'.

Gay, beautiful, inviolate, guardian of liberty and of public order – the attractions of Venice were too great for another Italian state to succeed her quickly in representing what Englishmen most valued in Italian civilization. There was long hesitation before their allegiance, hesitating between Naples and Florence, turned to the latter.

The social life of Florence was industrious rather than gay. Her beauty, certainly, had never been denied, but there went with it a massiveness, a severity that smacked distastefully of feudalism. One of the most valued characteristics of Venice was that she had never been successfully invaded: 'unravished', 'maiden', 'chaste', these were the favourite epithets of her panegyrists. Florence, on the other hand, had seen many revolutions, and her present rulers were themselves in power as a result of foreign conquest. As for liberty, the reputation of Venice was dead; it had depended on a particular view of her constitution, and did not survive a different view even as a legend. But before Florence could take her place, the great republican age of her mediæval liberties would have to be disinterred, a task that the eighteenth century did not seriously attempt. It was as nourisher of arts that Florence was to take the lead in a century more interested in art than in constitutions, in the Medici than the Doges.

Mentions of the Medici in the seventeenth century had concentrated on Leo X and Rome, with the result that Pope, in the *Essay on Criticism* (1711), made him responsible for a general revival of the arts.

> But see! each Muse in LEO's golden days,
> Starts from her trance and trims her wither'd bays,
> Rome's ancient Genius, o'er its ruins spread,
> Shakes off the dust, and rears his rev'rend head.
> Then Sculpture and her sister arts revive;
> Stones leap'd to form, and rocks began to live;
> With sweeter notes each rising Temple rung;
> A Raphael painted, and a Vida sung.

Not till 1755 was an Englishman sufficiently interested in the Florentine Medici to propose writing a history of the city under their rule.

The proposal was made by John, Earl of Cork and Orrery, when, in the course of a tour, he was kept prisoner in Florence by gout. He passed the time in reading Machiavelli, Varchi, Segni and Scipio Ammirato and with their aid writing his history, bringing it, at least in epitome, down to 1510. It was never published but to judge from the tone of his *Letters from Italy in the years 1754 and 1755* (1773), he probably did little to break away from the bad tradition of sensationalism. It was in this direction that his tastes lay. The letters included some of the most famous Italian scandals, the story of Bianca

Capello, for instance, and his impressions of the city reflect his study of a period chiefly attractive to him for its violent contrasts of good and evil. To the student of the Pazzi conspiracy, when Giuliano was killed and Lorenzo wounded in the Duomo, the Cathedral was 'a vast gloomy vault, fit for assassinations and deeds of horror'. And his description of the Palazzo Vecchio echoes the awful fascination of the story of how Vasari was witness from his scaffold of the incest of Duke Cosimo and his daughter Isabella. He presents, nevertheless, an age whose interest in Florence was to be as intense as that of an earlier one had been in Venice.

By this time, too, had come the idea that modern Europe awoke with a Great Age, many of whose characteristics were Italian. The feature of this age earliest dwelt on was the restoration of learning to a world grown ignorant, as sketched by Sir William Temple in his *Essay upon the Ancient and Modern Learning* (1690). When the Turks took Constantinople, he declared, many of the refugee Greeks fled to Italy with books under their arms and settled down to teach their language and to reveal a literature hitherto lost. They were patronized by princes and 'Thus began the Restoration of Learning in these parts'. The age of accomplishment was a short one, for, starting some two hundred years previously, 'the Arts of Painting and Statuary began to revive with Learning in *Europe*, and made a great but short Flight; so as for these last hundred years we have not had One Master in either of them, who deserved a Rank with those that flourished in that short Period after they began among us'. This notion of an age of cultural revival, 1450–1550, was by no means generally held as yet. The historians of art talked of a revival in 1250 if they followed Vasari, around 1500 if they thought in terms of the painting they actually admired, but the political historian was not yet thinking in periods. When he came to, much of his work had been done by historians of the arts.

A fuller picture of revival was given by John Breval, who

had travelled widely in Italy during the 1720s. A scholar, deprived of his fellowship at Trinity, Cambridge, for an intrigue with a married woman, his subsequent career as professional soldier and free-lance journalist left his interests in the history and arts of the countries he visited wide and thorough. He made a visit to Milan the excuse for writing the longest account of its history from the beginning of Visconti rule that had appeared in English; Florence attracted him to the Medici, especially to Lorenzo, whom he revered more than Leo. He subscribed to Temple's opinion of the significance of the Constantinopolitan exodus, but added, in deference to Vasari, that the arts had shown some signs of reviving before that city's capture by the Turks. 'The Mist of the Monkish Ignorance was not, however, intirely dispers'd till about the middle of the Fifteenth Century; when what had been only a *Dawn* of *Taste* hitherto, blaz'd out in the full Lustre of the *Augustan* Times, under the Auspices of *Laurence* of *Medici*.' Lorenzo patronized learned Greeks like Lascaris and Chalcondylas and collected classical works of art, and it was upon the glimpses thus given them of the beauties of antiquity that the styles of Raphael and Michelangelo were formed, and through them, of all painting of excellence since. Breval was not concerned with disparaging Modern, as opposed to Ancient, achievement, and gives no hint of decline in the sixteenth century.

Fuller still was Gordon, who began his life of Alexander VI with a brief view of the age. 'Certain it is, that no period of Time, since the Decay of the *Roman* Empire, has been so auspicious for good and remarkable Events, as that some Years before, and during the whole Sixteenth Century.' In proof he did not simply quote the fall of Constantinople and the influx of learned Greeks, though he mentioned them together with the revival of literature, but he added the invention of printing, the wider horizons opened by the discovery of the New World and the fortunate coincidence that there were, to take advantage of all this, more men of genius living than at any time since the Augustan Age. It was, moreover, the age of 'the Ballance of Power in Italy'. In spite of this catalogue, there is no suggestion that these inventions, discoveries, political revolutions had any effect on man's outlook. The world had been discovered, but the discovery of man had to wait for the Reformation, when at last ignorance and deceit yielded to knowledge.

Gordon was able to find more contributing factors to shape his new Augustan age, and to bring them all into the period 1450–1550 because he was not primarily interested in the arts. To mention Dante, Petrarch and Boccaccio or Cimabue and Giotto is to involve at least a preliminary stirring or false dawn; the new age was to be defined far more simply by dating the revival of literature from 1453, ignoring painting, and concentrating on the balance of power, first exemplified in Charles VIII's invasion of Italy in 1494, and on the Reformation.

The consolidator of these faint formulæ, Bolingbroke, was also more concerned with politics and religion than with the arts. Moreover, he believed, with his contemporaries, that history was only of importance when it directly concerned the present. To read the story of ages which were fundamentally unlike our own was an affectation if pursued too seriously; history was philosophy in action, but the action should run continuously into our own. It was in the interest of the historian to feel back along the thread of action till there was a break, and call this the beginning of modern history, even if the break from some points of view, the arts, for instance, was only a fracture.

'The end of the fifteenth century', he wrote in his *Letters on the Study and Use of History* (1752), 'seems to be just such a period as I have been describing, for those who live in the eighteenth, and who inhabit the western parts of Europe. A little before, or a little after this point of time, all those events

happened, and all those revolutions began, that have produced so vast a change in the manners, customs, and interests
of particular nations, and in the whole policy ecclesiastic and
civil of these parts of the world.'

The religious revolution had begun forty or fifty years
before the Reformation, when printing and the exodus
hastened on the resurrection of letters – a process of enlightenment which was hastened by the popes themselves who
patronized the learning soon to be turned against them, and,
by the immorality of their lives, provided it with ruinous
argument. In civil life the change had been prepared by the
growing centralization of the monarchy and national unity,
processes which produced another hallmark of modernity,
the notion of the balance of power. This, the first period of
modern history, Bolingbroke saw as coming to a close at the
end of the sixteenth century. The crucial generation was that
of the Reformation, and because the idea of starting modern
history with a generation fertile in great men, an Augustan
age, was a popular one, the historians enlisted the heroes of
contemporary taste and set at the beginning of modern times
the generation of Raphael, Michelangelo and Luther; the age
of Leo X.

As yet there was no hint of the speculations that were to fill
the writings on this period in the second half of the eighteenth
century: on the relation between wealth and culture, between
the revival of learning and the Reformation, or sociological
explanations of the causes of either. If Hume had had less
contempt for Italian politics and literature and been less jealous of its art, had not, in fact, despised the race, speculation
might have come sooner. One of his *Essays Moral and Political*
(1741–2) was entitled 'Of the *Rise* and *Progress* of the *Arts*
and *Sciences*'. In it he made two propositions: that the arts
and sciences can only flourish under a free government, and
that nothing stimulates the growth of manners and learning
so much as a number of neighbouring independent states

connected by commercial and political interests. Both apply directly to Italy, but he restricts his argument exclusively to the culture of the Greek city states, and takes no single example from those of Italy. There was, too, very little information available to the English reader about the Italian middle ages except in translations like Machiavelli's *Florentine History*. Largely repetitive and second-hand, English historians of Italy still had little material to offer a generation to whom speculation on cause and effect in history was to become a habit.

No one in England attempted the astonishing experiment of the Frenchman, Saint-Marc, who turned historian in 1761 with the first of six thick volumes of tiny print, the *Abrégé Chronologique de L'Historie Générale d'Italie*. The subject being little known, he decided to treat it in detail, and it is hard to believe that when he died before reaching the year 1315 it was not as a victim of his own conscientiousness. For in order to keep the stories of the Italian states distinct, as well as that of the Empire and of cultural events, he wrote them between parallel lines. This involved as many as seven margins running down the page with the effect of a nightmare Old Testament in which duplicated strips of references have encroached upon and finally banished the text. But in the first two years of Saint-Marc's fantastic task England produced her own General History of Italy, in the shape of five volumes in *The Modern Part of an Universal History*.

The *Universal History*, an attempt to gather all historical knowledge since the flood into one great work, was England's most dramatic tribute to the confident encyclopaedic temper of the Enlightenment. Its aim and its influence (in America, for instance, where the account of Venice guided the Founding Fathers to incorporate features from the constitution of that state in their own) were more impressive, perhaps, than its actual merit. In the accounts of some countries legend and fact lay side by side, some of the authors were of doubtful honesty, and, paid by the sheet, were suspected of padding for profit. But the space given to Italy was unprecedented and these volumes were the first to depend on the crucial collections of sources by Muratori, of which the most important, the *Rerum Italicarum Scriptores*, was published between 1723–38.

The tone of the work was that of the Enlightenment, optimistic, with a strong belief in progress and the power of science to perfect mankind, a rational approach to religion, a liberal one to politics. Wealth had brought refinement – and the authors stressed the rise of paper credit in Florence, the improvement of coinage, the elaboration of commerce, with a novel emphasis on economic matters. The Florentines had improved on the political lessons of the Romans, their exemplars, too, and the notion of progress was applied equally to the arts, though so academically as to make of Duke Cosimo I a greater patron than any prince of comparable revenue either since his day or before; greater than Lorenzo, even greater than the first Cosimo. The arts had then been in their infancy, the patron had poor material to encourage, and since by the sixteenth they had come to their full height and a patron is as great as the thing he patronizes, it is of the first grand duke of Florence that 'it would not be too bold to say, that he raised them higher than they had been since the *Augustan* age'.

'Progress' in religion meant progress from the superstitions that marred the last days of the Empire to a rational Protestant faith. There was no marked anti-clericalism, the faults of the papacy were pointed out without emphasis. Condemnation was saved for fanaticism, not for wickedness. Alexander VI was mildly blamed, but nothing qualified the damaging account of Savonarola as a mad and irresponsible enthusiast. Similarly, progress in politics meant a movement away from the tyranny of the emperors. States were judged by how much liberty their constitutions had allowed and still retained.

The government of Venice was described and praised (anachronously) for its stability, the swiftness of its justice, the experience of its senators, the methods of election; but when the description is over, and Harrington, Paruta and Howell laid aside, the conclusion is that in spite of these advantages, 'the excellences of the Venetian constitution are weighed down by faults of so gross and enormous a nature, as one would think less tolerable than the most despotic and absolute monarchy'. This is because of the interference by the state inquisition with the subject's liberty.

The five volumes constituted the most extensive survey of Italian general history yet made in English, and it remains the longest. Yet for all its size and the novelty of much of its material, it was a purely descriptive work apart from occasional reflections on the themes of progress and liberty. Massive and elementary, it was already old fashioned when it first appeared among the philosophizing small fry who came to it, nevertheless, for supply. It contained no echo of Bolingbroke's Period. The Florentines under Lorenzo were compared to the Athenians and the reign of Leo (as well as that of Cosimo I) to that of Augustus; the balance of power was mentioned, the lives of the Reformation popes outlined, but no generalization was hazarded; in no case were details from the steady flow of narrative selected to show the special character of a certain century, nor were ideas used to explain or correlate events. In the succession of lives of the popes, for instance, there was no suggestion that the course of the Reformation was in any way shaped by the revival of learning, nor that the popes of the late fifteenth and early sixteenth centuries had many problems in common. Their lives were treated just as the narrative treated those of the fourteenth century and when the Reformation came it was the result of one action by one man, the granting of Indulgences by Leo X.

The theme of liberty, too, was unvaried by speculation,

though the unprecedented space given to the middle ages, the time when Italian liberties were most strenuous, caused a number of contradictions to emerge that called for comment but received none. The result was a reference to 'Venetian liberty, if a people groaning under the tyranny of . . . a triumvirate can be said to enjoy liberty', or more serious uncertainties such as the effect of Medici rule; it had destroyed liberty, and it had made Florence great and creative, yet true greatness and creative power were the prerogatives of free peoples. No attempt was made to solve the dilemma set by Florence being greatest precisely when she was least free and the two statements were allowed to drift side by side.

If the *Universal History* did not speculate it did leave Florence supreme. The volume devoted to it was fuller and more vividly written than any other, and the histories of other states were deliberately made subordinate to that of Florence where there might have been duplication; Italian diplomacy was told in terms of Florentine statesmen. 'The elevated genius of the *Florentine* government' was set above that of Venice; Florence stood for liberty, and in Italian history Venice was treated as an exception, and not an admirable one. Voltaire's comparison of the Florentines with the Athenians was quoted; they were praised for their political energy and their lack of superstition. Florence under Lorenzo was the centre of arts, the peninsula's treasury, the pivot of the balance of power. It was she who was the commercial pioneer: 'Every page of the *Florentine* history produces instances of the glory attending the encouragement of commerce among a free people.' It was she, and not Venice, who cared only for herself, who saved Italy from being subject to one overgrown state. Florence gained even more from a study of her history in the fourteenth century than Venice lost through the study of hers in the seventeenth.

Travellers who had looked into the *Universal History* took with them no taste for the middle ages and discovered no new interest in cities whose monuments were Gothic rather than Palladian. The route Bologna–Perugia–Assisi and down to the main Ancona–Rome road remained a quiet one. Goethe took it, but for almost all eighteenth-century Englishmen, Italy remained the familiar Italy of the Tour, loved for fashion's sake and as the finest museum in the world. One of the exceptions, Sir Richard Colt Hoare of Stourbridge, wrote of his travels, towards the end of the century: 'A love for drawing and literature, induced me to visit this once happy and enlightened country; and a desire of examining the less-frequented and most picturesque provinces, obliged me to search for more detailed and satisfactory information than could be found in the usual track of modern tour-writers.'

Along the track there were some changes in the popularity of particular cities. The social life of Verona had become gayer, more tourists went to Vicenza for Palladio's works; Padua no longer attracted English students and was falling into a decay only little better than that of Pisa, where cattle grazed the weedy streets: Parma attracted large numbers to its gaiety and its Correggios, it was among the most popular of the smaller cities; Bologna's university still flourished, and a visit to the works of the great eclectics, the Caracci, and Guido Reni made the city, with its cultured and hospitable people, a crowded one; Naples became more visited than ever when the latter half of the century brought the hospitality of Sir William Hamilton as British Envoy, and the addition of Pompeii to the list of classical excursions; Ravenna was noticed at some length by Breval and even by more orthodox guides like Nugent's *Grand Tour*, but it was usually passed by as it had been before. Florence and Venice were obligatory as, of course, was Rome. With Greece in the hands of the Turks, Sicily scarcely visited and the classical monuments of Africa and Asia Minor buried in sand and scrub, Rome stood for the sum of Antique Art, both Greek and Roman. The city, besides, catered particularly well for Englishmen; things English were fashionable there and the traveller was made to feel at home. The south, apart from Naples and its environs, remained the source of dissuasive tales like this of Breval's: 'Near Cape *Palinure* we met with a Landlord that upon our disputing a Reckoning, barricadoed himself up in one Part of his House, that had been the Tower of an old Castle, and was preparing to fire at us from certain Loop-holes made on Purpose, if we had not been apprized of the Danger, and made haste to our Boat.'

Bad inns were no prerogative of the south, nor bad roads. Even the main roads were masses of ruts, and rain could make them impassable, but, lacking as they were, they were still preferable to the tracks leading off the frequented ways, and lack of recognizable comforts continued to keep travellers to the main routes. As it was almost obligatory to keep a record of one's journey, and fashionable to publish it, by the 'sixties there was a glut of accounts that could hardly avoid being stale and repetitious. Italy seemed to be exhausted as a source of interest and anti-Italian feeling began again to show itself. Travel there, it was claimed, was a penance rather than a pleasure, the Italians themselves were no better than slaves and barbarians; the *Critical Review*, in particular, seized on works that showed Italy in a bad light and acclaimed them. A book like Smollett's highly critical *Travels* (1766), it exulted, 'does more service to Great Britain than fifty acts of Parliament for . . . forbidding the exportation of foods, fops and coxcombs'. But the number of travellers remained as great as ever and though they saw little their ancestors had not seen, and brought no novel aspect of the Italian past to the notice of historians (as travellers in the next century were to encourage historians to write the stories of the newly popular mediæval cities), it was against a background of continued interest in Italy that the speculations of the 'fifties and 'seventies flourished.

Bolingbroke's location of the first great age of modern history was for a time unchallenged. Literary taste still concentrated on the sixteenth century, Tasso, Ariosto, and on Metastasio. Dante was only translated, and then in part, in 1785. The idea of the balance of power as the hallmark of modern times focused attention at the beginning of the sixteenth century, when Italy was the battleground of armies exemplifying this doctrine for the first time. And the Constantinopolitan exodus, together with the invention of printing, stood firmly at the period's beginning. From Temple's time the exodus had its supporters; they remained even when Hody had proved the existence of a vigorous cultivation of the classics well before 1453. They were not only men of letters, like Johnson, whose life of Ascham (1763) attributed the intellectual revolution of his subject's day to these two causes, but professional historians. Mosheim, whose influential *Ecclesiastical History* was translated in 1765, had read Hody and followed him in his account of the intellectual life of the fourteenth century, but this did not prevent his portraying the fall of Constantinople in terms that seem to make it the sole efficient factor in the subsequent revolution. The *Critical Review* accepted the convention for reasons of its own; it proved the worthlessness of the Italians, 'for had not their neighbours the Greeks been driven by the Turkish arms and conquests into Italy, and brought with them the only property they had left, that of books and knowledge, the Italians might have remained as illiterate and barbarous, as the nations to whom they were so liberal of these epithets'.

Much of this attention paid to Italy as the home of the revival of learning and the Reformation and the first battleground of the balance of power was quite remote from interest in that country itself. The character of Italian society was not used to add a flavour to Bolingbroke's period, which was concerned solely with the great events that affected Europe at large. It was still possible for historians of manners in the 'sixties and 'seventies to write chapters headed 'Progress and Effects of Luxury', or 'Of the Corruption incident to Polished Nations', without giving any illustrations from Italy at all.

As taste in history came to ask increasingly for explanations as well as descriptions of phenomena, the neat limits of an age, 1450–1550, became blurred at the same time that attention was forced ever more surely upon Italy, where not only great events, but the antecedents of those events were to be marked.

Already the creed was formed, natural to an increasingly industrialized country, that civilization depended on a taste for luxuries. Man's instinctive needs were simple, he did not have to apply to their satisfaction the extra effort on which alone improvement can be based, but until he did, he remained in a state of mental torpor and physical barbarism. In the next century the thesis was to accompany the doctrine of colonial expansion; for the present it was useful for explaining the civilization of the sixteenth century.

It had been suggested in general terms in one of Lord Lyttelton's *Dialogues of the Dead* (1760) – a series of imaginary conversations between illustrious shades. As dialogues they are uninteresting, as each character is entirely absorbed in waiting for opportunities to state his own case, but one, between Pericles and Cosimo de' Medici, names often coupled now the parallel between Athens and Florence had been established, launched a train of thought that was to become obsessional. Pericles, in giving his companion a cue for his next monologue, says: 'The Commerce which you carried on in all parts of the World, even while you were placed at the helm of the State, enabled you to do those liberal Acts, which rendered your name so illustrious, and endeared you so much to the People of Florence.' Commerce enabled patronage to foster the arts. But Pericles goes on to deny what was to be the second component of the fashionable sociological explanation of Italian, and any other culture, by

declaring: 'Your excessive Liberalities to the indigent Citizens, and the great Sums you lent to all the noble Families,
did in reality *buy* the Republic of Florence, and gave your
Family such a Power, as enabled them to convert it from a
Popular State into an absolute Government.' It is the dilemma
of the author of the Florentine volume of the *Universal History*: The Medici were despots, and the arts can only flourish
in liberty. Money and a rising middle class were the sociological keys to understanding culture, and the Medici used one
to destroy the other. Henceforth historians were forced either
to interpret Medici rule more favourably or pass over the
inconsistency as glibly as possible: the thesis itself was too
deeply rooted in the political and economic state of the nation
to bend.

The necessary facts relating to the mediæval period were
supplied in 1764 by Adam Anderson's *An Historical and
Chronological Deduction of the Origin of Commerce*, and five
years later Robertson, in his *History of the Reign of the Emperor
Charles V*, gave the issue a broad and judicious stare. The
work began with a preliminary section, 'A view of the Progress of Society in Europe, from the Subversion of the
Roman Empire, to the beginning of the Sixteenth Century',
that attempted to explain the sixteenth in terms of the previous centuries. He saw that the splendours of his period –
and foreign history should only concern itself with splendours
– owed their nature to the past, to the generally despised
middle ages.

The pattern was simple and appeared sound. Light began
to shine with the Crusades. They led to intercourse between
east and west in which the pachydermatous crusader was
seduced by eastern softness. Commerce sprang up to cater
for the taste for luxuries with which he returned. Towns
became rich and began to break their feudal bonds. In this
they were aided by rulers who needed their support and had,
in exchange, to give them some say in government. The

advantage was mutual. Nations became richer, could afford great armies, and from their struggles evolved the principle of modern statecraft, the balance of power, in terms of which Charles V was to fight and intrigue. And it was Italy, with her growing commercial power in the twelfth and thirteenth centuries, with her merchants who 'became the carriers, the manufacturers, and the bankers of all Europe' who contributed most. Robertson had nothing to say about learning and was scarcely concerned with Medicean rule, but he made the classical statement of the view that modern civilization was formed by a taste for luxuries fostered by the Italian cities, and a few years later his exposition was adopted and strengthened by Adam Smith.

While preoccupation with mediæval commerce was eroding the earlier limit of the First Period of modern history, another speculation was attacking the later: did the awakening, the opening of the mind to speculation of a modern cast, come before or after the Reformation? There was no doubt that the revival of letters came first. Hody's opening words settled that: 'Felici illo secolo, nempe xiv ab orbe redempto, quo renasci in Italia coeperunt literae amoeniores, expolirique incepit lingua Latina, quae jam diu in barbariem abierat, illucentibus ingeniis Dantis, Petrarchae, et Boccatii; eodem quoque, et in eadem regione, riviviscere coeperunt literae Graecae, quae multis jam seculis intermortuae per totum Occidentem jacuerant.' But did this fourteenth-century rebirth, or even the quickened tempo that followed the discovery of printing and the exodus amount to an enlightenment? Had the time come, properly to be called the beginning of modern times, when 'men roused from that lethargy in which they had so long sleeped, began to call in question the most ancient and most received opinions', when their minds, 'somewhat awakened from a profound sleep of so many centuries, were prepared for every novelty'? Not necessarily, for Hume in these phrases is referring to the Reformation. The battle between Ancients and Moderns had been decided in favour of modern progress. The revival of literature had simply reacquainted the west with the classics; the breaking of superstition in the sixteenth century freed inquiry and launched the modern scientific method.

The protestant historian used the word 'ignorant' with a religious bias. Modern times began with the destruction of ignorance, but not the ignorance of ancient literature – whose recovery, after all, was largely aided by the popes. Ignorance was equated with mediæval catholicism. When the foundations of this were challenged, and only then, could the fetters on men's minds be snapped and enlightenment come. The great ferment of intellectual life followed, and could not precede the Reformation. Even literature, according to Goldsmith, benefited from the wider horizons of this time.

This literary point was challenged, but the main argument widely sustained. It drew the attention of those who followed this path to the origins of modern history no further back than to the Reformation and its consequences. The argument, that religious conflict leads to intellectual freedom, was too general to be conclusive, and this was shown as early as 1785 by a remarkable work, *A Translation of the Inferno of Dante Alighieri, in English Verse. With Historical Notes, and the Life of Dante*. By Henry Boyd, A.M. In the 'Life' Boyd used this very argument to prove that intellectual ferment began not in the sixteenth but in the thirteenth century. It was the religious conflicts and the political rivalries of that epoch that produced the revival of learning and of the arts. He ignored those who took the Reformation as a starting point, and mocked those who fixed it at the exodus. 'Long before the taking of *Constantinople* by the *Turks*, which is looked upon as the common era of the revival of learning, she (Italy), like another *Athens*, saw the arts revive in the lap of liberty.' Not Leo and Luther, but the Guelphs and Ghibellines headed the pedigree of the modern mind. And Boyd had been anticipated by a work that placed the awakening at an even earlier period. Mrs Susannah Dobson, in the preface to her translation of Saint-Pelaie's *The Literary History of the Troubadours* (1779) took her own period, that of the Crusades, as the crucial one. This time it was the conflict between Empire and Papacy from the pontificate of Gregory VII which 'excited a general kind of fermentation, which opened, as it were, the faculties of the soul'. The Crusades produced 'new sensations, new ideas, new tastes', and with this advantage 'The Troubadours awakened Europe from its ignorance and lethargy: they reanimated the minds of men; and, by amusing, they led them to think, to reflect, and to judge.' All before the birth of Dante.

In these two instances it was the search for the seminal religious, or politico-religious conflict that took the writers into the middle ages. Usually the motive was different and had nothing to do with the relationship between religion and enlightenment. As soon as the causative nature of the middle ages was grasped, when it was seen that in some respects they stood in direct relation to modern behaviour, both private and public, they became, in due proportion, the care of the historian as well as the antiquarian. One manifestation of this was an interest in origins, which in art produced the Gothic revival, in national history a sudden leap into the past, clean back to the Norsemen and the Celts, in science and to a lesser extent in literature that went as far back as the Saracens. Anderson had praised them as the inventors of algebra, the improvers of astronomy, the importers of chemistry into Europe. They were praised by Adam Smith for their translations of classical authors, the sole means of keeping some of them alive; they played an important part in stimulating intellectual revival 'long before the Greek fugitives from Constantinople promoted a taste for eloquence and the *belles-lettres*', as schoolboys were already being told in the 'eighties. The middle ages, in fact, as the course of science, commerce, an energetic middle class, literature, religious conflict and intellectual curiosity drew off from the Italy of Bolingbroke's period the prestige it had gained as the source of modern civilization; the source was now seen either to have been before the Exodus or after the Reformation; Italy between these dates stood fair to be ignored.

William Russell's *History of Modern Europe* (1779) shows what was happening. It was written ostensibly 'In a series of letters from a nobleman to his son', but Russell, the self-educated son of a small Scottish farmer, confessed that he had adopted the character of nobleman and father simply to give weight to his reflections. He was concerned particularly with the progress of society (as potent a source of useful maxims for a son as the political history of nations) and pre-sented it as follows. First come the Crusades. These stimulate trade and, consequently, civic life. Especially true is this of the Italian cities, and 'the establishment of these communities may be considered as the first great step towards civilization in modern Europe'. The next point he made was a novel one, that the revived study of Roman Law in the thirteenth century led to a study of letters and of a variety of sciences useful in its interpretation; law became a respected profession along-side that of arms, which meant added prestige for the arts of peace. Thus was begun an 'ardent though mistaken' spirit of inquiry. Art was revived in Italy at the same time, and litera-ture, too, though the impulse came to Dante and Petrarch through the troubadours of Provence. By the fourteenth cen-tury there was a civilization not only intellectual, but elegant. And having made these points he has nothing more to say about Italian literature until Tasso, or politics until the in-vasion of Charles VIII. The Medici are not even mentioned. By their assumption of power the story of Italy's contribution to modern civilization is already closed.

The idea of a great age that began with the taking of Constantinople, and in the following three or four genera-tions freed Europe from ignorance and superstition, having

appealed for a while to original minds, declined into the textbooks, where stubbornly it lives on. At the beginning of
the 'eighties Alexander Tytler told his students at Edinburgh
University that learning and the arts began to be widely diffused in the fifteenth century, thanks to the dispersal of the
Greeks in 1453. A few years later Joseph Priestley told his
pupils at Warrington Academy that they should fix their
attention on the end of the fifteenth century as 'particularly
illustrious, and more distinguishable, as *a period*, than any
other in the whole course of history; according to the ideas
of Bolingbroke', because about this time 'happened the taking
of Constantinople by the Turks, which was attended with
the flight of several men of learning into Italy, who promoted the
revival of letters in Europe', and 'at this time politeness and
humanity are improved to such a degree as distinguishes the
present race of Europeans from their ancestors, almost as
much as men in general are distinguished from brute beasts'.
'*Felix qui potuit rerum cognoscere causas*,' he exclaimed, with a
justice that must have escaped some of the more up-to-date
readers of his lectures. His Illustrious Period, for all its
unfashionable ring, was akin to the Renaissance of lecturers
a hundred years later. But what led to a study of that period
for its own sake, and saved it for a fame that over-shadowed
any comparable period in the history of modern European
civilization, was not the echo of Bolingbroke in a textbook,
but the extraordinary rush of interest paid to the Medici by
historians of originality and power, of whom, if the Earl of
Cork and Orrery is excepted, the first was Gibbon.

CHAPTER THREE

Taste for Italian Paintings: (I)
Sixteenth to Late Eighteenth Centuries

An account of English taste for Italian art must begin by paying generous attention to Vasari. Though the *Lives of the Most Eminent Painters, Sculptors and Architects* were not fully translated into English until 1850–85, his views had interested and influenced every student of Italian art since their publication in 1550. Connoisseurs and historians found not only information about the style of individual artists but a judgment on the whole cycle of Italian art. For 250 years his views were virtually uncriticized, and to understand the prejudices that kept the early masters so long neglected, recourse must be made to the outlook of their historian; their reputation was affected so closely by the pattern of his book.

Vasari shared with his contemporaries the belief that human affairs never lasted in one state. From the glories of Rome the turning rim of fortune's wheel had borne the arts steeply down to oblivion, to the dark ages he so much scorned. He divided their recovery into three periods. The first ran from the mid-thirteenth to the early fifteenth century, from Cimabue and Giotto to Lorenzo di Bicci. Painting woke from its long drowsed subjection to the Greeks. The stiffness of the Byzantine style gave way to something like grace, figures began to cast shadows and to be foreshortened, their drapery revealed movement and their faces reflected feeling, fear, hope, anger or love. The second period ran to the late fifteenth century, ending with Signorelli. It was a period of experiment. Prompted by Masaccio artists made improvements in perspective and the rendering of landscape, making it possible to approach reality in objects as well as in the human body. But experiment involved a certain distasteful dryness, and painting still fell short of perfect imitation, of real grace.

These qualities were reserved for the third period, which ran from the work of Leonardo to that of Michelangelo, from the end of the fifteenth to the middle of the sixteenth century. Leonardo introduced the modern manner where at last force was combined with softness, where the rules of design were followed with results beyond those rules. Yet Leonardo was surpassed by Raphael in colour, in easiness and freshness. And he in turn was outstripped by Michelangelo who found nothing in nature that he could not portray. Even the antique yielded to him. And Vasari, Michelangelo's friend, realizing that fortune's wheel had brought the arts to their height again, turned with excitement and triumph to write down what he saw before the moment was passed and the inevitable decline began once more.

Art, in this view, was a progress from nothing to a fixed goal: the naturalism, philosophic energy and classical discipline of Raphael and Michelangelo. Progress towards this goal was the criterion of good art. He praised Cimabue, for instance, for breaking away from painters who were simply marking time, and lauded all other artists who contributed to the rendering of the human body as by his own contemporaries. Those who did not, however creative, were marked down for wasting time, as was Uccello, for instance, for his over-addiction to the study of perspective. Only Vasari's occupational pride in all artists, his patriotism and his love of anecdote preserved the non-contributors from oblivion; and these were qualities personal to him; though the seventeenth century had a taste for anecdote, later writers were more selective, and as the idea of progress came to mean more in philosophy, institutions and industry, Italian art was seen increasingly in terms of the few great contributions to perfection.

Akin in its effect to his notion of progress was Vasari's unfortunate analogy between life and art. Art is born, matures and dies: the artists of the sixteenth century were mature men: those of the fifteenth inexperienced youths: those of the fourteenth were children. However delightful the young, one does not take them too seriously. As a result grown men who happened to paint in the infancy of art – like the Giotteschi – were not taken seriously either. The phrase 'childhood of art' remains as destructive as it is pretty.

The birth itself was a miraculous one. Life began 'when, towards 1250, Heaven, moved to pity by the noble spirits which the Tuscan soil was producing every day, restored them to their primitive condition'. And this notion that art arose suddenly, practically without origin, cropped up from time to time to the middle of the last century, making the study of origins seem superfluous. Attention was also deflected from early art by Vasari's suggestion that it was to his patrons, the Medici, that posterity owed the culmination of art from the last part of the fifteenth to the middle of the sixteenth century. And his conviction, moreover, that the artists most worthy of note were Tuscan was partly responsible for the tardy recognition of, for instance, the schools of Ferrara, Siena and the Marches.

Behind much of this was a wider claim, one that has ensnared reflection on the Renaissance most seductively, the belief that the main characteristic of this revived art was its imitation of the antique. He painted it all most movingly. In the long silence that followed the decline of Rome, the ancient monuments, the finest paintings, the noblest sculptures sank one by one into the sands of time, into the vineyards of Tuscany and the Romagna. In the shade of olives whose roots, unknown to him, clutched the Medicean Venus or the Laocoon, the Italian learned from émigré Greeks an alien and barbaric rote. He copied this until the miraculous birth, after which 'the minds then awakened, becoming capable of distinguishing the good from the worthless, and abandoning old methods, returned to the imitation of the antique, with all the force of their genius, and all the power of their industry'. Attention was drawn, then, to the school (the Tuscan), and the period (the late fifteenth century) where classical art was most respected.

All these ideas drew attention from the masters before Raphael, and Vasari's word, that of a practising painter and a contemporary and fellow countryman of many of his subjects, was so respected that a work of 1817 that involved preferring original documents to one of his Lives could be termed 'a new kind of research'.

The first English account of Italian painting was given in the interests of a liberal education by Henry Peacham in *The Compleat Gentleman* (1622). This consisted largely of a list of names and anecdotes, with most space given to Cimabue, Taddeo Gaddi, Giotto, Stefano Fiorentino, Orcagna, Masaccio, L. B. Alberti, Filippo Lippi, Antonello da Messina, Raphael and Michelangelo, names selected for fame in the case of the last two, for the amusing stories to be told about the others. Since he is taking his information from Vasari, however, some notion of progress emerges. Italy was overrun with wars and the arts lay neglected until about 1240. Then painters were brought over from Greece to teach the Italians. Their most famous pupil was Cimabue, but he was surpassed by Giotto, outstripped in turn by Masaccio, who, 'broke the Ice to all painters that succeeded in Nakeds and foreshortenings, which before him were knowne but of few'. With the introduction of oil painting to Italy by Antonello, Peacham's connected narrative ends, though there are a few lines in another place referring to Michelangelo's Last Judgment as one of the best paintings in the world. Apart from these remarks, Vasari's anecdotes, not for the first time, led

to an author misleading his readers as to the relative importance of Italian painters. Buffalmacco has a page and a half,
Pietro Cavallini nine lines, while 'Fryer John of Fiesole, Pedro
di Perugia, di Botticello and Leonarde de Vinci' receive a bare
mention. And for over two centuries the names of Filippo
Lippi will be known because of his abduction of a nun, of
Alberti because of his ability to flick up a coin so that it rang
against the dome of the Cathedral at Florence, rather than
for their works. Here are the first wraiths of the Vasarian
haze of sentiment that was to drift, thicker and thicker,
between Italian canvas and English eyes.

The Italian paintings in England at this time were nearly
all by contemporaries of Vasari. We have not full details of
the great Stuart collections of Charles I, Buckingham and
Arundel, but there is no evidence that they contained anything earlier than Mantegna (the Triumph of Caesar at
Hampton Court) and Leonardo (the St John, now in the
Louvre). To judge from the inventory of the Arundel collection the most popular artists were the Venetians, Bassano,
Giorgione (a category rather than a name at this time), Titian
and Veronese, with Parmigianino and Raphael. The emphasis
on the Venetian school, disparaged for poor draughtsmanship
by Vasari, shows how the actual collectors heeded the political emphasis on Venice while art historians still reflected their
source's emphasis on Florence.

The paintings were obtained from agents on the Continent,
but also through amateurs. Arundel used his son's tutors and
his chaplains, and friends who happened to be going in the
right direction. On his death-bed he requested Evelyn, who
was passing through Florence, to go to a nobleman at Cas-
tellacchio and try for his Parmigianinos and Titians: 'I thinke
hee will sell any thing being old & having but one daughter
wch. is marryed.' It is true that Arundel had affection for the
un-Vasarian art of Dürer, but the Italians, the contemporaries
and seniors of Dürer, were his favourites. Of a Dürer

Madonna given him by the Bishop of Würzburg he wrote to
his chaplain: 'it is more worth than all the toyes I have gotten
in Germanye and for such I esteeme it, havinge ever carried
it in my owne Coach since I had it; and howe then doe
ye thinke I should valewe thinges of Leonardo, Raphaell,
Corregio, and such like!'

Dürer was really a little too near the Gothic. Arundel gave
Evelyn a 'Remembrance' of things worth seeing in Italy and
in it recommends the Cathedral at Milan although 'it hath
the misfortune to bee done on an ill designe of Gothick Architecture'. Evelyn shared this dislike of Gothic, save when it
made him agreeably melancholy, and took Michelangelo as
his hero not so much for his paintings, which he barely
explores, but for freeing architecture at a blow 'from the
trifling of *Goths* and *Barbarians*'.

Since the publication of the *Diary* in 1818, Evelyn's lack
of originality, and the ignorance and confusion of his ideas
about art, have been shown more clearly than during his
lifetime when he was respected as the author of a work on
architecture and the translator of another on painting. These
works contained two arguments designed to keep attention
from early art. One was the idea that thanks to classical
models architecture sprang suddenly away from Gothic in
the later fifteenth century and was only then made really
interesting. The other was the assertion that great art must
be learned; an artist's reputation depended largely on his education. Evelyn mocked the booby who had painted Adam
and Eve with navels. The *great* painter 'should be almost as
universal as the *Orator* in Cicero, and the Architect in *Vitruvius*:
But Certainly some tincture in *History*, the *Optics*, and *Anatomy* are absolutely requisite'. The idea was popular and the
next generation, reflecting contemporary taste for pictures
with profound or complicated subjects, added to the painter's
requisites a knowledge of Poetry, Philosophy and Divinity.
Where, then, were the early painters who probably had none

of these? Ignorance became increasingly a stigma until the noble savage reappeared in literature, and simplicity became a virtue.

Evelyn had leaned heavily on Vasari, especially in his evaluation of Michelangelo, and Vasari again was to be found prominently in Richard Lassels's *The Voyage of Italy*. Though a man of rather self-advertised independence of judgment, Lassels rarely gives his own opinion of a painting, quoting Vasari instead. At Siena for instance, he was told that the Duomo pavement was by 'Meccherini', 'but I had rather beleeve *Vasari*', and he gave it to Duccio and Beccafumi (unaware that Mecarino and Beccafumi were one and the same man).

It is interesting to see what works of art he looks at in his tours of Italy. In Florence he goes to S. Marco and mentions only the Fra Bartolomeos, ignoring Fra Angelico. In S. Croce he says nothing of the frescoes but describes the tomb of Michelangelo. In the Duomo the tomb of Cimabue prompts a familiar reflection: 'It was hee that first restored painting again which had been lost for many years in *Italy*, and taught it to *Giotto*, *Gaddi*, *Taffi* and others who carried it on to a great height.' But in the Duke's palace, where he could have seen these great heights, he mentions no paintings by name, and spends most of his time among the jewels and guns. He did not go to Ravenna and in Padua, ignoring the Arena chapel, mentions the Eremitani, but only to say that there are two Guido Renis there. Rome had St Peter's, the eighth wonder of the world, and the Sistine Chapel, though one visits this only for the Last Judgment. Of Raphael's work, the Loggie are only inferior to the divine history itself: the Maxentius is praised, the Stanza d'Eliodoro mentioned, the Segnatura omitted. But though Florence may have been the birthplace of the arts, the place to see the greatest number of rare paintings was not there, nor even Rome, but Venice. In parting company at this point with Vasari he was not left without a guide, finding one in Rodolfi's lives of Venetian Painters. And we leave him in Siena, admiring the Piccolomini library frescoes (which he attributes to Perugino) and being, for once, independent. For 'when all's done, give me bookes in a *Library*, not pictures'.

By this time, the established fame of the Bolognese Caracci (Lodovico, d. 1619; Agostino, d. 1602; Annibale, d. 1609) finally ensured that curiosity aroused by Vasari's mention of names earlier than Raphael would not be followed up. The emphasis was not to lie on his predecessors, or even his contemporaries, but increasingly on his successors.

The names to become so familiar to the eighteenth century, Guercino, Barocci, Guido Reni and the Caracci, first found extended notice in England in 1679, in a translation of Barri's *Viaggio Pittoresco d'Italia*. This took the English tourist to Ravenna, but it was to show him the Guido in the Duomo and a Barocci in S. Vitale, and in the Sistine, it is still the Last Judgment that alone was looked at. He did mention some of the paintings in the Medici galleries; for instance (due to the literal translation of *quadro*), he sees 'a Square with the History of the *Fall of Phatëon*, by the hand of *Leonardo da Vinci*', and 'likewise two Squares of *Naked Women*, by great Titian'. And the second important English account of Italian painting took notice of the late sixteenth-century revival and added it to the Vasarian analysis. It was published in 1685, nearly a hundred years after Peacham's book, and was far fuller. *Painting Illustrated in Three Diallogues, containing some Choice Observations upon the Art, together with the Lives of the Most Eminent Painters from Cimabue to the time of Raphael, and Michael Angelo, with an Explanation of the Difficult Terms*, was written by William Aglionby who was ashamed that of all the civilized nations of Europe, England cared least about the arts. The English knew little and collected little. He was going to try to inform and interest them, painlessly, as he hoped.

The lives were from Vasari and were chosen deliberately to mark the stages by which Italian art came to perfection, with Raphael and Michelangelo. He shortened them drastically but gave more information than any previous English writer about the names he selected: Cimabue, Giotto, Leonardo da Vinci, Andrea del Sarto, Raphael, Michelangelo, Giulio Romano, Pierino del Vaga, Titian and Donatello. The gap between Giotto and Leonardo was filled in by the second dialogue, which was devoted to a history of painting. He followed Vasari as to the importance of his artists, but not always as to their merit. He thought, for instance, that Michelangelo was overpraised, and that his power was spoiled by his lack of easiness. He took art through six phases, the first five of which are only a variation of Vasari's, and the last the cult of the Caracci, and as his outline is a representative one it is worth analysing in some detail. Thanks to the curiosity of Friend, which leads him indefatigably to pose such leading questions as 'How long was it from the time of *Cimabue* to the time of *Masaccio*?' the dialogue form permits the story to move briskly.

Barbarian savagery and Christian iconoclasm destroy classical art, and all is decay until the influence of a few Greeks that remained in Italy produced (Phase 2) Cimabue who, with the assistance of nature, outwent the dry gracelessness of his masters. His pupil Giotto lost yet more stiffness, and introduced some sweetness of colour and ease of composition; even the passions were represented by him, and crude perspective.

But not till Masaccio (Phase 3) was there a free imitation of nature approached. Towards this aim Taddeo Gaddi improved colour, Simone Sanese composition, Stefano Scimmia design. But most followed the manner of Giotto, like Spinello Aretino, Jacopo del Casentino and Andrea Pisano. The nude began to be studied and perspective improved, and at the same time Brunelleschi, Donatello and Ghiberti were

using their study of Roman antiquities to achieve new bold-
ness and accuracy of design.

Gradually colour became truer, ornament richer, figures
nearer nature. The main artists were Francia, Lazzaro Vasari,
Antonello da Messina, Castagno, Dom. Ghirlandaio, Botticelli, Mantegna and, outside Florence, the Bellini, Costa and
Ercole Ferrarese. But all lacked spirit and life and, above all,
an easy manner.

So we come to (Phase 4) Leonardo da Vinci, the father of
modern painting, who had a profound knowledge of the rules
of his art. Important among his contemporaries were these:
Perugino, a good colourist; Giorgione, who introduced Tuscan technique to Venice and was a fine colourist; Andrea del
Sarto, whose sweetness of colour lacked strength; Raphael,
the greatest painter that ever was, a student of the best both
in ancient and modern art, perfect in colour, easy invention,
richness and order; Correggio, exquisite with the nude, un-
surpassed in the natural rendering of hair; Parmigianino, so
good at landscapes and who painted with such sweetness and
grace that if he had spent less time at chemistry he might
have been the best painter of his age; Polidoro, an admirably
correct designer; Giulio Romano, who imitated Raphael
better than anyone else, and was an unexcelled student of
antiquity; Pierino dei Vaga, good at muscles and the grotesque; and, finally, Michelangelo, the greatest designer there
ever was and a specialist in the nude. But his manner is almost
savage, and lacks tenderness, nor do his figures distinguish
either age or sex, but all resemble one another. Nor is his
colouring good, he was a better sculptor than painter and is
much overpraised by Vasari.

However, after his time (Phase 5) painting decayed again,
for even the fine artists of this time, like Caravaggio, were
faulty, he, in particular, following nature with too little discretion, with good colour but bad composition.

Then (Phase 6) the Caracci of Bologna renewed Raphael's

manner to its former level. Annibale was greater than Agostino, though less learned. And they influenced a school which included Guido Reni, the most-sought-after of all, whose heads were as good as Raphael's; Sisto Badalocchi, the last great designer of the school; Albani, small in scale but excellently sweet; Domenichino, great in invention though deficient in easiness; Lanfranco, who had fire without correctness; Pietro Berettini da Cortona, who was above all a painter of landscapes, especially the antiquities of Rome which he rendered with great correctness. Among painters of other schools there are some of this time who should be mentioned. Titian was the best colourist, perhaps, who ever was, and he was also the finest portrait painter. Veronese was graceful, with good colour, but, on the other hand, his invention was poor and his colour gross. Tintoretto was too fiery, his vivacity outran his patience. The Bassani were only redeemed by their colour. And this is to have mentioned all the famous Italian artists.

There are only a few non-Italians worth mentioning: Dürer and Holbein, only kept by the gothicness of their world from being as great as the great Italians; Rubens and Vandyke. As for England – it esteems painters simply as it esteems 'Joyners and Carpenters'. Where are the patrons? Art cannot flourish without encouragement. Oh – and the peroration has the ring of true feeling in it – if only we would drink less and think more about art!

Partly, then, this work was to interest Englishmen, through Italian art, in painting in general, and hence to a support of their own. In 1598 Richard Haydocke, translating Lomazzo's influential treatise on painting, had complained of this indifference and lack of patronage and regretted that he had not the pen of a Vasari to eternalize such native painters as Nicholas Hilliard, Isaac Oliver and Rowland Lockey. And the theme was emphasized by the translation, a hundred years later, in 1699, of Pierre Monier's *The History of Painting,*

Sculpture, Architecture, and those who have excelled in them. For Monier, as painter to the King of France, patronage was a profitable and loyal theme. He traced its origins back to a visit paid by Charles of Anjou to Cimabue to watch him painting, an example that was somehow, he implied, one of the first causes of the revival of the arts. But this argument centred, of course, on the Medici, and the prime example of their patronage, Michelangelo, so a theme that might have resulted in the turning up of much that would interest readers in earlier periods simply emphasized the superiority of Michelangelo's contemporaries. The same effect was made by Monier's other main argument, that the arts are fostered by academies of painting. This was another convenient theme, for he was also Professor of Painting and Sculpture in the Royal Academy in Paris. Leonardo's Academy at Milan, he claimed, delivered the inhabitants from Gothic, and Vasari's Academy at Florence perfected the art of design, relegating the bad old art to the neglect it deserved.

Four years earlier Richard Graham had written the next English account of Italian painting, bound as fast to Vasari as Aglionby's. His account noticed 127 Italian artists from Cimabue to Luca Giordano but showed no independent valuations. Graham took the Vasarian pattern literally. Cimabue was 'FATHER of the FIRST AGE, or INFANCY of MODERN PAINTING', Masaccio 'The MASTER of the SECOND, or MIDDLE AGE of MODERN PAINTING', and Leonardo was the 'MASTER of the THIRD, or GOLDEN AGE of MODERN PAINTING'. His lives followed what was to become a formula for dictionaries of art. He took the Vasarian estimate. To this he added a spicy episode: Giorgione dying of plague caught in his mistress's arms; Signorelli stripping and painting the dead body of his son, unmoved; Paolo Farinato of Verona, cut out of his Mother's belly, just dead in labour. A further sentence is earned by those who 'invented' something, as Margaritone the art of gilding with leaf gold, upon bole armeniac; Jan van Eyk, oil painting; Fra Bartolomeo, the lay figure; Mantegna, engraving; Verrochio, the art of taking plaster masks of the face. Like Aglionby, he had fluent lists of early masters and even complimented a few, like Giorgione and Domenico Ghirlandaio, but it is doubtful if he or any other Englishman had yet looked closely at any of their works. Much more from the heart came the estimate of Annibale Caracci: 'All the several *Perfections* of the most eminent *Masters* his *Predecessors*, were united in himself alone.' Taste was not going to be changed one whit by the historians of Italian art: Vasari lay too authoritatively in the way.

So did the characteristic product of the learning of the age, the controversy between Ancients and Moderns. Had the modern world, with its command of the experimental method demonstrated by Bacon and its free ranging intelligence surpassed the Ancients in any department of learning? Had the Greeks and Romans done all things as well as they could be done, and must the reading of the classics remain the end as well as the means of education? The controversy ranged through all the arts and sciences and, unfortunately for painting, the strategy of the Moderns was to give in with regard to the arts and concentrate on the sciences. Here the discovery of the lodestone and of the circulation of the blood more than compensated for the failure of a modern artist to paint grapes so realistic that birds would peck at them, portraits so true to life that the subjects' dogs would fawn at them, figures so beautiful that men fell in love with them. These were the popular legends of classical painting and they were believed, though the paintings themselves had disappeared. It seemed impossible to rival the effect these works were supposed to have had.

When argument was attempted it was not on the score that modern art might be as great in a different way from classical art, but that the classical element in modern art challenged its prototype. So if the controversy did not politicly ignore

art it focused attention on the classicizing artists of the sixteenth and seventeenth centuries. An attempt was made to
trace back the most disparate elements in modern art to Greek
sources. Michelangelo and the Bolognese were supposed to
have followed the Athenian school, the French the Corinthian, the Venetian the Rhodian, while Raphael, Leonardo
and Giulio Romano had followed the most correct and easy
style of all, that of the Sicyonian school. So much did this
sort of comparison come to deplore anything but correctness
that even Michelangelo was adversely criticized for extravagance and immodesty. A beauty in William King's satirical
Dialogue of the Dead (1699) shows how hard it was for non-
classical art to get a hearing:

'*Calpurnia*. A Gentleman came one Morning with several
various readings upon *Vitruvius*, and from thence persuaded
me that the Frame of my Looking-Glass was the most inju-
dicious Piece of Architecture that could be, that the Bases
were Dorick, the Capitals Corinthian, and the Architrave
perfectly Barbarous, for which reason I went abroad without
Patches, till such Absurdities were entirely Mended and
Corrected by his Direction.'

At the same time that the Ancients and Moderns were
ruling a line behind which taste, in its search for classical
elements, could not profitably move, virtuosi were working
out formulæ about the painters of the sixteenth century
and a vocabulary to express them, formulæ beyond which
hardly an advance was hazarded during the eighteenth century, the same pictures being looked at in the same way
throughout.

Painting was divided into schools, each school being noted
for different qualities. When an artist did not conform to
these qualities he tended to be ignored. The school of Rome
and Florence was masculine and noble, not bothering about
details.

> In short, this College teaches *Force and Grace*
> And therefore justly claims the highest Place:
> It has produc'd Eminent *Elevees*,
> Julio Romano, Polydore Venise,
> Del Sarto, Perugin, *and such as these*.

The inclusion of Perugino in this gallery shows that lip-service was still sometimes paid to a great artist's (Raphael's) teacher, but no painting of his was discussed save the frescoes of the Piccolomini Library which he was erroneously supposed to have painted.

As for the Lombard school, it shows:

> How to give ev'ry Figure its true Station,
> And make them firm by *Æquiponderation*:
> Shews us the way each Object to *relieve*,
> And how the Eye, by *Shortnings*, to deceive.
> For this the three *Caratts* we are to thank,
> *Andrea Sacchi, Albano Lanfrank,*
> *Dominiquin, Corregio, Guido Rheni,*
> *Spaigniolet, Caravagio,* and *Guercini.*

Taste was formed, there was no room for exploration. The man of taste knew from reading jingles like this what was best, he went to look at them, and if at first they did not please he persevered until they did. We shall see how slowly travellers moved their eyes to pictures they had not been told to admire.

More and more did art appreciation become the preserve of a specially and narrowly indoctrinated circle. It had its own jargon, culled in part from the two fashionable modern languages, Italian and French. 'In *Invention* is to be considered, First, the *Gust of the Author*, whether it be *Grand* or *Petit*', the Carnations (flesh tints) must be studied, in a landscape table due attention must be paid to the *Gruppa* (group) and to the *Lointains* (distant parts). Conversation among virtuosi consisted of lengthy discussions as to the relative merits of different artists, conversations during which characteristics were further simplified into a series of labels. Late in the eighteenth century, Reynolds showed how far this had gone among ordinary fashionable travellers:

'With a gentleman of this cast I visited last week the Cartoons at Hampton Court: he was just returned from Italy, a Connoisseur, of course, and of course his mouth full of nothing but the Grace of Raffaelle, the Purity of Domenichino, the Learning of Poussin, the Air of Guido, the greatness of Taste of the Caraccis, and the Sublimity and grand Contorno of Michelangelo; and all the rest of the cant of Criticism, which he emitted with that volubility which generally those orators have, who annex no ideas to their words.'

Virtuosi liked artists with a sizable *œuvre*, something they could seize with blunt critical tools, for this vocabulary was not capable of seizing the difference between earlier masters, often anonymous, let alone different works by one of them. The words reflected what was expected only from a particular sort of art. The poet Gray, in a chronological list of artists he drew up for his own use in Italy in 1739, did not attempt to describe the nature of the work of the earlier artists, save Domenico Ghirlandaio whom the words fit very ill: 'Lively colouring genteel designing and good airs,' while with later artists he was quite at home. Against Lodovico Caracci, for instance, he noted 'Exquisite design: noble and proper composition; strong and harmonious colouring.' The words themselves are not precise but current taste would interpret them correctly. The anonymity of much early painting was in fact a great bar to interest. Pre-Raphaelite works were allotted to what seemed the most suitable among the half-dozen familiar names. Connoisseurship was concerned with describing and comparing established masters and there was as yet no vestige of the painstaking search among documents that is needed before schools, let alone names, can be handled with familiarity. The critic's reputation rested upon certainties, and he was not going to touch paintings he could not even put in their correct century; from this point of view the earlier period was not worth investigating. The virtuosi preferred to talk with vague grandeur about what was well known.

As their pretentiousness grew they were increasingly satirized, a necessary process before taste could break the vacuum in which they had confined it. Too few travellers were as independent even as the true-born Englishmen Boswell tells of, who, trapped into going round the Uffizi, submitted quietly to be shown a few pictures, 'but seeing the gallery so immensely long, their impatience burst forth, and they tried for a bett who should hop first to the end of it'.

Smollett, too, was an exception. He was at pains *not* to pose as a connoisseur and posed instead as a plain man. He made scornful remarks about the ancient Romans, made damaging criticisms of the Medici Venus, found Raphael's Parnassus ludicrous and Michelangelo's Pietà in St Peter's indecent. But for all this the painter he praised most was Guido Reni. If his dislikes were personal, his affections were guided by the taste of the connoisseurs he scorned.

The conventional frontiers of taste were not easily to be passed. The historians of art were bound by Vasari, the writers about art by the prestige of the ancients, the tourist by virtuosi at home and *ciceroni* abroad. Only the most open-minded traveller could find himself liking, even noticing, the work of the predecessors of Raphael.

Edward Wright has been hailed as one of the first travellers with a more catholic taste, which included a sympathy for primitives. But we shall see how little unconventional he was if we follow him, as we followed Lassels, round the monuments of Italy considered today most important from the viewpoint of pre-Raphaelite painting.

He was in Italy from 1720 to 1722 and published two volumes of observations on the country, with particular attention to its art, of which he was to leave a small collection on his death.

He preferred the new mosaics to the old in St Mark's, and he was disparaging about the mosaics of Ravenna, too. The Cathedral came as a relief, for this had a 'Chapel painted by Guido', and a statue with a 'very genteel attitude, and fine Air of the head'. He visited the Sistine Chapel in Rome, and after describing the Last Judgment, gave an opinion that can have cost but little crick of the neck: 'Upon the Cieling of this Chapel are also painted by the same master the Prophets, the Sibyls, and other Subjects.' A final glance around: 'On the Walls are painted, by *Pietro Perugino*, the History of the Old Testament on one side, and that of the New on the other', and *exit*. At Pisa he enthused over the Campo Santo: 'A most delightful structure, tho' Gothick.' He described the frescoes, too. 'The Painting in this fine Cloister is most of it hard, according to the Manner then in use; nor is there any great Observance of the *Chiaro Oscuro* . . . but many of the Countenances are very expressive and good, particularly in those of *Giotto* and *Benozzo*.' We follow expectantly to Florence but – nothing at all. No mention of painting in Sta. Croce or of the Benozzos in the Medici Chapel. Nor did he record a visit to S. Marco, Sta. Maria Novella or the Carmine. Only the Medici tombs and the Uffizi seemed to interest him. It is not quite clear, in fact, upon what his reputation for precocity rests. The earliest painting in his collections was a 'Leonardo' Virgin and Child which went for three pounds eight shillings. Apart from the flash of insight at Pisa he was conventional enough, repeating what he had been told, and not looking where there was no habit of looking.

It is true that he was not so brusque about the middle ages as was Burnet in 1685 with his downright assertion at Milan that 'The Dome hath nothing to commend it of Architecture, it being built in the rude Gothick manner', or at Venice that 'St Mark's Church hath nothing to recommend it, but its great antiquity, and the vast riches of the building', but fundamentally, Wright saw with the classically conditioned eyes of Addison.

With the publication of his *Remarks on Several Parts of Italy* in 1705, Addison affirmed that Italy was, first and last, a treasure house of classical monuments, and classical monuments alone. As his reputation as a writer grew so this attitude became more influential, and his work became the orthodox companion of young connoisseurs making the Tour. He took them to Milan and made no mention of Leonardo, to Rome and forsook inscription-raking only to praise St Peter's, to Florence and described only antiquities. His attitude towards the middle ages was conveyed clearly enough by his remarks on the cathedral at Siena. 'When a man sees the prodigious pains and expense that our fore-fathers have been at in these barbarous buildings, one cannot but fancy to himself what miracles of Architecture they would have left us had they been only instructed in the right way.'

Nor did Wright approach even the severely qualified admiration of the earlier masters shown by Jonathan Richardson. *An Account of some of the statues, bas reliefs, drawings, and pictures in Italy, etc. With remarks* (1722) was the first guide to the actual paintings of Italy written by an Englishman. Based on material gathered on the spot by Jonathan Richardson the younger, it was edited, and partly written, by his father, whose notable reputation as a portrait painter and wide circle of acquaintances, including Pope, Prior and Gay, increased its effect.

Richardson senior's earlier writings had shown that he was prepared to be tolerant towards even the predecessors of Masaccio, for 'this Bad Style had something Manly and Vigorous; whereas in the Decay, whether after the Happy Age of *Rafaelle*, or that of *Annibale*, One sees an Effeminate,

Languid Air, Or if it has not that it has the Vigour of a Bully, rather than of a Brave man: the Old Bad Painting has more Faults than the Modern, but this falls into the Insipid.' But for all this the chronological accounts he gives of Italian painting in his *An Essay on the Theory of Painting* (1715) and *Two Discourses* (1719) are as confused and conventional as those of his predecessors, and the anti-Gothic, pro-Classical bias almost as pronounced as Addison's.

It was his son, by going to Italy and actually looking at the works of the artists his father had been writing about, who produced references more stimulating to the traveller than the generalization quoted above. Richardson's tour was a whirlwind one, rather in the modern manner, for, as his doting father confessed, 'the Time my Son spent Abroad was indeed not Long, but he made the Most of it'. Familiar is the pace, for instance, of his first day in Rome. 'He enter'd *Rome* about Noon, after having Travell'd all that Morning, and the whole preceding Night, and Day, and that in the time of the Heats, consequently without Sleep. That being Fatal in those Seasons in that *Campagna*; yet the Same Day he visited the Works of Raffaele in the Churches of *S. Agostino*, and the *Pace*.'

Yet speed, the great enemy to independence in taste, did not prevent him from expressing some original opinions. His account of the Sistine Chapel is particularly interesting. He was immediately struck with the Last Judgment, huge, conspicuous and in good repair. Then, the first and last time anyone did this for over a hundred years, he raised his head and looked carefully and critically at the badly-lit vault. And he concluded that for all their faulty colouring and incongruities the compositions in the vault, especially the Prophets and Sybils, were better than the Last Judgment. This is because Michelangelo, 'being withal Reserv'd, and if not Melancholy, very Sombrous, and perhaps inclining to Savage', was best when he was painting something in which the excessive was appropriate: a Sybil rather than a human body rising to judgment. The rest of his comments were conventional, and after wrongly attributing the whole of the paintings on the walls to Perugino, and not his best work at that, he left.

Another instance of his originality was his appreciation of the thirteenth-century miraculous Annunciation at the Annunciata at Florence. He only looks carefully at this particular early work because it had the merit of having been finished by an angel, but as a result of this forced scrutiny comes the admission: 'Truth is, tho' the Style is *Gothic*, the Thought of the Picture is so fine, I wonder other Painters have not taken it in treating this Subject.'

This instance makes one wish that there had been some cause, miraculous or not, for his paying the all-important second glance to the primitives in the Duke's gallery. As it is, his remarks on Pollaiuolo, Filippo Lippi and Leonardo contain the usual phrases: 'hard manner', 'good Expressions, but very stiff and hard'. Giorgione, Andrea del Sarto and Fra Bartolomeo, on the other hand, he praises enthusiastically, and, in sculpture, the Ghiberti gates are 'of a much better Taste than one would expect to find in a Work 100 Years before Raffaele'. It is Raphael who receives more space in the book, though the conclusion is that he can be better seen at Hampton Court than anywhere else, for there are the Cartoons, and they are the finest paintings, probably, that the world has ever seen.

This conclusion is less surprising in that the whole of the long description of the Vatican frescoes was written by Richardson senior, who had never been there, but was working from reproductions. It is a useful reminder of the bookish nature even of comparatively *avant-garde* critics.

The artists who figure most largely, then, in the writings of the two Richardsons are, first Raphael, then Michelangelo, Andrea del Sarto, Annibale Caracci, Correggio, Giulio

Romano, Guido Reni, Parmigianino, Titian. The little space given to the Venetians is due to the fact that Jonathan junior did not go there, but his father noted that this was no great loss, as Titian, Tintoretto, Veronese – none of them was of the first rank. And the eighteen-day sale of his own collection contained comparatively few Venetian works, and hardly any school prior to 1500.

More than to Wright, more than to the professional connoisseurs, Richardson father and son, the praise for being the first Englishman to find pleasure in primitives should go to John Breval whom we have already noticed as the historian of the Visconti. After holding a captaincy in Marlborough's army and years of miscellaneous and pseudonymous writing following the Peace of Utrecht, he was a scholar well shaken out of the ruts of scholarship of 1720, when he went to Italy as tutor to George, Viscount Malpas.

The records of his travels in Italy and elsewhere were published in 1726 and 1728 and show that in several respects he anticipated the opinions of later generations. It was he who best emphasized the importance of Medicean patronage in the development of the arts, who praised Florence as, after Rome, the city of all the world where the greatest number of fine works of art were to be seen. Not content with the names of the early painters, 'My earnest Desire to see some original Production of *Cimabue* carry'd me to *Sta Maria Novella*', and though the Rucellai Madonna was too decayed to be judged properly, he admired – with still more independence – the Ghirlandaio frescoes in the chancel. Ghirlandaio was the subject of fuller admiration in the Palazzo Vecchio, though it is not clear that he distinguished between Domenico and Ridolfo. At Padua he admired the 'noble Fresco's' by Mantegna in the Eremitani, an opinion no Englishman had recorded before, I believe. And as novel was his attitude towards mosaic, and though he was content with barely mentioning their existence at S. Vitale and the mausoleum of

Galla Placidia, he goes so far as to say that those at St Mark's are 'fine'; such marginal praise was all they were to get until the publication of Lord Lindsay's *Sketches of the History of Christian Art*, in 1847. Add to this an appreciation of Perugino and Breval's originality is proved, in spite of the Addisonian point of view that guides him in most other respects. Even this is qualified, and Siena Cathedral is 'of a *Gothic* stile indeed, but very beautiful in its kind'.

For the next two generations nothing new was said on the subject of Italian art. Travellers went in as great numbers as ever, they continued to write about what they had seen, but interest was jaded, discovery at an end. Taste was thought to be complete and reviewers were tired of a class of literature that could do no more now than repeat familiar matters; there was scarcely anything new left for a traveller, however ingenious, to describe. Notice was taken only of what was established, mechanically interesting, or of notable size. Domenichino continued to be admired, cabinets of curiosities described, the dome of St Peter's measured, the capacity of the lantern on the Florentine Duomo estimated, the cost of the new Medici chapel at S. Lorenzo marvelled at. Increasingly the traveller yawned or joined the Dilettanti, a club, wrote Horace Walpole, 'for which the nominal qualification is having been in Italy, and the real one, being drunk'.

There was a new note of harshness, too, in Protestant distaste for the subject matter of Catholic art, a note that had not been struck by aristocratic tourists whose social contacts took much of the rough edge off Italy's foreign-ness. The increasing number of non-aristocratic travellers found more to worry about, discomfort, rudeness, tiresome formalities, and horrors. Thomas Jones, the landscape painter, was miserable when he went to Rome to study there in 1776. He was afraid of being knifed in taverns and 'at home I was shut up alone in a large Open Apartment, with a brick floor rougher than that of many of our English stables – the walls hung round with dirty, dismal pictures of Weeping Magdalens, bloody *Ecce homos*, dead-Christs and fainting Madonnas – by my bedside was fixt a kind of little Altar with a Crucifix . . . In this melancholy chamber, or rather Chapel, I retired to rest, and lulled to sleep by the pattering of the rain against the windows, sometimes dreamt of the many Enjoyments I had left behind me in London.'

And while travellers were finding either a classical education or religious prejudice a bar to cultivating new enthusiasms, the writers on art were affected in the same way by the historians who were telling them of the patronage of the Medici and helping them associate great art with great patronage. A precocious sociological interpretation of Italian art had been hinted at by Shaftesbury in 1712, where he suggested that the revival of Italian art was shaped by three things, patronage by Rome, the civil liberty of Italian states like Florence and Venice, and the fostering of taste by the discussions which took place in them. But he was speaking of the Italy of the late fifteenth century, the earliest period yet widely known about, and the conviction grew that the first great patrons were those of Michelangelo and Raphael. It was no good, then, looking for great art any earlier. Gaining force as more was written about the Medici, it passed into common knowledge in Mengs' article on Painting in the *Encyclopædia Britannica* (1771), where even the backwardness of Chinese art, which lamentably made no attempt to paint things as they actually were, was explained by lack of patronage.

During the 'seventies, however, there were signs of change. The first move was made by Thomas Patch, an English artist who from 1747 to 1755 was living in Rome. Here he came to know Reynolds, who included him in his parody of Raphael's School of Athens. Reynolds was a useful example for a pioneer of taste, who needed patience and the willingness to look many times at a work that at first seemed distasteful. When Reynolds first visited Raphael's stanze at the Vatican he was dismayed to find that he did not like them. 'Notwithstanding my disappointment, I proceeded to copy some of these excellent works. I viewed them again and again. I even affected to feel their merit; and to admire them more than I really did. In a short time a new taste, and a new perception began to dawn upon me; and I was convinced that I had originally formed a false opinion of the perfection of art; and that this great painter was well entitled to the high rank which he holds in the estimation of the world.'

This generous attitude depended on the previous fame of Raphael. What were the chances for an artist whom critics had never sung? When would anyone look twice at the Botticellis in the neighbouring Chapel?

Patch was banished from the Papal States for an offence whose exact nature is not clear. He fled to Florence where he found a patron in Horace Mann, Envoy Extraordinary, who had a lively interest in the arts. Patch lived mainly by selling conventional Views and by his better-known cartoons, but he also took an unusual interest in early Florentine painting.

He published an engraving of Uccello's Sir John Hawkwood in 1771, but most of all he was attracted by Masaccio, to whom he attributed the chief role in the restoration of painting. He drew and engraved heads from the Brancacci Chapel in 1770, delighting in an art so 'different from the disagreeable stiffness in the horrid spectres of the School of Giotto and of the modern Gretian Mosaicks'. His dislike of anything earlier than Masaccio did not stop him, fortunately, from copying what he thought to be the Giottos in the Minetti chapel in the same church, the Carmine; fortunately, because they were destroyed in the fire of January 1771, and his chiaroscuro woodcuts give the best impression of these compositions that remains: a cycle illustrating the Life of the Baptist which was, in fact, the work of Spinello Aretino. It was historical, rather than aesthetic zeal, that made him

publish them, desire to interest the student of the different
stages of painting rather than to show him something beautiful. He was, indeed, sceptical of Giotto's place in the revival
of painting, wondering if his work were really superior to
the great number of painters of his day from places other
than Florence. This was the first query raised as to the validity
of Vasari's formula, and Patch's prejudice reveals itself in
the way in which he 'improves' the paintings he is copying,
making them approximate to the canons of his day. He was
careful, though, to distinguish modern restoration from original work and to show spaces where the plaster had fallen
off, revealing the lines of the preliminary cartoon. He published these, together with twenty-six engravings from the
Brancacci Chapel and twenty-four of Fra Bartolomeo's
works in S. Marco, in 1772, in a work dedicated to Horace
Walpole and Horace Mann.

It is perhaps surprising that Mann should have taken so
great an interest in his work, praising and recommending it to
Walpole, for his own taste, like Walpole's, was conventional,
leading him to furnish his apartments with copies. The pro-
curing of copies of sixteenth- and seventeenth-century
masters for illustrious clients in England, like the Earl of
Northumberland, was one of the services expected of an
Envoy, and Patch not only showed a taste independent of
his patron's, but quite different from that of contemporary
Florentines. The typical approach to art was not that of Patch
but Botta's, whose reorganization of the Pitti was based on
one overriding principle: that none of the figures should have
its back to the Ducal throne: at least one famous Titian was
banished the throne room for this breach of etiquette.

Patch went on to make another contribution to the history
of art with his *Porte del Batistere di Firenze* (1774), which was
an illustrated account of the Ghiberti doors, the engravings
being so arranged that 'the impressions may be joined
together to form an exact half of the gate'. The example of

his works encouraged others to follow suit with further books of engravings – the effect of one of which, Carlo Lasinio's *Campo Santo*, we shall see. Nor was Patch's taste unique. Also living in Florence at this time was another English painter, Ignace Hugford, a man who could lavish praise on the florid and empty mannerist drawings of his master, Anton Domenico Gabbiani, and at the same time amass a small collection of primitives. But these men stood for a while almost alone.

The taste of their contemporaries was admirably represented by Sir Joshua Reynolds. Reynolds owned the Bellini Agony in the Garden now in the National Gallery, and he praised Masaccio in a *Discourse* of 1784, but in a *Discourse* of 1769 he drew a line dividing the curious from the admirable; it ran straight through the middle of the career of Raphael, 'the first of painters'. When Raphael saw Michelangelo's ceiling, Reynolds told his audience at the Royal Academy, 'he immediately from a dry, Gothick and even insipid manner, which attends to the minute accidental discriminations of particular and individual objects, assumed that grand style of painting, which improves partial representation by the general and invariable ideas of nature'.

CHAPTER FOUR

The Medici and William Roscoe: Late Eighteenth to Early Nineteenth Centuries

Before his vision in the Capitol, Gibbon had thought of describing not the end of ancient, but the beginning of modern times. In 1761 he was considering the French invasions of Italy, in the following year a joint scheme, *The History of the Liberty of the Swiss* and *The History of the Republic of Florence, under the House of Medicis*, which would provide a grand commentary on liberty, how it was won by the Swiss and lost by the Italians. Even when his subject had changed to the decline and fall of Rome it was with the later part of the narrative, where the story was Italian rather than Roman, that he was most concerned, reading the mediæval records of Muratori till he 'almost grasped the ruins of Rome in the fourteenth century, without suspecting that this final chapter must be attained by the labour of six quartos and twenty years.' When it finally appeared in 1788, his views on Italian history were subordinate now to another theme, and used to illustrate it, and had changed: he spoke no longer of an Italy 'whose courts and families were perpetually defiled with lust and blood, with incest and parricide'; Italy was the home of noble contrasts to the sloth and servility of Constantinople, of republics which vindicated the human rights she habitually betrayed. While Byzantium lay sluggish, her population dwindling and her vigour drained by satiety or indifference, Italy was the scene of a commercial activity that crowded her cities and improved material life to a point where elegance and genius, too, could flourish.

It may have been true that it was the arrival of Greek scholars both before and after the fall of Constantinople that was crucial to the revival of letters, but this would have been useless if Italy had not been prepared to receive them. The miracle was not in the sowing but in the soil. 'The Greeks were stationary or retrograde, while the Latins were advancing with a rapid and progressive motion.' As her poet, Petrarch, had been the first harbinger of day, so it was Italy who in 'the resurrection of science . . . was the first that cast away her shroud'. At every turn, Italy gained from his denigration of Byzantium.

The Medici, in this view, no longer illustrate the loss of their country's liberty but the growth of its strength and prestige. Cosimo was no longer the founder of a line which muffled the republic with its wealth, he was 'the father of a line of princes whose name and age are almost synonymous with the restoration of learning: his credit was ennobled into fame; his riches were dedicated to the service of mankind; he corresponded at once with Cairo and London; and a cargo of Indian spices and Greek books were often imported in the same vessel'. Against the blaze, too, of Lorenzo, genius and Mæcenas, was illuminated not the straitened coffers of Florence, but the desperate decline of the eastern Empire. These splendid hints were not lost on the attentive readers of Gibbon's great work. One in particular, William Roscoe of Liverpool, resolved to act upon them and to produce a work that would bridge the gap between the last chapter of Gibbon and the first of Robertson, a gap which would be closed in the name of the Medici.

Within a generation, Roscoe's name was as internationally famous as Gibbon's. The son of an innkeeper, he came through his works on the Medici to be ranked among the greatest scholars of his age. His books earned large sums and the patronage and friendship of men like Coke of Holkham, the Earl of Derby and Horace Walpole. Through him Liverpool became a rendezvous for men of letters as well as merchants. Washington Irving tells how, curious to know who was the stranger with the impressive air entering the Liverpool Athenaeum, he asked his name, and on being answered: William Roscoe, 'I drew back with an involuntary feeling of veneration. This, then, was an author of celebrity; this was one of those men whose voices have gone forth to the ends of the earth; with whose minds I have communed even in the Solitudes of America.' The centenary of Roscoe's birth, in 1853, was celebrated in Liverpool with a breakfast presided over by the Lord Lieutenant, which was attended by 560 persons, who listened to eight distinct panegyrics. This homage, and the existence today of an annual oration in his honour, was directed in part to the public figure, the man of principle who started, or helped to start, all Liverpool's learned foundations, who stood out for Abolition and Emancipation in a city of slavers and anti-Catholics, and who interpolated (with permission) in a translation of an Italian poem, a glowing description of the advantages of breast-feeding as exemplified by the Duchess of Devonshire. But he became so notable a public figure because he first became an international one, and this was due to his work on the Medici.

It was the first to satisfy, on a large scale, the interest aroused by the constant brief references to them in histories of Italian art since Vasari, by references since Voltaire to a Medicean Age, and, most recently, by the glowing contrasts of the last volume of the *Decline and Fall*. Roscoe wrote at a favourable time, and by presenting the Medici in a wholly favourable light he ensured the success of his subject, though at some loss to his later reputation as a historian.

The origins of his interest in the Medici were literary and artistic. They appealed to him as the half-legendary patrons of the arts he most admired. He practised them, too. When his first poem, *Mount Pleasant*, appeared in 1777, Sir Joshua

Reynolds wrote to congratulate him, and in the first public exhibition of painting in Liverpool two of his own hung among those of Fuseli, Paul Sandby and Angelica Kauffman. These, like all his works, were the result of a serious but circumscribed self-education. Formal schooling stopped at twelve, when he was taken away to help in his father's market garden. During this time he studied painting on china at a nearby factory, and in spare time from his later jobs as book-seller's assistant (at fifteen), and solicitor's clerk (at sixteen), he learned Latin and Italian with friends, especially Francis Holden, whose habit of reciting Italian poetry on their walks acted as a spur to his envious companion.

The preoccupations of the citizens of Liverpool at this time were still almost exclusively commercial. Roscoe and his friends resolved to change this, and when he was twenty founded a Society for the Encouragement of the Arts of Paint-ing and Design. As if this were to aim too high for the son of 'The Bowling-Green', his friend, Miss Maria Done, dis-patched the following warning:

> Teach Pride to own, and owning, to obey
> Fair Virtue's dictates, and her sacred laws:
> To brighter worlds show thou the glorious road,
> And be thy life as moral as thy song.

The exhortation was not likely to be wasted. Roscoe was in a ponderous mood at this period, with something of the pomposity and lack of humour common to the self-educated. His learning had been gained strenuously and he valued it in proportion, whether in a youthful work on Christian moral-ity or in his letters to his future wife, Jane Griffies, another poetess, of like tastes. 'To feel with one heart, to judge with one mind, and to look to the same high and pure sources for happiness, are the most beautiful links in the golden chain of domestic union.' But he was not just a dull young man with one or two precocious talents. As his interests widened, and came to deal with more important issues, his temper became more elastic; the greater the load placed on his intellect the more easily it seemed to bear it. From the turgid verse of his first political pamphlet *The Wrongs of Africa* (1787) he proceeded, as his confidence increased, to the vigorous lampooning of his opponents in rhyme doggerel. The man who had surrounded the prospect of matrimony with portentous moralizing wrote for his large family one of the most popular jingles for children of its time, *The Butterfly's Ball and the Grasshopper's Feast*. Not one of Roscoe's enthusiasms soured; each publication brought enough success to increase his assurance and the number of his friends: the popularity of *Lorenzo* and *Leo* enough to tide over bankruptcy and the loss of his parliamentary seat.

He began practising as an attorney in 1774 and using his salary to collect Italian books and prints. This expenditure, he knew, was helping to postpone his marriage, and on one occasion, when he was in London for a trial, he was smitten with remorse for spending forty shillings on prints. 'Be assured,' he wrote to Jane at once, 'I am not without a full sense of the danger I run in the many temptations which surround me in this line, but my affection for you is the great security which must prevent me from trespassing in this respect, as well as in all others,' They married in 1781.

The Society for the Encouragement of the Arts of Painting and Design had foundered by this time, and Roscoe formed a new Society for Promoting Painting and Design. The society was an early patron of Fuseli, who became Roscoe's firm friend, sharing his interest in the history of Italian art, and it encouraged Roscoe to write a number of lectures on painting. The fostering of this interest led him about 1785 to write a poem on 'The Origin of Engraving' which contained his first mention of Lorenzo dei Medici. Talking of painting, he wrote:

> Long droop'd the sacred art – but rose at length
> With brighter lustre and redoubled strength;
> When great Lorenzo, midst his mild domain,
> Led the gay Muses and their kindred train.

And in a footnote on Lorenzo he sounds firmly the note of the later book. 'To the munificence and taste of Lorenzo is principally to be attributed the sudden progress of the fine arts in Italy at the close of the fifteenth century. But this is only a small part of his praise. If a full inquiry he made into his life and character, he will appear to be not only one of the most extraordinary, but, perhaps, upon the whole, the most extraordinary man that any age or nation has produced.' Roscoe made this inquiry and came to this conclusion. The little time he had been able to give to reading history in general made it hard for him to change opinions once he had formed them. He had seen it hinted that Lorenzo was a great man, and also Leo, and he developed these hints to their limit. Similarly, he reflected none of the discussions about the nature of the period he chose that were so common during the previous two generations; he had no taste for philosophical history and there is no evidence that he had read any. To the end of his life he believed in the sudden progress of the fine arts after 'the middle ages – that long and feverish sleep of the human intellect', and this in spite of his conviction that Vasari was wrong in stating the same thing. He saw that there were artists of merit before Cimabue, his own collection bore it out, but this did nothing to alter his determination to make enlightenment wait for the Medici. Florence under Lorenzo, Rome under Leo, these he came to know well, but he knew them at the expense of knowing where they stood, either in the history of Italy and Europe in general or in the debates of his fellow historians.

Work on Lorenzo continued. In 1791 he printed a few of

his poems, referring to him as 'vero Mecenate, e restauratore delle belle lettere nel secolo decimo quinto, e da molto tempo l'ogetto di mia somma reverenza, ed ammirazione'. Two years later the biography was ready for the press.

In spite of numerous earlier references to the Medici such a work was a novelty. The scanty Italian literature on Lorenzo was based on the short early life by Valori, whose opinion of his hero was too guarded for Roscoe's taste. Varillas he rightly rejected and, in fact, the only books he found of real use were a Latin life by Fabroni, printed in 1784, and Tenhove's *Mémoires Généalogiques de la Maison de Médici*, which only appeared when the first sheets of *Lorenzo* were already at the printers, and was, besides, only briefly concerned with Lorenzo. This lack of precedent was encouraging; however much the critics might wish to rend him, they would not be able to, a great comfort for an amateur historian. As it turned out, they were universally approving. The book became popular at once. Roscoe sold the copyright for £1,200, and a third edition appeared in 1799, three years after the first. Lord Orford took it for granted that Lorenzo was now 'one of the most excellent and greatest men with whom we are all acquainted', and added to a correspondent his belief that Roscoe had shown himself the greatest of modern historians. Lord Lansdowne praised it in the Lords, the Earl of Bristol offered him the use of his apartments in Rome and Naples, the reviewers fawned. The poet Thomas Mathias rallied the attention of his readers:

> But hark, what solemn strains from Arno's vales
> Breathe raptures, wafted on the Tuscan gales!
> LORENZO rears again his awful head,
> And feels his ancient glories 'round him spread;
> The Muses, starting from their trance, revive,
> And at their ROSCOE's bidding wake and live.

By 1799 it had been translated into French, Italian and German, in 1803 an edition appeared in the United States. But most surprising tribute of all was the decision of Fabroni, the author of the Latin work on Lorenzo, and the greatest living Italian authority on the Medici, to cancel his project of translating his own work into Italian and to arrange for the translation of Roscoe's instead. In flattering correspondence with scholars all over Europe, Roscoe moved to a large house, Allerton, in the country north-east of Liverpool, where his father was said once to have been butler, gave up the law and became partner in a bank. His fortunes were at their height.

It was significant that the parts of the book that were most commended were the most subjective, and therefore the most subject to a change of opinion. He was praised for his liberal ideas, his love of humanity, his defence of the principles of freedom and virtue; readers felt warmly that they had been made to know him, his pure taste, his charity and benevolence; they admired the harmony and elegance of his style. As Roscoe had foreseen, they did not know enough to appraise his treatment of Lorenzo, and were forced to turn their approval on his biographer instead. And Roscoe had challenged no one, he was humble. Repeating the belief that all the roots of modern Europe dwindled back to the beginning of the sixteenth century and the close of the fifteenth, he declared himself dazzled by the complexity and radiance of the time and retired to a period where the light was dimmer, where the closing middle ages exonerated the historian from being too minute: 'It appeared to me', he excused himself in the preface, 'that the mere historical events of the fifteenth century so far as they regarded Italy, could not deeply interest my countrymen in the eighteenth.' He had only turned to history at all because a love of literature had forced him. He explained how his interest in individual Italian authors had led him to a study of Italian literature in general, and this had brought him back, time after time, to the figure of Lorenzo, around whom the arts and sciences revolved as about their true centre. With *Lorenzo*, in fact, Roscoe had satisfied widespread interest with little risk. It is not an experiment that can safely be repeated.

Hardly had *Lorenzo* appeared than Roscoe's admirers hurried to urge him to a task that would stretch his powers further than they could reach: the reign of Leo X, in the centre of the period Roscoe had exclaimed against as being too bright for him. Having portrayed the Pericles of modern times, he was now to be pitted against the Augustus.

One of the difficulties in writing *Lorenzo* had been the lack of a public library in Liverpool. Roscoe had to buy whatever he could afford on his visits to London. Fortunately, Italian books were cheap, and there were two important sales, of the Crevenna and Pinelli libraries, which helped him to stop a number of gaps, but there seemed no chance of going beyond printed sources, and he was without many even of these. Then in 1789 a friend of his and of Holden's, William Clarke, had to go to Fiesole for his health. Roscoe appealed for his help, and Clarke at once plunged with ardour into research. He was lucky in that in Florence alone was a bribe unnecessary to gain access to the archives, and Clarke browsed freely in the Riccardi and Laurentian libraries, and in the Palazzo Vecchio. Here he copied and extracted whatever he thought Roscoe would find most useful. Lorenzo's poems arrived in one of these budgets, and Roscoe's edition was dedicated to him, but Clarke was not a scholar, and his industry was no compensation for the absence of the historian himself, who had to accept what was sent him, with no knowledge of its accuracy or of what had been passed over. The difficulties that *Leo* offered were, of course, much greater. There was the Vatican library, there was material in Venice, and in the *Bibliothèque Nationale* in Paris lay the crucial diary of Paris de Grassis, Leo's master of ceremonies.

Roscoe was not deterred. Lord Holland paid Penrose, Chaplain to the British Embassy at Florence, to transcribe documents there, and before long two bulky folios arrived. A complete stranger, John Johnson, wrote from Rome to say that he had heard of Roscoe's project and would be glad to collect material for him at the Vatican. Roscoe agreed unconditionally. 'With respect to the pontificate of Leo X,' he wrote, 'every thing that refers to it will be of importance to me – whether it concerns his political transactions and negociations, his encouragement of literature and art, his conduct, both in public and private life; in short, whatever has any connection with his history, or with that of any branch of his family.' A large assignment, and how impossible to control! Similar generosity came from Italians themselves, who gladly provided materials for a work in English, written by someone who had never been to Italy, and which they would have to translate back into their own tongue. Even the problem of the de Grassis MSS. was solved when his friend the Rev. W. Shepherd went to Paris and volunteered to copy any parts that seemed as though they might be relevant.

Though at the mercy of his copyists' whims, Roscoe was not much worried. He did not find an undue restlessness at devoting years of thought to a country he would never see. His friends, when abroad, were used to receive from him poems written by his fireside describing scenes they had actually under their eyes. Clarke, at Lisbon, for instance, received this apostrophe from Liverpool:

> Ye hills and towering forests crown'd,
> Ye plains by sultry suns embrown'd,
> Ye vales along whose vine-clad sides
> The Douro rolls his rapid tides.

Roscoe had never seen a sculpture by Michelangelo, but he declared, nevertheless, that an illustration of a bust of Lorenzo 'cannot be mistaken for the work of any other hand', in which he was unfortunate, for the bust was in fact by another hand. It was only in keeping with his writing about a country he had never visited and judging a work he had never seen that he elected to study an order of plants which could not be made to bloom in this country, and of which specimens had to be sent from as far afield as Calcutta.

It must be thought that Roscoe was alone in this belief that the writer need not visit the country he was concerned with. It was the habit of English historians at least as late as Grote, whom Taine anathematized for his writing a history of Greece without setting foot there. While Roscoe was selecting from his correspondents' selections, Mrs Radcliffe was writing the scenic passages upon which the effect of her novels so much depended, out of travellers' accounts of Italy, descriptive works like John Smith's *Select Views of Italy, with Topographical . . . Descriptions* (1792–6) and reproductions of the landscapes of Salvator Rosa. Roscoe's contemporary and adversary Sismondi, however, made a point of visiting nearly every spot he described, going so far as to travel through Germany to visit its historical monuments, because her history was so bound up with that of Italy.

Roscoe was flattered by disciples, as well as assistants. The Rev. W. Parr Greswell claimed that his classic pen had stimulated rather than allayed the curiosity of the public, and produced his own *Memoirs of Angelus Politianus, Joannes Picus of Mirandola . . .* etc., in 1801. Shepherd, the transcriber of Paris de Grassis, was similarly inspired by *Lorenzo* to write a book of his own. 'From the perusal of that elegant publication, I was led to imagine, that the history of Poggio must contain a rich fund of information respecting the revival of letters.' In 1802 appeared his *The Life of Poggio Bracciolini*. He was more interested in causation than Roscoe and explained the intellectual vigour of Italy in the fifteenth century in these terms: the disappearance of feudalism released men from the bonds of strict subordination, a process that was aided by the precarious titles of rulers who were forced to sue to their peoples for favours; the hazardous life of the time led to a development of energy and genius; the division of Italy into petty states meant that diplomacy was important and learning necessary; finally, once intellectual activity was aroused, there were copies of the works of the ancients at hand which could excite and direct it. But this explanation is no more than an aside, interpolated to explain the disappointment Poggio felt at the poor state of literature he met in Britain, and why the two countries differed so much in this respect. Again, when Tenhove's *Mémoires Généalogiques* were translated, they were arranged on the plan of Roscoe's book. He had inspired a play, William Rough's *Lorenzino de Medici* (1797), which was dedicated to him. The only work dealing with Florentine history at this time which did not acknowledge a substantial debt to Roscoe was Mark Noble's *Memoirs of the Illustrious House of Medici*, which was published, to the author's concern, a year after *Lorenzo*. He was careful to say that 'After I had completed my work, and not till then, I had an opportunity of perusing Mr Roscoe's Life of Lorenzo de Medici, surnamed Il Magnifico', and his book, certainly, is very unlike Roscoe's. It runs from the beginning of the fifteenth century to 1737, and contains only one chapter on Lorenzo himself. He believed, moreover, that the Medici, and Lorenzo in particular, deliberately sapped the independence of the Florentines, an opinion whose exact opposite Roscoe passionately espoused.

As work on Leo proceeded, there were signs that its reception might not be entirely favourable. *The Edinburgh Review* in 1803, its second provocative year of issue, attacked Shepherd's *Poggio* as one of the unfortunate results of the 'too splendid reputation' of *Lorenzo*. As a result of the flattering reception given to Roscoe's book, the reviewer goes on, 'the enlightened and scientific philosopher of the present day is

called upon to peruse the annals of an ignorant and superstitious age, to study the effusions of scholastic ostentation,
and to enlarge his understanding, by contemplating the
exploits of monks, in plundering half-demolished libraries,
and cleansing their mouldy treasures . . . Dry details, interspersed with trifling incidents and silly stories, are eked out
into expensive works, which are, however, recommended to
the taste and judgement of a very large class of readers, by the
beauty of the typography, and the vast expanse of margin.'

When *The Life and Pontificate of Leo the Tenth* appeared in
1805, it was in four volumes, carefully printed, with wide
margins, and adorned with frontispieces, vignettes and med-
allions. The *Edinburgh* was ready. *Leo* was too long, contained
ridiculous minutiæ, was the vehicle for despicable cant and a
remarkable degree of prejudice. It was sad that a subject that
had been contemplated by Collins the poet, and Warton the
literary historian, and Robertson, should have been actually
written by a man who had no eye for form, who whitewashed
Lucrezia Borgia and reviled Martin Luther. Other reviewers
were no kinder. To the *Christian Observer* Roscoe 'had received a retaining fee from the Pope'. The *Critical Review*
warned its readers that 'to approve of the moral and religious
part of his work, would render a person obnoxious to the
Society for the Suppression of Vice'. More bluntly still, the
Literary Journal opined that 'a well informed child of ten years
of age might give him the lie direct'.

Roscoe was directly responsible for these strictures, which
had little to do with the historical value of the work. He had
insisted on making it a *confessio fidei* as well as a biography.
His stature as a public figure had grown, since *Lorenzo*, and
his confidence with it, and, as he explained to a friend, he
had used the events of Leo's life to convey, as he was in duty
bound to do, his most earnest thoughts on politics, morals,
religion and taste and a variety of topics of less importance.
As a result, the *Edinburgh*'s crushingly charitable conclusion

was deserved: 'his writings impress us with one uniform conviction, that he is a truly amiable and benevolent man.' After
reading the book it seemed easier to form an estimate of
Roscoe and his times than of Leo and his.

The impetus of Roscoe's initial success, however, was too
great to be seriously slowed by the reviews. He sold half the
copyright for £2,000, an unusually large sum even for the
whole of it, and it was translated as a matter of course into
German, French and Italian. The last was promptly placed
on the *Index*, a sufficient answer to the *Christian Observer*.
His patrons were satisfied with the mass of new material he
produced referring to letters and social life, his Italian col-
leagues were grateful for such extended notice being taken
of their country when its political prestige had disappeared.

With *Leo*, Roscoe declared that he would write no more
of the history or literature of Italy. And this decision he
adhered to, except when goaded to reply, in 1822, to the
steadily accumulating criticisms of *Lorenzo*.

His opinions on morals and politics had put mortality deep
into his historical works, but they widened the opportunities
for public ones. His sentiments and his character had become
well known when in 1806 he was asked to stand for Parliament against generals Gascoyne and Tarleton. And it speaks
much for his repute that he was elected in spite of the unpopu-
larity of his programme: Catholic emancipation, Parliamentary reform, and the abolition of the Slave Trade. He saw
this last aim achieved, though his share in it might have cost
his life; on making his public entry into Liverpool on the
dissolution of Parliament, his procession was waylaid by
gangs of seamen, mostly from slaving ships, who fell on it
with bludgeons. In the mêlée a friend's horse was stabbed
with a knife, but Roscoe was extricated and escorted in safety
to the bank. To prevent such extravagant feeling, he declined
to contest the seat again. Another honour he had to refuse at
the same time was the Deputy Lieutenantship of the County

which the Earl of Derby offered him. Roscoe replied regret-
ting that the test laws excluded him as a dissenter.

His political life, which he continued through pamphlets,
and his business with the bank, left him little time and he
spent that not on history but on his earlier love, art. Politician,
whose theme was peace and tolerance, banker, whose aim
was to soften commerce with letters, he seemed to have the
image of his youthful hero, Lorenzo, always before his eyes.
By now he was an established patron of artists. He supported
Stubbs and Bewick's pupil, Henry Hole, Gibson the sculptor,
and Fuseli, and forgotten figures like the Mr Crouchley
'whose sketch of the transfiguration received the commen-
dation of Mr Roscoe as a more consistent work than that of
Raffaele, inasmuch as the group was more in unity of design
than that of the great Florentine painter'. Like Lorenzo, too,
he was a collector. The purchase of prints and paintings, once
so hesitant and remorseful, had never stopped, and he came
to own the most representative collection of Italian works in
England. He had paintings attributed to all the important
masters of the sixteenth and seventeenth centuries, and many
of the fifteenth, though those attributions were in many cases
wrong. He was repeatedly asked to write the history of Italian
art, its rise and decline, and though he always refused, his
attention was constantly brought back to the subject.

He had bought a tract of waste land, for instance, at Chat
Moss, near Manchester, where he experimented in an attempt
to bring it into cultivation. That he had some success was
indicated by Mrs Barbauld, who mentioned in her otherwise
pessimistic *Eighteen Hundred and Eleven* the place

> Where Roscoe, to whose patriot breast belong
> The Roman virtue, and the Tuscan song,
> Led Ceres to the bleak and barren moor
> Where Ceres never gain'd a wreath before.

But more important than the notice of a minor poetess was the interest and friendship of Coke, with whom he stayed at Holkham. He was later to catalogue the library there, but at first his artistic rather than his literary appetite was whetted by the discovery of a volume of Raphael's drawings of the architectural remains of ancient Rome, and a manuscript in mirror-writing where, as he exclaimed:

> . . . Da Vinci's genius strives
> Through nature's works to trace the cause,
> The water's rapid course describes –
> Its weight, its current, and its laws.

But before the drawings or the treatise on hydraulics could send him back to contemplate a history of Italian art, his collection, which would have illustrated it so well, had to be sold. His bank broke, suspended payment, and Roscoe, as a bankrupt, was forced to fly to Chat Moss, where he had to ponder experiments for getting rid not only of surplus water but the creditors who were preventing him even from leaving the house. It was clearly necessary to sell his library and the pictures.

On the sale catalogue, which was his epitaph as a Mæcenas, he lavished a necrophagous care. It was scrupulously printed and reflected, like the sonnets which peppered the weeks of gloomy preparation, Roscoe's intention to make even a personal disaster a thing of beauty. The sale realized over £11,000, of which £2,825 was fetched by the drawings of paintings. The best paintings went to Holkham, where he could see them again, and many of his favourite books were bought by friends who presented them back to him. But research was no longer possible. The fortunes of his family of ten were dependent on his pen, but having neither time nor opportunity for accumulating facts, he had to depend on accumulations of principle. He became interested in penal reform and wrote a series of pamphlets on the question, kindly, sensible and strongly reasoned, as always, his object being to persuade society not to revenge itself on the criminal but to reform him. He retained his interest in the cultural life of Liverpool, assisting in the foundation of the Institution for the promotion of literature, science and the arts, giving the inaugural address 'On the Origin and Vicissitudes of Literature, Science, and Art, and their Influence on the present State of Society'. And as a little more money came to hand he was able to offer protection and advice to the needy, as he had always wished to do, whether it were the tattooed man at a neighbouring circus with literary ambitions, or a half-savage prodigy from Wales. The latter, Richard Roberts Jones, was the subject of a *Memoir* by Roscoe (1822) who described the disadvantages of having a guest whose knowledge of Hebrew philology was extraordinary, but who persisted in sleeping under the bed; whose knowledge was fascinating, but whose conservatism was such that 'it was with the utmost difficulty he could be persuaded to submit to those ablutions which were absolutely necessary to render a near conversation with him agreeable – or, indeed, safe'.

It is not surprising that the *Illustrations, Historical and Critical, of the Life of Lorenzo de Medici*, published in the same year, contained little that was new, and offered no changed point of view but an exaggeration of an old one. It was written to answer critics whose opinions as to the greatness of Lorenzo were more temperate than his own. He was accused, notably by Sismondi and Thurot, Roscoe's French translator, of being led by his own political convictions and the constitution of his own country, to ignore the evils of a hereditary despotism in Florence; it had looked like the English monarchy and Roscoe assumed it was excellent for that reason. His riposte was to make the same charge against Sismondi, and to accuse the Swiss author of being misled by his own love of republicanism. Lorenzo, he repeated, had not only been a great man, and a liberal one, he had 'set an example, which, if it had been successfully followed, might have prevented ages of contention and bloodshed, and enabled us to date from the commencement of the sixteenth century the great career of human improvement'. But, in fact, the *Illustrations*, for all its copious documentation, and bulky appendix, is more than ever a record of Roscoe's feeling rather than his learning.

It had been only an interlude in a life devoted now to other concerns. As honours flowed in which recognized the historian of twenty years before: associate membership of the Royal Society of Literature, its gold medal, a corresponding membership of the Academia della Crusca, he continued to work on monandrian plants, and on an edition of Pope. His latest honour did not come from a literary body at all, but from the Horticultural Society of New York. In 1831 he died.

For only fifteen of Roscoe's seventy-eight years was he mainly concerned with history. *Lorenzo* and *Leo* were written in the leisure hours of a man with a large family and a business. He had had no critical training, his friends and correspondents were amateurs of arts and letters like himself. His aim was one in which objectivity is hard to achieve: the description of periods of literature. He had his special axes to grind: that the Medici were heroes and that history must instruct and reform. He was unconscious of a dilemma when he stated that his motive in writing *Leo* was 'to deduce, from the unperverted pages of history, those maxims of true humanity, sound wisdom, and political fidelity, which have been too much neglected in all ages, but which are the only solid foundations of the repose, the dignity, and the happiness of mankind'. Roscoe tended to skip the pages which would have contradicted the story he was determined to find. Because he came to know Florence and Rome through their literature, he saw the Florentines and Romans too much in terms of the books they read and the poems they wrote. The roar of commerce and the cries of political rivals are muffled by library doors, and Roscoe's one original plea, that no detail is too small for the dignity of history, was wasted when those details were devoted only to the part of man's personality which sits with pen in hand.

His insistence on the relevance of the late fifteenth century to the late eighteenth led him to bridge the 300-year gap too easily. His desire for a wider suffrage, for instance, and his belief that the more persons have a stake in government the more industriously they work, led to an erroneous picture of Florence, where industry thrived because 'every citizen was conversant with, and might hope at least to partake in the government'. The position of Lorenzo in the constitution was described, as Sismondi complained, too readily in terms of that of George III. A more personal, but equally misleading, parallel was one between the Medici and himself. His son Henry wrote: 'All that he became was the result of his own exertions.' The same had been true of his heroes, and it was one of the things that commended them to Roscoe and his contemporaries. 'They were beholden only to themselves for their grandeur,' wrote Noble, 'they have shown what arduous tasks may be surmounted by unwearied perseverance.' Roscoe had persevered, had become, in his smaller way, statesman, patron, poet, the centre of a literary circle, the gilder of commerce with arts. But to read the development of the ruler of an important state in terms of the development three centuries later of a self-made private citizen, however unconsciously, was to circumscribe the historian's view too far. Roscoe was drawn to Lorenzo by too much hero-worship, was too undisciplined as an historian to resist reading himself into his subject. And as a zealous citizen the parallel between Liverpool and Florence came naturally too. Like the Italian cities, he said in his Royal Institution inaugural address, the cities of England are seeing 'the beneficial influence which commerce and literature have on each other', and of these Liverpool was the first. It was not simply a dream of Roscoe's. His works, wrote a contemporary, issued 'from this great mercantile city, as from a second Florence', and another dedicated a history of art to 'those who delight in seeing their country become the seat of the Arts and Sciences, and the reign of George the Fourth rival the period of Lorenzo de Medici'.

These very faults as an historian go a long way to explain the popularity of Roscoe, the extraordinary vogue of the Medici. The subjective part of his work suited that very Spirit of the Times which he pooh-poohed as 'only another phrase for causes and circumstances which have not hitherto been sufficiently explained'. His anti-mechanist view of history, his insistence that the individual alone counts, fell sweetly upon many early nineteenth-century ears. Chance and the turn of fortune's wheel were phrases which flattered men's irresolution. To believe in an inevitable decline was 'to subject the powers of the mind to the operation of inert matter' and give the lie to the vigour and initiative every man felt in his own breast. Progress was accelerating. Hence the need for institutions to keep pace with new discoveries, and Athenæums to humanize them. Hence the importance of the Medici, the prime exemplars of the successful union of commerce and culture, both attained through individual effort.

That Roscoe spent far more time on cultural than on commercial, or political, or religious matters was another fault that pleased his audience. The majority of them were more interested in literature and painting than in history; the middle ages to many were only tolerable for their dying contribution to art, a pontificate only for the artists and writers who lived during it, whose work was as beautiful to Protestant as to Catholic eyes. Most of Roscoe's friends and patrons were dilettanti, grateful for information about the highest exemplars of their order, especially when comfortably expressed, with eloquence and high principle, and indifferent to other sides of the subject. Another section of Roscoe's audience was also avid for more news of the Medici, but for a different reason. An age of patronage was dying; writers and artists were finding it increasingly hard to get support. Especially the painters felt this; with French and Italian painting in the doldrums and the growth of an English school of history painters, like Benjamin West, it was felt that if only the auspicious moment could be taken advantage of, if only it could be *patronized*, British art might spring with a bound to the level of the great continental schools. The greatest period of Italian art had been produced by great patrons. Great patrons could bring a similar fortune to Britain.

'Perhaps on the face of the earth there never existed a family to which the fine arts, and the general interests of learning, have been so much indebted.' This judgment was made by the Rev. Robert Bromley in his *A Philosophical and Critical History of the Fine Arts* (1793–5) and was one of many that whetted the appetite for Roscoe's large-scale treatment of the two most famous Medici. Bromley's work is interesting because it is precisely the theme of patronage that lifts his work above the level of trite dependence on Vasari and Félibien it shows in other respects. He not only gives a fairly full account of the patronage of the Medici but explains its nature in sociological terms, and claims that to understand the nature of a painting one must understand the particular demands of the patron. Raphael's frescoes in Rome, for instance, reflect the two outstanding needs of the papacy: to exalt their temporal glory, and to foster the growth of superstitious reverence for their divine powers. Thus, says Bromley, while 'the justification of Leo III' and 'the miracles of Leo IV' celebrate the irresistible nature of the pontificate, the 'Mass at Bolsena' 'fixed the church in the possession of its sheet-anchor, the doctrine of transubstantiation'. The power, then, of the patron, is dangerously great. We must be thankful that when the mediæval church wanted representations of martyrdoms and judgment days, the powers of their artists were so small.

Patronage of this time is something to shudder at, but 'when we speak of the house of Medici, the name sounds sweetly to every ear'.

More important was the effect of Roscoe's championship of Lorenzo on the interest taken in the last part of the fifteenth century as a whole, in maintaining the belief that it was a period of crucial significance. The middle ages were still under fire. The old prejudices continued to speak in textbooks like the Rev. John Adams's *View of Universal History* (1795) to the effect that 'till the sixteenth century, Europe exhibited a picture of most melancholy Gothic barbarity'. The new prejudice spoke in the *Edinburgh* with its fad for the doctrine of usefulness. 'Let us not, in the nineteenth century, deify works of the fifteenth, when the present age furnishes subjects infinitely more worthy of those immortal honours.' The objection is not simply to the first part of the century. 'It is not from the barbarous ages of the Medici,' went on the reviewer in 1803, 'that improvements in the modern art of government, or the principles of modern policy, are to be derived. Nor is it in those dark and superstitious periods that we are to search for models of imitation, either in public or in private life.' The same plea, that life with a revolution just behind and a Napoleonic victory possibly just ahead was too earnest for anything but *useful* history to be written, was levelled at the historian of a single family; two years after *Leo* had been struck, a similar work confronted the reviewer in Cox's *History of the House of Austria*. 'No man,' came the opinion, 'no man has a right to fill three quarto volumes with the history of the house of Austria, or of any other house whatsoever.' And as the war continued, the tone became stricter, and the *Quarterly*, too, added its demand that history should be written for no frivolous reason, but only when it illustrates and encourages that public virtue without which a free nation cannot weather its crises.

Nor had the importance of Lorenzo's lifetime to be

reasserted only against the enemies of political and religious mediævalism; the lovers of letters themselves, in seeking for the most significant cultural period, were tending to look earlier or later than that of Lorenzo.

Interest in the troubadours and the Arabs continued. Berington's *Heloise and Abelard* (1789) showed that there had been independence and learning in the eleventh century, and in 1798 Charles Philpot produced his influential *Introduction to the Literary History of the Fourteenth and Fifteenth Centuries*, a work which showed how amply the culture of the fifteenth and sixteenth centuries had been prepared for in the eleventh, twelfth and thirteenth. The revival of letters was due in the first place, he wrote, to the Arabs who had absorbed Greek learning and retransmitted it to Europe from the Near East, Africa and Spain during the tenth and eleventh centuries. Their texts of Aristotle and mathematical and physical works stirred men's faculties and prepared them to receive classical literature. The Crusades, with the Troubadours, introduced a taste for poetry which prepared for the reception of Dante and Petrarch, and the revived study of civil law sharpened men's reasons and gave them a sense of style. Commerce was growing, and, with commerce, a taste for luxuries and the encouragement of the arts. There were patrons, as there was learning, centuries before the Medici: Frederick II and his minister Petrus de Vimeis, Charles of Anjou, Alexander III. This earlier period, then, the dawn of the revival, was with all its wide promise, 'the proper subject of historical and critical consideration'.

Since the last volume of Gibbon, attention was also drawn to this period, in admiration of the democratic valour of the Italian republics. It was an interest that was to grow with the appearance of Sismondi's *Histoire des républiques italiennes au Moyen Age* (1807–18) and with increasing interest in electoral reform, but already in 1794, John Adams, one of the drafters of the Declaration of Independence and later President of the

United States, had brought out his *History of the Principal Republics in the World*. The work was tendentious. Its aim was to find what lessons old republics had to offer the new. He investigated over fifty of them, paying particular attention to Italy, for 'There once existed a cluster of governments, now generally known by the name of the Italian Republics of the Middle Age, which deserve the attention of Americans, and will farther illustrate and confirm the principles we have endeavoured to maintain.'

While these arguments were tending to show that the origins of modern thought were to be found in the early middle ages, the argument – Enlightenment: Reformation: which came first? – continued to emphasize the mid-sixteenth century as the point of origin. The point made in works like George Thompson's *The Spirit of General History* (1791) was that since the Roman Church was synonymous with superstition, enlightenment could not come until its power was broken. Literature had revived long before, it was true, but its slavish dependence on antique models, its barren preoccupation with style, debars it from all claim to freedom of thought. The book is a bad, ill-informed one, but the argument was common to anti-Catholic writers with inadequate knowledge of literary history. How far terms now applied to the Renaissance could be used of the Reformation is shown in Coleridge's remark that 'The Reformation sounded through Europe like a trumpet; from the king to the peasant there was an enthusiasm for knowledge; the discovery of a MS. was the subject of an embassy.' Roscoe himself hesitated between the two opinions. He emphasized the benefits of the Reformation in enlarging freedom of inquiry, but he deplored the shrinking of patronage it entailed, and pointed out that the Reformation itself was the work of men whose minds had been liberated by the earlier revival of letters. But though he gave more favour to the view that enlightenment came before the Reformation, he gave ammunition to the opposing view of doing so much to encourage interest in sixteenth-century literature.

Italians and Italian books were out of favour at the end of the eighteenth century. Travellers continued to be disparaging in spite of the efforts of John Moore in *A View of Society and Manners in Italy; with Anecdotes relating to some Eminent Characters* (1781) to clear the Italians from charges of gross immorality, violence and superstition made by other English writers. The lack of interest in Italian books was charmingly illustrated by Mozart's librettist, Lorenzo da Ponte.

In 1800 he lost his position at King's theatre and was walking along the Strand in a state of deep depression when he was aroused by screams and saw a bull, escaped from a slaughterhouse, charging up the street towards him. To save himself he slipped inside a nearby shop. When the animal had thundered past and da Ponte had recovered his breath, he saw that the shop was a bookseller's. It recalled an earlier scheme he had had for selling Italian books in London. He asked the owner if he had any. 'Only too many,' was the reply. 'You will do me a pleasure if you will come and take them off my hands.' So little was the demand that da Ponte was able to buy this man's stock, and Italian books from other shops, for a very small sum, and with these he opened a shop himself. One of his steadiest customers, and the one who did most to popularize his wares, was Roscoe. And from the publication of *Lorenzo* and *Leo* there was a renewed demand for Italian texts as well as a steady flow of translations and accounts of Italian poets and prose writers, several of the most influential being by Roscoe's son Thomas. But it was natural that this reawakened interest should dwell on the literature of the sixteenth century, beginning with Ariosto, one of the heroes of *Leo*.

The result of Roscoe's work was to regain for Bolingbroke's period much of the attention it had lost. He did this not by harnessing two generations of speculation into a general explanation of the period, or even by describing it as the period in which modern man awoke; his speculations were reserved for matters of principle, the treatment of slaves, or of religious minorities; his interest was in individuals, not in individualism. On the question of periods, Roscoe went no further than to say that he saw history as a landscape, largely desert, but interspersed with glades and luxuriant valleys where the traveller would gladly pause. The source of the underground streams that fed them, the provenance of the seed which had provided such grateful shade were matters of indifference; the traveller's role was to describe, not to explain. His distaste for those Burning Ghats, the middle ages, made the sudden appearance of the Laurentian oasis seem like a theory as well as a statement. But it was not. When Roscoe thought of the middle ages in the congenial terms of art, he could see that there had been wide cultivation, and it was the same with literature; it was only his veneration of Lorenzo and minute interest in all his circle that gave the impression of civilization suddenly appearing at his court. But his abrupt marshalling of a host aroused an interest in the late fifteenth and early sixteenth centuries that has lasted as firmly as the habit of seeing that age in terms of its great men. When the concept of a Renaissance arrived, the forces it was invented to explain would have to group themselves round the Medici as about a monument, inconvenient but sacred, to the hero-worship of the innkeeper's son who became the Sage of Liverpool.

CHAPTER FIVE

Taste for Italian Paintings:
(II) Late Eighteenth to Early
Nineteenth Centuries

Since the effect of the Gothic Revival was to awaken interest in the middle ages at least to a further extent than this had yet been achieved by historians, it might have been expected that mediæval art would find a new sympathy.

In England, it is true, continuity with the past was felt more naturally in literature than in art. The achievement was greater, and however much taste had changed, the past was seen there to have contributed to the present, whereas the line of English art had been violently crossed and broken by Italian influence; the affinity recognized by Pope in his parodies of Chaucer and Spenser could not have been felt by Gainsborough for the artist of the Wilton diptych. Yet the habit of comparing the art of poetry with that of painting became so persistent that it seemed hopeful that the sort of literature admired would affect the sort of art admired, that when there was a growing appreciation of 'barbaric' literature, this would attract attention to 'barbaric' art, too.

To some extent this happened, but the art affected was only that of architecture; painting, lower in the artistic hierarchy, remained unaffected. There was a nationalist element in the mid–eighteenth century interest in the middle ages that was partly responsible for this. The publication of the *Niebelungenlied*, the translation of the *Edda*, the appearance of the Ossianic poems, these events had directed proud attention to the past of the countries concerned. Among the arts, the one most suited to remind the present of past glories was architecture, mileposting the middle ages with castles and abbeys which, if alien, were undeniably impressive. They could even be fitted into the important category of the Sublime through their melancholy and majesty, and from gracing a landscape came to be tolerated for their own sakes. In 1762 Richard Hurd wrote in his *Letters on Chivalry and Romance*: 'When an architect examines a Gothic structure by Grecian rules, he finds nothing but deformity. But the Gothic architecture has its own rules, by which, when it comes to be examined, it is seen to have its merits, as well as the Grecian.'

How complete was the failure of this taste for Gothic architecture to spread to painting of the same period was shown by Horace Walpole, who, having gothicized Strawberry Hill ten years before Hurd wrote, housed a large collection in it; in the preface to the catalogue he prepared, he was faced by Cimabue and his successors, 'but as their works are only curious for their antiquity, not for their excellence, and as they are not to be met with in collections', he passed them by.

The taste, too, was almost exclusively for the Gothic of the north; the mixed styles of Italy and Sicily defied analysis, and as their times were unwritten by the historian they were unable to appeal through sentiment. At home, the Englishman was led by Gothic architecture to mediæval history, in Italy he needed a knowledge of history before he could appreciate mediæval buildings. The Gothic revival, in fact, did no more for the popularization of early painting than to foster a general interest in the mediæval past, and less was done by Englishmen and Germans, who had seen a revival of interest in Gothic, than by Frenchmen, who had not. Some of Hugford's collection may have passed into the hands of Artaud de Montor, who had amassed a collection of a hundred and fifty primitives by 1808 and who published in that year *Considérations sur l'état de la peinture en Italie, dans les quatre siècles qui ont précédé celui de Raphael*. In his defence that such a treatment was needed in order properly to explain the greatest of all painters, Raphael, he was less devoted to his subject than his inspirer, Séroux d'Agincourt, who loved those centuries for their own sake.

D'Agincourt's is a considerable name. Born in 1730, this ex-army officer who knew Voltaire and had travelled in England, Belgium, Holland and Germany, came in 1778 into Italy and remained for the rest of his life. There an enthusiasm for antiquity yielded to one for the middle ages and he resolved to be their interpreter. 'Yes,' he is quoted as saying, 'I have bidden adieu to the beauties of Venus of Medici in order to devote myself completely to the simplicity of the Madonnas by Cimabue, by Giotto, and by the old Greek masters.' He employed numbers of artists to make copies of these works for him and accumulated a mass of material which he did not live to see through the press. It eventually appeared in 1823 as *Histoire de l'art d'après les monuments depuis sa décadence au IVe siècle jusqu'à son renouvellement au XVIe siècle*. A version did not appear in English until 1847.

He had influential pupils apart from de Montor. Paillot de Montabert, in a book on mediæval painting in 1812, even criticized Raphael for diverting art from its primitive simplicity, and one of d'Agincourt's copyists, William Young Ottley, was one of the pioneer English historians of Italian art.

He published two works, in 1823 and 1826, illustrated by examples of his own collection of drawings, which preached a familiar theme, but were useful in that they did so with the aid of numerous examples. The period from Cimabue to the end of the fifteenth century is meritorious largely in that it prepared the way for the perfection of the early sixteenth, with Leonardo, Fra Bartolomeo, Michelangelo and Raphael. Decline followed, only qualified by an attempt by the Caracci at the end of the century to reform painting, an attempt that though earnest was unsuccessful. His fellow collectors would probably have written the same sort of thing, had the occasion arisen, but they would not, like him, have bought according to it. Lip service to Leonardo did not mean that his drawings fetched a fraction of the price of those of the Caracci, or that a Michelangelo would be preferred to a Domenichino. And half of Raphael's own *œuvre* was in eclipse. The agent of a London art dealer wrote in 1802: 'All I could see in passing [through Florence] was a pair on wood, said to be certainly by Raphael in his first manner (or rather between his first and second manner), and which are admirable in their way; but I have some fears of acquiring even Raphael's works of this time.'

Even Ottley arranged his purchases on a didactic principle, rather than solely for the aesthetic pleasure they gave him, and this was certainly the case with Roscoe. The title of his 1816 sale catalogue was 'Series of Pictures Illustrating the Rise and Progress of Painting in Italy'. But it contained works that have been looked at since with great joy for their own sakes, like the Simone Martini in the Walker Art Gallery at Liverpool, and the Ercole de Roberti Pietà in the same place.

The list of names in the catalogue was remarkably representative. It even started with four paintings of the generally despised Greek school, though one could plead the distinction of having been painted by St Luke. Then, from Cimabue and Giotto onwards, scarcely an important name was missing from Angelico to Zuccarelli, the emphasis being on the quattrocento and early cinquecento, and there are some really remarkable names for the time: Castagno, Pollaiuolo, Baldovinetti, Ridolfo Ghirlandaio, Jacopo and Gentile Bellini. Certainly a good number of the attributions were wrong. The Pollaiuolo was the Ercole de Roberti, for instance, and the Giorgione has become a Dosso Dossi.

At the sale the later paintings went and the primitives were left behind or sold at a minute price. As Roscoe's son said afterwards, 'though highly curious as illustrating the history of art, (they) were little interesting to the ordinary collector'.

Though a few others, like William Beckford, the author of *Vathek*, and John Strange, whose collection contained works by Bellini, had come to share Roscoe's taste, the ordinary collector still preferred Annibale Caracci, who 'was unquestionably, take him for all in all, the most perfect painter that Italy ever produced', and Correggio, who painted 'the most splendid and harmonious of all pictures, the Christ in the Garden', which is now in the National Gallery. An early periodical, the *Annals of the Fine Arts*, had nothing to say of anyone working before Raphael, and when speaking of the sixteenth- and seventeenth-century Italians, its tone was hardly critical: 'It would be superfluous and arrogant, to criticise these deified productions of the pencil.'

But the best picture of average intelligent taste came from James Northcote, the portrait painter, protégé and biographer of Reynolds. In 1807 he wrote a short work entitled *The Dream of a Painter* which amounts, in fact, to a history of Italian art *en charade*.

He tells how, in the course of a ramble round the Vatican, he fell asleep 'on the steps of an altar in a small oratory built by St Pius the Fifth, situated immediately beyond the *stanza* of Raphael'. Dreaming in this auspicious place a figure appeared to him, the Genius of the Fine Arts, and led him into a huge room at one end of which stretched great golden tapestry curtains. A blast of trumpets – Apollo is revealed on Parnassus – a procession of Greek and Roman sages pass before his throne.

'After these had passed, there entered on the stage one of the most enchanting and graceful female figures I had ever beheld. She was encompassed by a splendour, or rather glory, that sparkled with every colour of the rainbow; in her hands she bore the implements made use of by painters. But what appeared ludicrous and unaccountable to me, was to see with

how much sollicitude this charming nymph encouraged and
enticed to come forward the oddest group I ever saw, and
the most unlike herself. Their number was considerable, their
manners timid, and they paid her great homage: this assembly
was in general composed of figures, lean, old, and hard fea-
tured; their drapery hung about them in so formal a manner,
that it fell into nothing but straight lines, and their sallow
complexions appeared well to correspond with the dingy hue
of their gothic monastic habits. Several amongst them were
females, with half starved and sickly looking children accom-
panying them, but not one of the whole group had beauty
sufficient to attract much attention. However, their modesty
and diffidence were such, as rendered it impossible for them
to offend the most fastidious spectator; for their manners
were natural, simple, and perfectly unassuming. They displayed no airs of pretence to self-importance, no violent con-
tortions of affectation, nor the grimace of forced expression;
but, on the contrary, such a degree of strong and distinct
meaning in the countenance, and in their actions, such strict
propriety, judgment and simplicity, as altogether gave them
a peculiar air of dignity.'

These figures, the Genius informed him, were the earliest
revivers of the fine arts, and after they had quit the scene
there was a long pause.

Then in a chariot of his own devising, came Leonardo,
Francis I seated beside him, horses and smiling followers.
Next, each with appropriate air and entourage, came Michelangelo, Raphael, Titian, Correggio, the Caracci ('Annibal, I
saw, boldly took the lead in the procession, although not the
first in age'), Guido Reni, Barocci, Rubens, Claude, Nicholas
Poussin, Rembrandt, Salvator Rosa, Van der Velde, and,
finally, Reynolds, not named but welcomed by the Genius
as his favourite and latest pupil.

'I was enraptured with pleasure, when on a sudden a dreadful burst of thunder that seemed as if it had torn the earth in

twain brought me to my original state, and I found myself reposing on the steps of the altar in the little oratory of St Pius the Fifth.'

The earlier actors may have seemed lean, old, and hard-featured to Northcote, but there were kindlier visionaries. Lanzi's *Storia Pittorica dell' Italia* joined Vasari in 1809 as an authority of almost equal weight, and emphasized the merits of Giotto and Cimabue, 'the Raffael and Michaelangelo of their day', a phrase that found quick acceptance in England.

In spite of the popularity of a book like Lanzi's, a great obstacle to the wide appreciation of early art remained: the public's unfamiliarity with the works themselves. Illustration had hardly helped. Until the technique of reproduction was improved it involved a simplification of the original. This was a subjective process, and the Arundel prints of the 1850s, like the engravings of Patch and Ottley, reflected not only the original painting but the contemporary way of looking at it. There were large numbers of drawings, it is true, in the hands of a few collectors, but the stiff price often charged for admission kept them out of the public eye. The purchase of panel paintings was virtually nil.

Purchase, of course, follows, and does not determine taste. But wavering taste may be encouraged to buy when pictures emerge dramatically from deep obscurity, are cheap, are exhibited openly and discussed. All these things happened as a result of the Napoleonic wars, and if collectors did not stop collecting the Caracci, Guido Reni and Domenichino, they at least changed their copies for originals and began to speculate cautiously in earlier wares. For the wars sliced through the roots of nearly every collection on the Continent. Even if the flowers remained in the soil they could easily be lifted out.

Especially was this true of Italy. Certain domestic measures, such as the suppression in Tuscany of a number of churches, as well as *Arti* and religious companies, had shaken a number of pictures free before the wars, but now the process was immensely hastened by political treaty and private bargaining. Treaty made with state after state in Italy provided the French with compensation in terms of works of art, including some 1,150 pictures. The Treaty of Tolentino alone, signed by the Pope in 1797, made over about a hundred paintings, busts, vases and statues from Rome, and other works from Ravenna, Rimini, Pesaro, Ancona, Perugia and Loreto. The author of *Hints to Travellers in Italy* warned his readers in 1815 that 'Since the late system of spoliation has taken place in Italy, the connoisseur in painting and sculpture will find little to detain him, I fear, in many of those cities where weeks were scarcely sufficient to satisfy his ardent curiosity.'

Triumphal processions accompanied the loot to the Louvre when it arrived in Paris. Among the works fêted by the crowd were the bronze horses of St Mark's, the Apollo Belvedere, the Laocoon, the Capitoline Brutus and Raphael's Transfiguration. And more caravans were on their way, bringing Rubenses from Belgium, Rembrandts from Holland, the cream of the royal and ducal collections of Germany. Wagonload after wagon-load still came from Italy, from antique busts to the Marriage of Cana by Veronese, which was so large that it was too hazardous to return and remains in the Louvre today.

On the heels of the public commissioners (Stendhal was one in Brunswick) came the dealers, the representatives of private collectors. One of them, William Buchanan, has left an account of his activities.

As soon as peace was declared in 1802 his agents in Italy got to work. Many families, as a result of Napoleon's constant demands for cash, had been forced to sell already; more were only holding on with difficulty. Buchanan's agents used every means to force them to let go. They engaged priests to use their influence on families who were loath to part with some cherished portrait. They scented and waited for death with vulturine rapacity. 'In some houses,' one wrote, 'where there are several sons to inherit, there are hopes of doing something should the old boys step off, but during their time I am told there is little chance of success.' Another, barely waiting to let the coffin pass him round the corner, hurried in to pick off the Sampieri collection. He was forestalled, however, by the appearance of the 13-year-old heir who declared that he was fond of painting and would not sell. Another agent had bargained with the bishop and priest concerned for the purchase of a Domenichino altar-piece from a small church near Genoa. He had hardly removed it when the infuriated peasants threatened to march on the church and pull it down over the heads of those responsible for the sale. This work was returned, but the toll was great, and among other works we owe to Buchanan's method is the Titian Bacchus and Ariadne in the National Gallery.

With the treaty works, a series of magnificent exhibitions was held in the Louvre. The old French royal collections were added, too, so the result was a concentration of masterpieces that has never been paralleled. There were together on the walls at one time 25 Raphaels, 23 Titians, 33 Van Dycks, 31 Rembrandts and 53 Rubens. After the reannexation of Tuscany in 1812 a large number of primitives arrived. But the predominant taste of the confiscations had been traditional: 26 Guercinos, 23 Guidos and 33 Annibale Caraccis showed that. The taste of the purchases had been the same. Buchanan's lists are headed by the favourite names of grand tour collections: the Caracci, Gaspar Poussin, Domenichino, Claude, Guido, Guercino, and so on. From other sources came the same sort of pictures; of the twenty major sales in London and Paris between 1795 and 1810 only three contained pre-Raphaelite paintings, and two of these had only one each. But whereas on dispersal of the treaty pictures the great names went home, the earlier ones often stayed because they were unwanted.

The return was largely due to the Duke of Wellington who was determined to have justice done to the injured nations, who seemed dangerously on the point of doing their own. Blücher would not wait for negotiations to finish, and is described as marching up and down the gallery, claiming this and that, and silencing the pleadings of the dismayed officials in favour of some picture which had never breathed the balmy air of Berlin or Potsdam with a thundering 'Halt's Maul!' So in 1815 the packing began. The exhibitions had been seen by enormous crowds, and some of the English visitors were there to see it break up. Andrew Robertson, the Scottish miniature painter, vainly remonstrated over the way in which a cartload of uncrated Rubenses might lead to damage, and, still more desolating, 'when the (Medici) Venus was put in the cart on Monday, Sir T. Lawrence, Mr Chantry, and Canova burst into tears; but a German officer who stood by kissed her and laughed at them'.

There was no one yet to weep for the primitives, though some found their way into various provincial museums, like Tours and Toulouse, and a few remained in the Louvre. Others went back to Italy to find their owners dead, and for these local picture galleries were formed, easily accessible to the tourist.

A major convulsion seemed to have produced little effect. But publicity and proximity helped the revaluation that had begun. The composition of the collection at Christ Church, Oxford, shows what was happening. It is chiefly composed of Italian paintings from two main gifts. The first was the group of paintings left by General John Guise in 1760. This consists almost entirely of works (or copies) of the sixteenth and seventeenth centuries. The second was the Fox-Strangeways gift of 1828, consisting mostly of works of the fourteenth and fifteenth centuries.

In 1820 the Reverend J. T. James wrote the first scientifi-cally organized treatise on *The Italian Schools of Painting*, for, as he said, 'It is upon the historical criticism of the art alone that a classification of the various knowledge necessary to form a good *connoisseur* can be securely founded.' And he arranged his work by schools and dates within them. True, in each section he hurries towards the accepted great, dutifully leaving a trail of earlier names behind, but there are some independent judgments, and the historical method led, like a spring-cleaning, to an unexpected discovery of two. Masaccio, Filippo Lippi and the Ghirlandaio, for instance, 'by no means deserve to lie in that oblivion to which they have generally been consigned by posterity'.

Greater enthusiasm for early painters, with some quite ferocious prejudices, mark Henry Fuseli's *History of Art in the Schools of Italy*. This was published in 1831 but seems to have been based on notes taken in 1802 and earlier, but if it were actually composed shortly afterwards, Fuseli, rather than James, should be credited with writing the earliest large-scale history of Italian art in English.

He was a friend and regular correspondent of Roscoe's, and though no friend of the Medici, he believed that they had had great influence on the progress of Italian art in its climb towards Raphael. To get there he ranged wider than James. He did not start with Cimabue but mentioned Guinta Pisano, Guido of Siena, Duccio, Buffalmacco and Margaritone, and although each man was judged for what he contributed to the course of art, he recognized that from time to time a Giotto or a Masaccio did something, achieved a certain sort of expression, that was as good as it could be. Fra Angelico, the hero of the next generation, he scorned as 'a name dearer to sanctity than to art', and the walls of the Sistine Chapel were still without a champion:

'The superintendence of the whole the Pope, with the usual vanity and ignorance of princes, gave to Sandro (Botticelli), the least qualified of the group, whose barbarous taste and dry minuteness palsied, or assimilated with his own, the

powers of his associates, and rendered the whole a monument of puerile ostentation, and conceits unworthy of its
place.'

These two writers, who relied largely on feeling plus
Vasari, worked in a decade that also saw the conclusions of
a great scholar, Rumohr. His *Italienische Forschungen* (1827–
31) dealt solidly and critically with the early names that appear
in James and Fuseli, and many besides. Ruskin, the English
hare, would have found the German tortoise in front of him
if he had cared, in the 'sixties, to look.

Even the *Edinburgh Review* was coming round. One of
their contributors said in 1828 (reviewing Thomas Roscoe's
translation of Lanzi) that 'there is much both of absolute
beauty and of technical excellence in those early productions'.
For generations young artists copied the works of the conventional masters with small and often grotesque results.
They 'should return to the oldest masters, and copy their
works'.

English taste was now well ahead of that of the Italians
themselves, and concern was felt about the condition of the
monuments. It would be ironical if they dissolved at the very
moment of admiration, discovered, like virtue in a Jacobean
play, too late.

Already in 1740 Gray, depressed by the poverty and ignorance of the Romans, had doubted whether the place would
be worth seeing in years to come. It was not only unpopular
works that were neglected. The French commissioners over-
looked Titian's Assumption in the Frari because it was effec-
tually disguised by smoke and dirt. Raphael's Madonna di
Foligno was described as 'Split, wormeaten, immensely
warped, and incredibly filthy, with much of the paint fallen
off, and the rest falling'. And though certain frescoes, like
the Giottos at Santa Croce were to some extent preserved by
being whitewashed, others were less fortunate. Some at Assisi
were almost entirely defaced. Damp was causing the Vatican

Raphaels to flake in the *loggie* and bulge in the *stanze*. In 1845, in the very shrine of the rediscovered Primitives, deterioration was rapid. At the Campo Santo, said Ruskin: 'Nobody cared for the old plaster and nobody pretended to. When any dignitary of Pisa was to be buried, they peeled off some Benozzo Gozzoli or whatever else was in the way, and put up a nice new tablet to the new defunct.' Two years later, an aggrieved tourist saw three distinct streams of rain pour over Giotto's Last Judgment at Padua, and Lord Lindsay solemnly warned the rulers of Italy that scarce one of their old frescoes would last the century.

Foreign reproaches, scholarship and purchases had their effect, and the governments of Italy became careful not to lose their great early masters. For a while zeal outran information. When the Tuscan government refused to let Sir Charles Eastlake buy a Ghirlandaio for the National Gallery on the score that it was the last one left in the country, he was able to retort with a long list of extant works, many copied straight out of Murray's Guide. The Guide, indeed, may have helped to form the argument it was used to defeat, for its outspoken editor, Sir Francis Palgrave, a friend of Eastlake's, had trounced the Tuscan as the outstanding culprit among the governments of Italy for the neglect of national monuments. The episode showed, moreover, that a guide-book could lead and not simply repeat traditional opinion.

Murray's *Handbook for Travellers in North Italy* was first published in 1842 and no work has ever done more to direct public attention to Italian art before Raphael. What had been needed was a popular work that would simply record the neglected names and show where the works were to be found. Even these dispassionate entries would have an effect: the tourist would find his attention drawn as of course; the habit of looking at them would become established, might become positive enthusiasm; and Palgrave was anything but dispassionate. His partisanship of the early masters was so vigorously expressed that he was at once replaced, as we shall see, by a more conventional editor.

Tourists from the seventeenth century had taken books with them which were in effect guide-books, combining information about roads and inns with outstanding works of art and (especially in the seventeenth century) objects of *vertu*. Sir Thomas Browne's son Edmund depended on Francesco Scoto (translated by Edward Warcup in 1660 as *Italy. In Its Original Glory, Ruine and Revival*); Lassels (1670), as we have seen, was popular; Addison used Misson's *New Voyage to Italy*; Smollett relied on Keysler's *Travels* and Nugent's *Grand Tour*; and from 1800 Mariana Starke taught tourists to think in terms of exclamation marks just as Baedeker was to teach them to see merit in terms of stars. At the Uffizi look out for 'St John in the Wilderness! ! ! – Pope Giulio II! ! – and three other pictures, all by Raphael – Titian's Venus! ! !' In Palazzo Farnese 'The centre-piece represents the triumph of Bacchus and Ariadne! ! ! !' and in Villa Borghese '*Sixth Room* – the Hermaphrodite, one of the most celebrated pieces of sculpture in Rome! ! !' The use of the exclamation mark to convey worth rather than censure or astonishment took perhaps some getting used to, but otherwise the tourist found no cause for surprise. Her opinions are those of her predecessors, and even when the work had reached its last transmogrification and appeared in 1833 in one volume, double columns and with much of the subject matter of the modern guide, these opinions were unchanged. Guido still reigned (! ! ! ! !), Raphael and Michelangelo still made possible the triumphs of Domenichino and the Caracci. On only two scores are her opinions worth recording. She exclaimed five times at the vault of the Sistine Chapel, and in Pisa, though conventional in praising the frescoes of the Campo Santo for promise rather than for worth (no exclamations) she was moved, nevertheless, to end her account in verse:

'*The solemn grandeur of this Burial-Ground
gave birth to the following*
SONNET, TO GRIEF:
*Which I am tempted to insert, because it is
descriptive of the Campo-Santo.*

Structure unmatch'd! which braves the lapse of Time;
   Fit cradle the reviving Arts to rear!
   Light, as the Paper-Nautilus, appear
Thy arches, of PISANO's works the prime.
Fam'd *Campo-Santo!* Where the mighty dead,
   Of elder days, in Parian marble sleep
Say – who is She, who ever seems to keep
Watch o'er thy precincts; save when mortal tread
Invades the awful stillness of the scene?
   Then, struggling to suppress the heavy sigh,
   And brushing the big tear-drop from her eye,
She veils her face – and glides you tombs between.
'Tis GRIEF! – By that thick veil the maid I ken,
Which hides her from th' unwelcome gaze of men.'

Mariana was published, very profitably, by Murray, and
it is fortunate that she was not used as a basis for his new
Italian Guides. Since the publication in 1837 of the *Handbook
for Travellers in North Germany*, Englishmen abroad had
become increasingly dependent on their Red Books, and it
would have been a pity if they had been catered for as though
their taste were identical with that of their great-great-great-
great-grandfathers.

Palgrave had made a break from his own forebears by
changing his name from Cohen and from the educational
convention of his class by being brought up at home under
an Italian tutor. As a result an almost native facility in the
language enabled him to make the most of his short visits to
Italy and to be independent of Guides and the time-worn

routes. Knowing that many of the places to which he was urging a visit would be unfamiliar to Italians, he warns travellers not to be put off with *'non c'è niente da vedere'* or *'bah! è una porcheria'*, but to follow the guide-book in the teeth of the guides.

As a contributor to the *Edinburgh* and *Quarterly* since 1814 he had early become friendly with John Murray the elder and his son, the inventor of the hand-books, and in 1838 the proposal was made that he should be responsible for the volume on North Italy, which was then to include South East France. Next year he began writing. The Veneto and Lombardy he knew well but was less fully acquainted with Tuscany, and Murray, in a hurry to anticipate rivals, would not agree to leave Tuscany to a later volume on Central Italy. So that section was written partly from books, books that contained the errors on which Ruskin was soon to pounce.

Of Palgrave's ideas, some warning had already been given in reviews, particularly in an article on 'The Fine Arts in Florence', published in the *Quarterly* for June 1840, from which he took some paragraphs *verbatim* for the Handbook. Here he was champion of the early religious masters, formed by the craft guild, great because of their simplicity and in spite of their lack of technical sophistication. Great, too, because they represented an age that was simple and sincere, and he wished to communicate the feeling of that age. 'I should like to make it really a good and truth-telling book,' he told Murray in 1838 and bade him pay particular attention to the Preface and Preliminary Observations. It was here that he warned his readers against being like those who 'pass through Italy, guided merely by conventional opinions, without caring to bestow the time on examining the works of artists whom they do not previously value: still less to give themselves the trouble of judging them with impartiality', and revealed himself as a teacher in his statement that 'the principle of describing not what *may* be seen, but what *ought* to be seen, has been strictly followed by the author of the present work'. Classical and Palladian Italy is no longer going to obscure the Italy of the middle ages, whose sculpture, painting and architecture must not only be recorded but preached. It is the attempt to reveal a creed through a form not far removed from a catalogue that makes Palgrave's the most personal and exciting of guide-books and, in its original form, the object of such strenuous blame.

His traveller was expected to see as he saw. In the interior of the Duomo at Florence:

'all is solemn and severe; plain, almost to nakedness, and dark; for all the very fulness and richness of the brilliant stained glass adds to the gloom, and this gloom is doubly felt when you enter this dark cavern-like shadowy pile, whilst the bright hot sun of Florence is glowing without.'

This was tidied by his successor into:

'*The interior* is rather dark, owing to the smallness of the windows, and the rich colours of the beautiful stained glass by which they are filled.'

He was expected to feel as he felt, so that looking at the Ghirlandaio frescoes in the chancel of S. Maria Novella, 'You never can turn away from these walls without wishing to turn to them again. You do not know how to leave this choir', and to share, even if in trade, a prejudice like this, expressed in S. Lorenzo: 'One mesh of Verrocchio's net-work is worth all Birmingham and Soho, and Sheffield into the bargain.' This remark is exorcized from the second edition.

Deliberately he broke down the old bad habits of tourists. Their attention had been drawn too exclusively by galleries; he diverted them to frescoes. He was enthusiastically full about the mosaics of Ravenna. Whereas Mariana had not mentioned the Giottos of the Arena Chapel in Padua at all, Palgrave gave them seventeen columns. He described the Fra Angelicos at S. Marco which she had ignored. He was much more detailed in his account of the Campo Santo and insisted

that the visitor should consider the frescoes there as records
of the religious feelings of their period as well as specimens
of art. Palgrave, of course, is better known today as an historian than as the author of an anonymous guide-book, and
it is as an historian that he recommends the tourist to examine
the Pisan frescoes in order of artists, however inconvenient
this may be, and reproaches Englishmen for ignoring the
sources of art history in spite of Rumohr's successful use of
them. To know Italy in the time when she was producing
her greatest artists the tourist must visit places that offered
little in terms of modern comfort, must study the artists of
Brescia, Verona and Cremona. Later he suggested that rail-
ways should be made the basis of the guide routes instead of
roads, so that even more unfamiliar ground could be covered,
and that tourists should take cameras with them, to preserve
records of ancient buildings. 'It is provoking to think', he
wrote to Murray in 1851, 'how the aid of photography is
neglected.'

Any or all of Palgrave's ideas exposed him to criticism,
and, moreover, together with his personal and somewhat
leisurely style, they meant that little space was left for practical information, for the compiling of which he had little taste.
Lifting his head from the pile of correspondence about hotels
sent on by Murray in 1844 he mildly complained 'that your
father advised me to make it as much a reading book as I
could'. Next year came two public attacks.

The first, and less important, was Francis Coghlan's *A
Handbook for Italy*. Coghlan, already piqued by the success of
Murray's earlier guides, implied that Palgrave was not only
too superior to give pounds-shillings-and-pence information
but had simply picked the brains of the printed authorities
for his ideas. Copious about doctors and lending libraries,
Coghlan had little to say about art, a topic on which he was
ignorant and reactionary, and what personality was possessed
by his ill-bred and misprinted work was derived from a series

of gibes at Palgrave. None of this could hurt, but a deep
wound was to come. In June, the *Quarterly* printed a review
(anonymous, as was the rule) of Richard Ford's *A Hand-Book
for Travellers in Spain*, another of Murray's guides, which
contained an assault the gist of which was that while Palgrave
was a learned and speculative person, he ought never to have
been entrusted with a guide-book, which should convey
more information than personal idiosyncrasy.

This attack in a Murray journal on a Murray author was
in fact by another Murray writer, Lockhart, who had even
collaborated in some sort with Palgrave by sending him
material from Italy for the second edition. It was also the
first public disclosure of Palgrave's name as author of the
Hand-Book. Hardly had this unlooked-for blow fallen when
a series of letters began to arrive which ensured that the next
edition would be given to someone else.

They came, at Murray's request, from Ruskin, who was in
Italy in 1845–6, and the blows fell heavily. The chronological
arrangement of the frescoes in the Campo Santo in the *Hand-
Book* was so inconvenient that Ruskin had to buy the locally
printed guide. Most of the information, what is more, seemed
to come rather from Lasinio's reproductions. 'Your writer,
however, is a man of good taste and judgement – or at least
of *fair* average taste – but he has not had time at the Campo
Santo.' He characteristically adds: 'I was a fortnight on lad-
ders and frames, at work on these frescoes.' So he moved
on from place to place, precisely where Palgrave was most
vulnerable: Carrara, Lucca, Pistoia, Florence. Of Santa
Croce: 'the book has made as nice a mess as could be wished
of the geography of it'. 'The account of the Uffizii (*sic*) is
particularly queer.' Sometimes it was only a matter of one
man's taste versus the other's ('The praise and importance
given to Bronzino are the worst features in the criticism of
the book.' A matter on which Palgrave rather than Ruskin
anticipated future opinion), but the burden of the arguments

was that the book was insufficiently convenient for the hurried, ordinary purchaser of Red Books. So in 1846, for ·the second edition, Palgrave was replaced.

This correspondence is of considerable interest, partly because Ruskin's *Modern Painters* had been turned down by Murray shortly before, partly because in important respects the ideas for which Ruskin is famous had been anticipated by Palgrave. It was not only that Palgrave admired and sympathized with the period of art that Ruskin was to 'make his own'; he believed, as Ruskin came to believe, that art declined fatally in the sixteenth century with the decline of earnest religious inspiration; he was repelled by the exclusively aesthetic, the reckless choice of subject. Ruskin himself could have written: 'It may be said that no one believes in Leda's swan or in Danæ's shower; but the swelling outlines and the forms rising from the glowing canvas, become a part of the mind into which they have been received.' And again, Palgrave believed that a great source of strength in Italian art before the sixteenth century was the craft connection. Art was always *used* and this removed the temptation to extravagance and affectation, bombast and rant. The tone, again, is very close to Ruskin.

'It is our *civilization* that has degraded the artisan by making the man not a machine, but something even inferior, the part of one: – and above all, by the division of labour. He who passes his life in making pin's heads wi!l never have a head worth anything more.'

Yet in all Ruskin's writings there is expressed no hint of affinity or debt. It is the more intriguing, therefore, to find them bedfellows in the second edition, where in Palgrave's chastened text lie passages of Ruskin, mostly descriptions of frescoes, as subjective and discursive as the peccant originals and soon, as edition followed edition, like them to be subdued and pruned.

Maule, the new editor, spread his responsibility by introducing quotations from several authors beside Ruskin, from Westmacott, for instance, and Flaxman. After all, he commented primly, it would be most unfortunate 'if the editor of a Hand Book of Italy were ambitious of compassing an original work'. But Palgrave's work had been done and he had drawn attention to certain artists whose names at least were permanently retained. In 1846 a note disclaimed his responsibility, but as change after change was made, opinion shrinking and information growing until even what was left of Ruskin was absorbed unacknowledged into the text, the creed remained: that the early masters were there, and there, and there, to be looked at, great not as precursors of the great, but in their own right.

CHAPTER SIX

Prejudice and the Term Renaissance: Early to mid-Nineteenth Century

As the century advanced, the champions of the Medici, rallied with increasing faintness by successive editions of Roscoe's books, became fewer. Their allegiance was sapped by the complex appeal of Romanticism. To whose who had already turned to the middle ages because they found in their chivalry, learning and faith the first motions of modern life, were added those who were attracted precisely by their remoteness from modern life, by a time when, as it seemed, faith was secure, the destiny of nations safe from the selfish demands of mighty individuals, liberty supreme and art at its most devoted and refined.

The artistic side of Romanticism did least to divert interest from the age of the Medici. A love of religious art, a revulsion from eighteenth-century classical canons, did not lead to a neglect of the century of Perugino and the young Raphael. The Gothic revival, which symbolized growing national feeling in Germany, France and England, did not affect the interest of these nations in the past of a country which had never been one, and whose history had been interrupted too often to be seen as a whole. At the time to which these nations were looking back so fondly for their own origins, Italy was filled with tough, matured units whose rivalry was the negation of nationalism. It was not through a change in taste, but through history and, in part, through romantic fiction that Englishmen came to dwell increasingly on the Italian middle ages.

History was impelled there mainly by liberalism, by the
Romantic hatred of tyrants and affection for small peoples
battling for their rights – this far more than the negative
appeal of the middle ages to the reactionary. Some indeed saw
in mediæval corporate life a grateful contrast to contemporary
social unrest; the Napoleonic wars and their aftermath had
caused the people, as well as tyrants to be feared; the catholic
revival helped to idealize the middle ages, but English history
books showed little of this. Mediæval Italy was loved for the
examples of men fighting for liberty, and so ardently was the
theme dwelt on that by 1840 Palgrave was able to remark
of the Medici that 'it really becomes difficult to understand
how the world has so long sat easy under the *prestige* of their
name'. The men whose love of liberty had forced them to
flee from Italy were gladly received in England, especially
by the Whigs. Holland House and Lansdowne House were
opened to them, political hostesses were proud to favour and
display an exile. Even Foscolo, rudest and least controllable
of guests, was welcomed, his patriotism standing him in
better stead than his reputation as a poet.

The tone was set by Sismondi's *Histoire des républiques Italiennes au Moyen Age* (1807–18), first reviewed in England,
before its completion, in 1812. Sismondi was formed to be
the historian of the Italian city states, and their partisan. His
family name was Simonde, and his early work was published
under that name. But noticing that his coat of arms was the
same as that of a Pisan Ghibelline family called Sismondi who
had fled to France, he chose to assume descent from it, and
became Simonde de Sismondi. In 1795 his identification with
Italy became more than a matter of name. The aristocratic
connections of his family forced them to flee from Geneva
to Tuscany, where Sismondi, leaving the others in Florence,
set off on foot to search for a refuge in the countryside where
his ancestors had once, he believed, held sway. He found a
small farm, the *podere* of Valchiusa, near Pescia, and bought

it. It was neglected, but beautiful, 'une gorge ombreuse, arrosée par un ruisseau toujours claire, pure et chaste naïade dont l'urne ne s'épuise jamais l'été', and so skilfully did he use this urn that the farm prospered, and his experience proved the basis of a detailed work on Tuscan agriculture. Why, his readers might ask, had he brought French attention to Italian farming? The answer was the same that he would give if challenged about the usefulness of his historical work. 'Les Italiens formés, il y a plusieurs siècles, à l'école de la liberté, nous ont précédés dans la route des beaux-arts, des sciences, de l'industrie et des richesses.' And he criticized Arthur Young for having concluded, on his travels in Italy, that her wealth had been founded on agriculture. The true story, he countered, was this: wealth flowed first through the commerce of the free republican cities. This enabled them to win back the countryside from feudal obscurantism. For a while commerce and agriculture prospered side by side. Then came the tyrants. Trade decayed and by the sixteenth century Italy had become the land that Young saw, without industries, supported by its agriculture.

He made no attempt to disguise these republican sympathies. No state can be great without liberty: from the thirteenth to the fifteenth century the story of Italy was the story of liberty being lost, masked for the gullible by the thickening veneer of culture. It was not culture, he declared, but laws that indicated the condition of a people; law is a more important factor in the development of civilization than culture or even religion. The splendour of letters and arts under the Medici did not save them from the reproach of having perverted the law. None of his writings is without this republican bias. A lecture on the philosophy of history ended with a clarion call to youth to be worthy of their political inheritance, Geneva. He wished modern Italy to retain the disparate nature of its greatest days, and was unable to enthuse when Napoleon told him that through war he had united Italy.

The *Histoire* was accomplished and sound enough to bear these prejudices without losing its value. It remains useful as the fullest attempt to combine the history of the Italian republics in one work – a challenge in arrangement met in part, Sismondi claimed, by his experience of double-entry book-keeping, learned when he was reduced to earning money as a clerk in Geneva. For twenty years he worked eight hours a day, writing three versions, hampered by a bad memory that obliged him to look up the same date five or six times in the course of the work, and the variety of languages, from Provençal to Portuguese, in which he found his material. The almost exclusive topic was political life. Even the economic side was briefly treated. It was bare of cultural history; his extensive learning in this direction was skimmed off into the *Littérature du midi de l'Europe* (1813). The contrast with Roscoe's approach was therefore complete. And though they met amicably, and Thomas Roscoe translated Sismondi's book on the literature of the south, their views remained irreconcilable.

Sismondi's views were hailed in England with enthusiasm. If history has ever been of use, said the *Quarterly* in reviewing the first part of the work, it can never have been more so than now, 'when we stand so greatly in need of all those resources that are to be derived from the example of past ages for our safe conduct through circumstances of unparalleled danger and difficulty. In this view, the history of Florence presents more objects of importance than that of almost any other nation – we mean, not the history of Florence under the Medici . . . but during the ages of her *real* greatness . . .' And the same review in the following year in noticing an edition of the Villani *Istorie Fiorentine* displayed a general enthusiasm for this period quite divorced from exact knowledge of it – Dante (d. 1321) and Brunelleschi (b. 1379) were quoted as illustrious contemporaries. The *Edinburgh*, in reviewing Hallam's *Middle Ages* (1818) which was itself based on Sismondi for its Italian part, went so far as to say that Florence's free constitution 'fell a sacrifice to the cunning arts of the Medici, whose patronage of letters and encouragement of the arts cannot redeem their name from the infamy of having subverted the most splendid republic that has existed since the days of Athens'. This statement incorporates three distinct changes of opinion since the previous century; Florence, not Venice, is held to be the most splendid republic; it is in the early fourteenth not the early sixteenth century that she is likened to Athens; the Medici have become infamous. In 1832, the year of the Reform Bill, *Gardner's Cabinet Cyclopaedia* catered for the spirit of freedom in the air by bringing out a translation of Sismondi's shortened and more specifically propagandist version of the main work, *Histoire de la Renaissance de la Liberté en Italie.* History has to be written anew from one period of crisis to another, for each age, as the *Edinburgh* said on welcoming the work, 'has its appropriate wants, and some problem or other more peculiarly its own'.

Once the splendour of mediæval Italian liberty was established, it could be used to point a moral for Englishmen. The first English work to reflect the tone of Sismondi was George Perceval's *The History of Italy from the Fall of the Western Empire to the Commencement of the Wars of the French Revolution* (1825). He was a violent critic of the Medici. The whole work is bent towards its moral, a moral taught by reflection on the long tragedy of Italy. 'And among a free, and happy and intellectual people, that tragedy will speak with a deep-fraught and awful application. By Englishmen it should never be forgotten, that it is only the abuse of the choicest bounty of Heaven, which has brought a moral desolation upon the fairest land in the universe.' Let Englishmen beware, lest like the improvident Italians, they fail to associate their talents with virtue and true religion. So far did admiration of the middle ages go at this time that arguments were even advanced to counter the reproach that this liberty was accompanied by little of the classical learning which was, after all, another factor in the emancipation of modern man; this ignorance of classical literature was, in fact, an excellent thing, as when it was eventually revived it came as an invigorating surprise, a shock more salutary than a long quiet course of absorption could have been.

This praise of the Italian republics had gone to grossly uncritical lengths before Dennistoun, in his *Memoirs of the Dukes of Urbino* (1851), pointed out how much their liberty had been exaggerated, largely owing to the influence of Sismondi. The Italians had neither personal freedom nor self-government. All they had was national independence. It was independence, not freedom, communal spirit, not personal liberty, that made Italy great. Dennistoun joined Sismondi in deploring attempts to unite Italy, to contradict the condition under which she became great in the middle ages, because independence, for all the wasted effort it involves, also stimulates what is highest in man. But Sismondi's Utopian interpretation of that independence he rejected. And he pointed out that even if there had been some approximation to democracy in some of the Italian cities, the expansion of genius had not depended on them; art and letters progressed as well under a despot as in a republic. This was to trap a contradiction that had so often slipped past the historian; the arts, as one writer had put it, 'can no more live out of free air than a sparrow in an exhausted receiver'. Yet the arts and letters of the middle ages were still largely ignored; the merchant-despots of the fifteenth century, the popes and grand dukes of the sixteenth – these were the authorities whose reigns saw the flourishing of the arts that the early nineteenth century most admired. Contemporary taste in art gave the lie to the theory that genius depended on freedom, and showed how far the glorification of the Italian middle ages had been shaped by a special interest, liberalism.

Taste in literature, on the other hand, did much to support the liberal historian's attraction to the thirteenth and fourteenth centuries. The other side of Romanticism, a love of the remote and strange, paid no more than the scantiest attention to the times of Leo and Lorenzo. The culture of their age had been so preoccupied with the study of the ancient world, and had since been hailed so emphatically by classical enthusiasts, that for those who were reacting from these canons it was tainted. The age of the Medici, the revival of learning – from these preserves of the formalizing, classicizing past romantic writers turned to the mediæval struggles of Guelf and Ghibelline, or to the bandit-haunted defiles of the seventeenth century.

There was no hint here of the sunlit colonnades, the wide *piazze* and fountains, the rational architecture of the fifteenth and sixteenth centuries. Bravoes lurked in the damp cloister of the earliest church it was possible to find, and escaped through the narrow passages of the *trecento*. There was no sign of the landscape admired by earlier travellers, wide plains, slow rivers, wooded slopes dotted with the graceful summer villas of the aristocracy. Instead the land was heavily forested and mountained after Salvator Rosa. It was a country of ruined castles and lonely convents whose lancet windows did not dismay the furtive ladder. Monks, robbers and immured maidens, taciturn strangers and loquacious servants; Venice in carnival time – masks, gondolas and bodies in the Grand Canal; these were the settings for the treachery, lust and violence of novels set in Italy. More and more crowded on the heels of *Leo* but none took any notice of the Medici. From 1807 there were seven novels in as many years: *The Castle of Rovigo, an Italian Romance*; *The Fatal Revenge, or The Family of Montorio*; *The Mysterious Florentine*; *The Italian Marauders*; *Angelo Guicciardin, or the Bandit of the Alps*; *Isidora of Milan*; *Barozzi, or the Venetian Sorceress*, without mentioning cheap books like *Horrible Revenge*; *or, the Monster of Italy!!*

This return to a black view of the Italian character coincided with a notable revival of the study of Italian, with the publication of new grammars and a new dictionary, a host of Italian teachers and an unprecedented number of reprints of the Italian classics. Hundreds of exiles had turned for a living to publishing, translation, and to catering for the fashionable desire to learn their language. Travelling was the rage; whenever there had been a lull in the wars – in 1802, in 1814, and finally in 1815 – the English had hastened across the Channel eager to display their knowledge of the tongue of Tasso, Ariosto and the Italian Opera in the Haymarket. Italian was not only heard in London but at the universities and in country towns. This interest in Italian language and literature did nothing to counter an avid reception of a distorted view of Italian life. An undercurrent of suspicion there had always been. Then, with the increasing interest in Elizabethan drama since the publication in 1744 of Dodsley's *A Select Collection of Old Plays*, authors began to see the Italians once more as Ford, Tourneur, Marston and Webster had seen them. Nor did travellers provide the evidence that this was absurd. No reproach was too vile for the petulant or self-glorifying protestant, and so far had the alliance of fiction and 'fact' gone by the beginning of the nineteenth century that in spite of the sympathy felt for an Italy dominated by Napoleon, in spite of renewed admiration for her past, there was 'a distrust and antipathy toward the Italian nation', as one writer put it.

There was little specifically Italian about the tales of horror set there. The scenery itself was rather that of Switzerland or Bavaria or Wales, the buildings and the cities similarly unspecific, for as the authors were interested only in what would induce a vague disquiet or apprehension, they found little use for the products of Italian civilization which were essentially lucid and definite. Most were romances more suited psychologically and scenically to the north, transferred to Italy to take advantage of its undeniable bandits and ruins, and its traditionally assumed blend of violence and refinement. For the same reasons, plays as well were set there. *The Italians* (1819) has a cast with Italian names but International Gothic habits and environment. The last scene is set in a grove 'with a ruinous edifice in the background'. Albano, on the brink of a precipice, utters his last distraught words:

> If innocent to Heaven! – If guilty down to Hell.
> I hear thee, Martyr! – Yes – I come – I come!
> Now for life's masterpiece!
>> (Stabs himself, and falls from the precipice into the sea beneath. THE END.

And Thomas Doubleday, for his *The Italian Wife* (1823), transferred the story of Fair Rosamund entire to Italy, with Florence taking the place of Woodstock.

The fashion continued. Of the fifty-two tales in the first volume of *The Romanticist, and Novelist's Library* (1839) more are set in Italy than in any other country, and again no mention is made of the Medicean age. The stories are set in the time of Boccaccio or after the Reformation. None, save *The Florentine Lovers*, by Leigh Hunt, who had a wide knowledge of Italian literature, makes any attempt at historical accuracy. Genuine historical novels were rare, and none gave an accurate portrait until with *Romola* (1863) George Eliot took advantage of the fact that there was more material available for a detailed reconstruction of Savonarola's lifetime than there was before (as Lytton's *Rienzi* (1836) showed) or after. The few attempts were not of much merit. One was *The Pope* (1840) by An Old Author (John Richard Best). Set in the early sixteenth century, there were a host of familiar names: Bayard, Vittoria, Colonna, Michelangelo, Correggio, Giulio Romano and Benvenuto Cellini. But the atmosphere was somewhat chilled by the presence of the English hero, Tilton, and his friend de Whittingham. Supping with Cellini and

Michelangelo one night, their host told the story (from the Autobiography) of how he brought a beautiful lad to a banquet dressed so cunningly as a woman that Michelangelo had kissed him. When he had finished:
'"Are you a married man, Signor Buonarotti?" enquired de Whittingham – "not", he added, "that the question has anything to do with the story we have just heard."'

On the border between history and romance were a number of popular works that gave sensational accounts of some of the more lurid episodes in the Italian past. Again, the thirteenth century and the sixteenth and seventeenth were the most popular, though the fame of the Borgia and, to a lesser extent, the Medici, brought some attention to their age. Miss Holford's *Italian Stories* (1823) were typical. Her account of the Cenci is weakened by her reluctance to name the crime associated with their name, but the opening sentence of her chapter on Cesare Borgia is full of promise: 'Of those fiends who have from time to time walked upon earth to the disgrace of the human form, no man has acquired a more notorious pre-eminence than Cesar Borgia.' Through books like this, English readers regained an acquaintance with the sensational aspects of Italian history which had been largely driven underground since the Counter-Reformation by the classical tinge of Italian studies.

The grafting of instruction on to the taste for lurid romances became a popular *genre*. Far better than Miss Holford's book was Charles MacFarlane's *The Romance of History: Italy* (1832), which gave, in three volumes, a series of tales representative of the country from the seventh to the seventeenth century, with an historical summary prefacing each group. Roscoe's son Thomas employed it too. His *Legends of Venice* (1841) were addressed to those who were wearied of the all-too-familiar institutional history of the city. Its political life was well known, 'but it is different with its traditional and legendary character, so fraught with strange and romantic incidents'; though in fact some of his stories, like that of Marino Faliero, or the Foscari, were already known to readers of Byron's plays or Moore's travels.

Foscolo had resented the way in which fashionable travel literature, like Eustace's *Classical Tour* (six editions between 1813 and 1821), diverted attention from the *quattrocento*, 'the very century in which the restoration of literature and the fine arts was accomplished in Italy'. But the same effect was given by a work quite different in intention, the *Italy* of his patron Samuel Rogers. In this series of verse meditations on Italian themes, Rogers claimed that he was breaking with convention; all other travellers, he declared, had praised the monuments of the first age of Italian greatness, 'while those of her latter have, comparatively speaking, escaped observation. If I cannot supply the deficiency, I will not follow their example.' But in fact he, too, largely ignored the *quattrocento*. Though he was familiar with the works of Patch and Ottley he favoured sixteenth-century painting and from a love of violent deeds and romantic scenery was led back to the age of barbarous virtue and forward to the era of the banditti. When he came to Florence, for instance, he recounted the thirteenth-century origin of the feud between Guelf and Ghibelline and traced the progress of the joyous company of the *Decameron* from the plague-stricken city into the fields and back again, but then, leaving out the age of Cosimo and Lorenzo and Savonarola, he described the murder by Duke Cosimo of his son Don Garcia. Instead of showing any interest in fifteenth-century civilization he devoted two chapters to bandits and included a long passage on the more furtive Assassin, who

> Wandered with restless step and jealous look,
> Dropping thick blood.

And he reminded his readers that

In every Palace was the Laboratory,
Where he within brewed poisons swift and slow,
That scattered terror till all things seemed poisonous,
And brave men trembled if a hand held out
A nosegay or a letter.

What is more, much of the finest poetry in this work, which sold nearly four thousand copies of the first illustrated edition (1830) within a year, was evoked by the classical remains of Rome, Naples and Paestum, the very subjects he set out to treat less prominently.

All this class of writing did nothing to fasten attention on one period of Italian history; all it did was to draw it away from the generations most studied by the previous century. Right up to the eve of the publication in 1860 of Burckhardt's *Kultur der Renaissance in Italien* with its dramatic focusing of attention on that period almost to the exclusion for a while of others, these popular works continued to describe a road mile-stoned by little more than regularly occurring acts of violence. It was soon to be unthinkable to write a history of Italy, however slight, without a mention of a special sort of civilization in the fifteenth and sixteenth centuries, or of a special sort of personality found only at that time – but not yet; in 1859, Miss Manning's *The Story of Italy* moved from one exciting event to another, the only original touch being found in asides like the one forced from her lips at the spectacle of the bloody brawls of the early fourteenth century: 'Oh! friends, had the Florentines but kept their tempers, what a different story might have been told of them!'

As a result of political admiration, and partly because of literary taste, more was written about Italy in the thirteenth and fourteenth than in the fifteenth and sixteenth centuries. And this was in spite of the prejudices against the middle ages that still remained. In England, the mediæval peasantry

could be castigated in retrospect for not having done anything
to improve the deplorable state of husbandry, and the insistence on progress still rendered 'the dreary course of the
middle ages' anathema in other respects; the editor of a work
on architectural antiquities in 1809 felt obliged to apologize
that the author should have confined his talents to a discussion
of so limited and partial an interest; the familiar reproach of
irrelevance was levelled at an author in 1829 who tried to
interest his audience in the Byzantine Empire. 'The history
of Great Britain has little, if any, connection with that of
Constantinople,' said the *Edinburgh*, and confessed that 'we
are somewhat unwilling to inquire into the annals of declining
states, to consult the historians of a dying empire.' But Italy
at this time was not dying, her arts were awakening and the
state of her agriculture was glossed over in admiration for
the volume of her commerce. Even in the thirteenth century,
Italy, alone of the states of Europe, was relevant to modern
times.

It was left for those historians whose study embraced all
Europe, not just Italy, to continue to stress the later period;
it was in their work that the Renaissance concept began to
show itself. They could dislike the Medici without recoiling
altogether from their age. The loss of freedom in fifteenth-
century Italy was less important than its growth in Europe
generally. The end of the Italian republics was less notable a
theme than the beginning of nations elsewhere. Hallam, in
his *View of the State of Europe during the Middle Ages* (1818),
denounced the Medici as enemies of their country's freedom.
But when he came to draw the line between mediæval and
modern times he did not place it at the accession to power
of Cosimo in Florence, or with reference to the internal policy
of any Italian state. He placed it in 1494, when the Italian
wars of France, Spain and the Empire first began that system
of alliances whose repercussions were still felt in his own day:
'here, while Italy is still untouched, and before as yet the first

lances of France gleam along the defiles of the Alps, we close the history of the Middle Ages.'

Hallam had nothing to say of the specific temper of any age. He did not suggest that there was anything remarkable about the fifteenth century's place in the history of civilization. He was concerned, as were all historians of Europe, to find a point at which the middle ages stopped, and modern times began. Only when the link was looked at as not a single moment, but as a period of transition with a quality of its own, would 'the Renaissance' arrive. Until one period had been decided upon which saw, in the rebirth of much that was very old, the birth of more that was new, would the various strands – freedom, letters, independent thought – be brought together. Till then 'la renaissance de la liberté' would be set in the thirteenth century, the revival of letters in the fifteenth, the shaking off of superstition in the sixteenth. If the historians who were preoccupied with Italy in the first half of the nineteenth century had invented this period, if Sismondi's title had gained general acceptance, then the Renaissance in Italy would have covered the thirteenth and fourteenth centuries; more easily defensible, in fact, than the period fifteenth-and-sixteenth-centuries that was felt for by the historians of Europe. And a cause of their hesitation and the reason for much consequent confusion was this: Italy had been so universally considered as the home of the rebirth of one thing and of another, it was inevitable that Europe's rebirth should be identified with hers – and that hers should be made to wait for that of Europe.

Political history and the search for the origin of the Balance of Power placed the change at the end of the fifteenth century. And in spite of the rival claims of the middle ages, the political support for the later period was aided by conservative literary histories, which continued to dwell on Medicean patronage, and by the bulk of current taste in art, which continued to favour the painting of the early sixteenth century until the

Renaissance was firmly established there in the 1860s. Sismondi's indignant pen had no effect on the Rev. Joseph Berington, whose uncontroversial *Literary History of the Middle Ages* (1814) ended with a panegyric on Cosimo, or on the bard of the *Gentleman's Magazine* who in 1816 welcomed the return to Italy of her looted works of art:

> Athens of Italy! once more are thine
> Those matchless gems of Art's exhaustless mine . . .
> Oh! high in thought, magnificent in soul!
> Born to inspire, enlighten, and control:
> Cosmo, Lorenzo! view your reign once more,
> The shrine where nations mingle to adore!

The most interesting of the literary histories that emphasized the early sixteenth century was *The Travels of Theodore Ducas in Various Countries in Europe at the Revival of Letters and Art* (1822), by Charles Mills. Mills affected to be the editor but was in fact the author of these imaginary travels of a Greek student in the Italy of Leo X. The idea was excellent, as Swift and Barthélémy had shown, but in Mills's hands it became tedious. He had only just set foot in Italy when the news of Napoleon's escape from Elba sent him hurrying home. For this reason Ducas was not able to describe the countryside he passed through or the cities whose great men he visited save in the tritest and most general terms. Ducas, besides, faithfully reflected the industrious humourlessness of his creator. Mills, who had taught himself shorthand as a youth to take down the sermons of a favourite preacher, ripened without deviation into an intellectual snob. His gift to the fiancée of a friend whom he wished to see elevated to their common plane of culture was a composition of his own, a 'Brief Summary of some of the Events of the Greatest Magnitude in the History of Continental Europe, from the Subversion of the Western Empire by Odoacer till the Subversion of the Germanic Empire by Buonaparte'. This industry he continued throughout his life, letting no moment pass without extracting a useful toll of fact. When dressing he learned some poetry and in the course of successive breakfasts he read the whole of Bayle's dictionary and proceeded to do the same with Johnson's for the benefit of the quotations it contained. Ducas was similarly thorough. Whenever he approached a city behind whose walls a learned man might be sitting, he recalled its past achievements in literature and art, summarized those of the present and only then entered to put his leading questions to the sage – to Ariosto at Ferrara, for instance. There was no attempt to make the character of Ducas interesting, the fictional element could have vanished with a day's erasure if his publishers had wished, and an exhaustive literary history from 1522 to 1562 would have been left.

Somewhat disingenuously (he had originally intended writing of Dante and Petrarch) he began: 'Next to the delight of living in the days of the Grecian sages, no man of letters would wish to breathe any other air than that which gives life to the literary heroes of the sixteenth century.' And fortified by copious draughts from Roscoe and Vasari, his hero breathes it for nearly nine hundred pages. But the book's reception showed how much interest remained in sixteenth-century letters. Though the fictional element was deplored at once, by 1828 it had become 'a text book for the scholar, and a manual for the learned dilettante'. But if one special interest could see man's intellect as burgeoning in the sixteenth century, to another it could burst forth at quite a different time. Two years after *Ducas* Frances Moore in her *Historical Life of Joanna of Sicily* insisted that 'the fourteenth century was the period when the intellect of man, like that beautiful insect which has furnished the most striking emblem of its immortal nature, burst forth from its temporary slumber'. For a historian of sixteenth-century Italian letters to see an awakening then, and a biographer to see it in her heroine's lifetime, was of little relevance to a historian with wider views. He sought not precocity in one particular direction, but 'the universal motivity of the human mind'. All else were but clues, and some false ones, to this central discovery.

The phrase was used by Sharon Turner, in his *History of the Reign of Henry VIII* (1826–9), and sums up the burden of his first chapter, or 'Sketch of the Intellectual Excitement; Spirit of Novelty and Invention; and General Disposition to Change and Improvement in the Fifteenth and Sixteenth Centuries'. Turner is best known for the pioneering quality of the Anglo-Saxon volumes of his history, which Palgrave praised as containing probably more new information than a history book had ever contained before. But he was as truly a pioneer in this later volume where he attempted a description of the period of accelerating flux, 'a new aera in the mind and history of mankind', which joined mediæval to modern times.

He dwells on qualities which were to become the familiar components of the Renaissance. For the first time universality is suggested as a criterion. As early as 1711 the *Spectator* had hailed Leonardo as a 'Universal Genius' but there had been no attempt to generalize about the nature of Italian civilization in the fifteenth century from this. Nor does Greswell try to make of Pico della Mirandola a figure in any way representative or symbolic of his time. Turner's assertion that 'the mind began to act with a universality and with an emulous diversity which preceding ages had never equally witnessed' was infectious; familiar, too, was to become his claim – or claims like it – that 'the intellectual principle, which animates and guides the human frame, displayed in all things an excited and an investigating curiosity; awakening from the sleep of its former contentedness, and never to be deadened or satiated again'. And he emphasized that curiosity was not simply extended to belief and letters, but to science, the study of nature instead of metaphysics. 'The enriching study of nature' – another familiar note was struck. And yet another occurred in his comment that a salient quality of the time was man's search for distinction, his desire to excel and achieve glory in some line of action. Universality, scientific interest in nature, *virtù*: these qualities, though not expressed with the clarity Burckhardt was to give them, were at least suggested. Nor were they tied exclusively to Italy, or even to the revival of letters. He attempted no full explanation for man's changed outlook, but was clear that the revival was not responsible. He followed closely Guicciardini's picture of the decline of Italy's fortunes after the death of Lorenzo in 1492, the end of her prosperity and glory, but when he came to generalize about the state of Europe at that time, his metaphors were of growth, expansion and discovery. While Europe is beginning to live, Italy, in some respects, is dying. But as she is part of Europe, and included in any formula general to an age of European history, her culture is looked on as a youthful one; because of her prestige it is even looked on as typical, and passed on the puzzle of an age of birth that could contain so much that was sophisticated, whose excesses often have the stamp not of youthful excitement but of senility.

Among historians of Italy confusion as to her period of awakening continued. Thomas M'Crie, in his *History of the Progress and Suppression of the Reformation in Italy in the Sixteenth Century* (1827), was quite sure that it was the Reformation which represented the awakening. After this, superstition and ignorance were put to flight. The beginnings were in the fifteenth century, but only in its latter half. He restored the myth of the Exodus to its old position as a dogma; without the fall of Constantinople Florence would never have become a new Athens, in spite of what historians of literature had said to the contrary. The discussion of literary questions had, indeed, obscured a more fruitful theme, the progress of religion. Both persuasions were drawn to the revival of letters, Catholics because it fostered infidelity, Protestants because it helped to destroy infidelity; and though the revivers helped create a demand for Church reform, the effect of this preoccupation had been to attribute to the literary revival phenomena more accurately to be ascribed to the religious one.

Political histories did not yet concern themselves as a matter of course with social or cultural affairs. Smedley's long *Sketches of Venetian History* (1831–2) had nothing to say about manners or art, save one passage on Titian. And William Spalding's three-volume *Italy and the Italian Islands* (1841), although it claimed to be a pioneer work in respect of completeness as a popular survey, made no attempt to define the nature of Italian civilization at a particular period other than to divide the middle ages into two at 1300. Of the next two centuries he noted the contrast between piety and irreligion, progress in the arts accompanied by political violence, but leaves these impressions disunited. Even writers who were far more explicit about the reasons for change remained content with 'revival of letters' or 'Reformation' as a formula to cover that change. George Miller gave in his extensive *History, Philosophically Illustrated, from the Fall of the Roman Empire to the French Revolution* (1832) a striking list of factors that shaped the late middle ages, but which did not help him to a reinterpretation: 'the invention and use of gunpowder and the modern artillery, the great plague of the fourteenth century, the appearance of the gypsies in Europe, the practice of card playing, the introduction of the venereal disease, the restoration of the fine arts, and the invention of printing'. The apparent discrepancy between the relative importance of some of these he dispels when he comes to explain their sociological implications. Gunpowder and printing explain themselves. Card playing, though less obviously, was almost as far-reaching in its effects. It encouraged increasing familiarity between the sexes, thus preparing the way for modern social life. The venereal disease, on the other hand, by investing this intercourse with a certain hazard, forced the development of a strict morality. Miller was an uncritical historian who discussed the inevitable improvement of man's lot as though *Candide* had never been written. But his catalogue was not unique. More and more reasons were being produced for the changed nature of man and society at the end of the middle ages, but, for want of a better phrase, they were all piled uneasily upon the 'revival of learning' a base too narrow to support a conception of total change, not just a literary one.

Even an elementary textbook like Thomas Keightley's *Outlines of History* (1830) shows a crowd of isolated factors waiting awkwardly for a synthesis. At the end of the middle ages, he noted, learning had returned, the study of law had sharpened men's wits, travel had enlarged their knowledge of the earth, the use of the mariner's compass had made their voyages bolder, gunpowder had revolutionized war, paper and printing diffused knowledge at an unheard-of rate, the fall of Constantinople scattered the knowledge of the East throughout the West, schools and universities were becoming numerous, there was a love of classical philosophy and an admiration for the institutions of Greece and Rome, Wycliffe, Huss and their followers had taught men to question religious orthodoxy, the discovery of India and the New World filled men's hearts with aspirations after adventure, wealth and yet further knowledge. As he concluded: 'A universal fermentation was going on.' In spite of this idea of universal fermentation he did not see it as constituting something so different from what had gone before that it deserved a period on its own. He was simply concerned to find the date when mediæval times stopped and modern history began. And he found a precise one: In 1498 Vasco da Gama landed at Calicut and 'The middle ages here terminate'.

So many other revivals were being attached to the 'revival

of learning' that it came to be used very much in the way that 'Renaissance' came to be. In his *Lectures on Modern History* (1840) William Smyth claimed that the two greatest events of modern history were 'the Revival of Learning and the Reformation'. Unfortunately the phrase was tethered so securely to Italy, and to the age of Dante, Petrarch and Boccaccio that it could not liberate the repressed multitude of details concerning Europe in general in the age of Caxton, Francis I and Columbus.

By the 'forties enough had been written to show that the end of the middle ages was of such a special nature that it merited a separate name, that even if modern political behaviour dated from 1494, the modern temperament as a whole was to be explained by forces operating during the whole of that century. The only historian, and the last, to show no trace of this suppressed desire to periodize was Henry Napier. Overshadowed by the fame of his brothers, Sir Charles, conqueror of Scinde, Sir George, governor of the Cape and Sir William, historian of the Peninsular War, Henry Napier's *Florentine History* (1846) is yet of great interest. It is very long, six large volumes, and much of this bulk was pioneer work; he wished to give not only the political narrative but a full description of the character, manners and customs of the Florentine. There are long 'Miscellaneous Chapters' on social conditions, century by century, dealing with roads, harbours, ships, arms, commerce and agriculture, and also with dress, morals, anecdotes, food and festivals. He celebrated Leonardo as the complete man very much as Burckhardt was to celebrate Leon Battista Alberti; the miscellaneous chapters, if put together, would comprise a history of Italian civilization not very different in material from *The Culture of the Renaissance in Italy*. But in Napier there was no idea of a Renaissance. Each century was simply later than the previous one and earlier than the next. To readers accustomed to a Renaissance, the presentation of his material appears

invertebrate, lacking a theme. He did not even see the fifteenth century as particularly important. He rather preferred
the fourteenth and gave it more space.

Sober, conscientious and objective, Napier was unique in
his insulation from the current restlessness. The insulation
was partly due to his interest in the Florentine constitution
at all stages of its development – it was to decide upon its
merits that he studied the social milieu so closely – partly to
a temperament unvolatile and precise. The future spoke with
Mrs Jameson, impressionable and subjective. In the previous
year she had written of the fifteenth century as 'a period
perhaps the most remarkable in the whole history of mankind; distinguished by the most extraordinary mental activity, by rapid improvement in the arts of life, by the first
steady advance in philosophical inquiry', a passage in which
the '15th century' is almost 'the Renaissance'.

All that was needed was a term, whether an English or an
imported one. Abroad, in the arts there had been Vasari's
rinascita since 1550; Félibien had written in 1660 of Cimabue's
age as that 'lorsque le Peinture commença de renaître'; then
came *Wiedergebuhrt der Mahlkunst* (1675), *La renaissance des
beaux arts* (1701), *Risorgimento delle belle arti* (1795), a *Wieder-
auflebung* in 1798 and a *Renouvellement* in 1809. In letters there
had been a similar crop of equivalents, from Leland's reference to the *renascens doctrina* in his praise of English humanists,
and Paolo Giovio's account of the happy century *quo renatae
literae Latinae existimantur* (1546) to *la renaissance des lettres* of
Bayle's Dictionary (1695–7), and from the *Wiederaufblühens*
of 1827 back in 1843 to *la renaissance des lettres* without definite
result. We have noticed Sismondi's *Renaissance de la Liberté*
(1832). England had used both 'revival of letters' and 'resurrection of letters', which was Bolingbroke's preference, in
the eighteenth century. The Rev. J. T. James had referred to
'renascent art' in 1820; Ottley had 'regenerate arts' in 1823
and 'restoration of the arts' in 1826 and in 1840 *renaissance*

arrived in England when T. A. Trollope, in his *Summer in Brittany*, came face to face with the sixteenth century church of St Thégonnec. He did not admire it. 'It is built in that heaviest and least graceful of all possible styles, the "renaissance"', as the French choose to term it.'

In the same year Eduard Kolloff showed that the term had reached Germany when he published an article on the development of modern art from the antique to the *Epoche der Renaissance*. And Palgrave wrote in 1842 of 'the period of the *Renaissance*' in his handbook on North Italy. Both men were still applying the word to a style of painting or architecture, but it was beginning to break free. In 1845, Murray's guide to Spain, by Ford, referred to 'the bright period of the *Renaissance*' again, and Ruskin naturalized the word out of its italics in 1851 when he wrote in *The Stones of Venice* of 'the art commonly called Renaissance'. But still the word had not been used of the period as a whole, despite the long train of images that had shown painters and writers and sometimes the common man breaking bonds, straining against shrouds, starting from sleep, vaulting from tombs and the like during the periods of the *renaissance* of arts and letters. Dennistoun went so far as to say in 1851 that 'assuming the close of the fifteenth century as the zenith of Italy's glory in letters and arts, in politics and arms, the only word specifically indicating that period is *cinquecento*'. Even that he rejected, deciding that the term 'mediæval' could be stretched a little to serve instead.

In 1855, however, the year in which Burckhardt in the *Cicerone* was still using the word in its art-historical sense, came the decisive publication of the seventh volume of Michelet's *Histoire de France* which he entitled simply *Renaissance*. Burckhardt adopted the term in 1860 with his *Kultur der Renaissance in Italien*. Following Michelet, John Addington Symonds wrote his Oxford Prize Essay, *The Renaissance*, in 1863, and in 1869 Matthew Arnold tried to give the word a native English look as 'Renascence'. Soon it was used of other periods altogether. In 1866 Symonds wrote of 'the English Renaissance' in the Elizabethan age, in 1872 Morley referred to 'the Renaissance of the eighteenth century', and in the next year Pater, in his preface to *The Renaissance*, invented a 'medieval Renaissance', 'a Renaissance in the end of the twelfth and the beginning of the thirteenth century'. By 1882 the term was being bandied about with such freedom that the *Athenæum* could talk of 'a theatrical renaissance'.

By the 'sixties, then, the term was ready for use. Books like Adolphus Trollope's *History of Florence* (1865) were exceptional in their avoidance of it, and this can be explained from the author's affection for the twelfth and thirteenth centuries and dislike of the Medici, whose splendour and glory 'was but as the phosphorescent light that may be seen to float above the putrescent remains of organic matter in process of dissolution'. The claims of the earlier centuries to be a period of rebirth had been generally put aside. There were no traces left of the point of view that would make a rebirth wait for the Reformation. The growing conviction that the late fifteenth and early sixteenth centuries constituted a period of ferment in Italy of special significance for Europe, had triumphed, and had won a name – The Renaissance. By 1879 the *Quarterly* was already complaining of the vagueness of the word; 'there is a large class of writers, and a far larger class of readers, with whom it stands as the symbol of something very grand, but very vague, and so, very misleading.'

CHAPTER SEVEN

Taste for Italian Paintings: (III) Early Nineteenth Century to Ruskin

Towards the middle of the century protestant prejudice against the arts of the middle ages was almost at an end. Sometimes it still spoke up as in Josiah Conder's *Italy* (1831) where even the apses in the churches of Ravenna were criticized as showing how early Christianity had deserted the simple commemorative nature of the sacrament and tried to dramatize it. But revulsion from Catholic subject matter was fading, and, more important, the conviction was growing that great art was necessarily religious art.

This notion, only fully established in England during the 'forties, arose on the Continent at the end of the previous century in a book with a passionate title: *Herzensergiessungen eines kunstliebenden Klosterbruders*, and a sentimental message that art should appeal to the heart, not to the head. And the art that could touch the heart most movingly, most deeply, was religious art. Wackenroder's touchstone was also used by Friedrich Schlegel, one of the most important names in early German romanticism. He found that in the calm assurance of the older masters, whose faith had not compromised as yet with classical paganism, was the most directly communicative religious spirit. But the writer for whom the identity between religious and great art led to the widest and most influential sympathy for pre-Raphaelite painters was Alexis-François Rio. He, too, loved art only till its religious content became alloyed with a debasing element of scientific or pagan interest. Fra Angelico was for him the greatest of

painters before Raphael; the art of Siena, almost totally neglected by others, had charm for Rio, and even the rough
paintings of the catacombs breathed the spirit he loved, the
poetry of Christianity.

His *Poésie Chrétienne* was published in Paris in 1836 and
translated in 1854. But Rio had become well known here
before that. He married an English woman and was a frequent
visitor to England, and had, besides, made important converts. For Mrs Jameson, seeking something to fill her mind
after a miserably unsuccessful marriage, and already affected
by tractarianism, a meeting with Rio in Paris was one of the
great events of her life, and it inspired her to spend the rest
of it describing early sacred art. And Ruskin, who read his
work in 1844 or '45, found that on his first Italian journey
he had been 'a blind bat and puppy' and resolved, with Rio's
guidance, to see Pisa and Florence again before writing
another word of *Modern Painters*.

Nor had feelings for the religious simplicity of early painters remained textbook pieties. To re-create something of the
spirit of the artists earlier than Raphael, artists formed groups
of which our own pre-Raphaelite Brotherhood was but the
latest and most erratic.

A group of David's students were known as 'Les Primitifs'.
Ingres, who once exclaimed in a letter about the Campo Santo
'it is on one's knees that one ought to copy these men', was
one of them. To their love of simplicity and dignity a group
of German artists added a religious fervour that made them
try actually to reproduce the conditions in which early art
arose. Deeply affected by the ideas of Wackenroder and
Schlegel, a number of German painters in Rome went to
live and work in the monastery of S. Isidoro. There, under
the leadership of the artists Cornelius and Overbeck, they led
a communal life of work and prayer, some of them going so
far as to wear mediæval clothes. For them, Raphael, the early
Raphael, was the last of the masters before art was stifled by

the Renaissance, though some preferred to draw the line after Giotto. Known as *Die Klosterbrüder* or, after 1815, as *Die Nazarener*, they remained a considerable element in Roman cultural life into the 'forties, though they made few actual converts. When antiquaries, questioning Vasari's account of Raphael's burial, got permission to open the tomb in the Pantheon, Overbeck, as the skeleton was brought to light, had still to sigh: 'Alas! the spirit of the great artist remains buried far deeper than his bones.'

Certainly it was not brought a spadeful nearer the surface by the activities of Rosetti's group. It was not the religious candidness that they were after. The P.R.B. manifesto on the back page of *The Germ* declared that 'the endeavour held in view throughout the writings on Art will be to enforce an entire adherence to the simplicity of nature', or as John Seward put it in an article in the second number, of February 1850, 'an entire seeking after originality in a more humble manner than has been practised since the decline of Italian Art in the Middle Ages'.

In spite of its name, the movement, which originated in Rosetti's enthusiastic perusal in 1848 of Lasinio's engravings of the frescoes in the Campo Santo, did nothing in the way of history or criticism to rehabilitate the loved centuries. Seward's article was the only one in its organ, *The Germ*, which tried to defend the early masters, and he did this merely by saying flatly that they are *not* all gloomy, insipid and unsublime. For a serious periodical the woolliness and near-illiteracy of *The Germ* is almost spectacular and suffices to show how little importance the P.R.B. attached to the theoretical or historical basis of their pre-Raphaelitism.

One contribution, however, is worth discussing.

It is a story by Rosetti called 'Hand and Soul' and appeared in the first number, in January 1850. It is about a certain imaginary painter of Arezzo, Chiaro dell' Erma, who lived, one deduces, in the thirteenth century.

From his boyhood he was troubled by an 'extreme longing after an invisible embodiment of his thoughts' until 'he would feel faint in sunsets and at the sight of stately persons'.

Eventually, after a mystical and rambling narrative of his spiritual and artistic pilgrimage, told in tiresomely archaic language, he succeeds in externalizing with great effort, his own soul. It turns out to be remarkably like Lizzie Siddal:

'A woman was present in his room, clad to the hands and feet with a green and grey raiment, fashioned to that time. It seemed that the first thoughts he had ever known were given him as at first from her eyes, and he knew her hair to be the golden veil through which he beheld his dreams. Though her hands were joined, her face was not lifted, but set forward; and though the gaze was austere, yet her mouth was supreme in gentleness. And as he looked, Chiaro's spirit appeared abashed of its own intimate presence, and his lips shook with the thrill of tears: it seemed such a bitter while till the spirit might be indeed alone.' He then paints her, or it, and that is the end of one part of the story.

The other describes how the author himself suddenly came on the painting, stacked among many others during a rearrangement of the Pitti. It was hung immediately under a Raphael. The story now becomes interesting from the point of view of contemporary taste, for Rossetti, having been asked to move out of the way to enable an Englishman to copy the Raphael more conveniently, asks him what he thought of the one underneath.

'He did not laugh, but he smiled as we do in England. "*Very* odd, is it not?" said he.'

Englishmen were beginning to smile less at the thirteenth century, however, though this was not due to the English pre–Raphaelites. It was the German example that was more persuasive and alarming. Overbeck, in search of a devotional purity of design, had gone over to Catholicism; to certain temperaments the study of early Italian painting had simply to be denied. This is clearly shown by the case of the Rev. M. H. Seymour. In his *Pilgrimage to Rome*, published in 1848, he told how powerfully, and how dangerously, he was affected by it. Not so much by the drawing, for he found it stiff and awkward, nor by the composition, which was often absurd and grotesque, but by the idea behind the work. He was moved by Giotto, by Pinturicchio, Francia and the earlier works of Raphael, but especially by Fra Angelico and Perugino. With mounting enthusiasm he describes his emotions and then pauses, shocked. Is what is happening altogether good? Lulled by the quiet unearthliness of these rapt figures he is being drawn towards the sensations of a recluse rather than of an active, stirring Christian. Worse, he is being led to sympathize with the religious temperament inspiring these works, that of Rome! He hardens his heart against them, reminded of the consequences by the example of so many of the German painters in Rome, who in the course of careful study of early painting had become Catholics, and mariolators at that.

It was not a fear of the proselytizing power of the primitives that hampered a true understanding of them so much as a haze of sentiment, a by-product of religious feeling, that was causing them to be approved as a class by persons who were still ignorant of them as individuals. Illustrations, save Ruskin's, continued to soften angularities and smooth out the differences between the techniques of different artists. The Arundel prints were so ugly that they could convey pleasure only to the already converted, to those who knew that primitives were something which gave a nice feeling of devout nostalgia.

The authorities were not blameless. Mrs Jameson was the most widely read exponent of the primitives, apart from Ruskin who believed her absolutely without knowledge of painting or instinct for it. She followed Rio and she followed her heart, and its *Ergiessungen* earned her a pension from the

Queen. Even Lord Lindsay was affected. His *Sketches of the History of Christian Art* (1847) was the most scholarly work on the subject yet written in England, but his judgment again was the heart's, in terms of the feeling expressed by the artist rather than of colour, draughtsmanship or historical background. For him the three ages of art paralleled the three parts of man: Egypt – the body; Greece – the Intellect; Christianity – the Spirit. As the spirit is higher than body or intellect, so Christian art must be higher than pagan art, and that of the Christian primitives highest of all. 'The old masters I plead for', he wrote, 'knew how to touch the heart', and he called on his readers to love them. Toss to the winds your jargon, was his advice to the young artist, listen and kneel humbly before these men and your eyes will be touched by the magician's salve and all about you will be a world of undreamt of beauty. We must go back to them, he cried a year before Rossetti opened Lasinio's engravings; only by studying them can art become great again. Ruskin, reviewing the book for the *Quarterly*, poured cold water on this: 'the voice and the gesture must not be imitated when the innocence is lost', but he himself was not always on guard against sentimental extravagance, and in the same review admitted that any terms of description applied to an artist like Fra Angelico must seem derogatory. And while Lindsay was chanting about 'a holy purity, an innocent naïveté, a childlike grace and simplicity, a freshness, a fearlessness, an utter freedom from affectation, a yearning after all things truthful, lovely and of good report', Dickens's Rome correspondent of the *Daily News* was studying the feud between *Puritani* and *Classicisti* at the Caffè Greco, where to order a *Carlo Dolci* was to get syrup and the way of obtaining a stiff tumbler of grog was to call, somewhat oddly, for a *Pietro Perugino*.

In saying that English artists could learn from early Italian painting, Lindsay was repeating a popular belief. The competition organized for the frescoes in the new houses of parliament caught the public imagination and for a while high hopes were entertained of a new spirit infusing English art. Mrs Jameson compared the contest to that held for the gates of the Florentine Baptistery and the second edition of Murray's *North Italy* contained a special section on fresco painting to meet the new demand for information; the traveller was now directed more than ever to the great early cycles so that he could decide whether they did not indicate the best way of elevating public taste in England. While panel and canvas tended simply to please, fresco could elevate and purify the mind.

Sentimental and ethical prejudices were not without their uses. It is easier to love than to understand, and, besides, they helped combat other purely destructive prejudices. The middle ages had not yet been given pratique. Of a great exhibition of mediæval and modern art at the South Kensington Museum as late as 1862, 'We have in our retrospective glance over the Loan Collection', cried the terrified reviewer, 'backed upon the very verge of that deep and steep gulf which parts the art of the Middle Ages from that of the Renaissance'. Another test which most artists before Raphael were forced in their critics' pages to sit and usually fail, was for Progress. Painters were marked for progress as sharply as inventors in the biographies of Smiles. Ottley, for instance, was not ungenerous to some of the early masters, but could not help being angry with them for not doing more to hasten their art in the direction of exalted naturalism – that of the sixteenth century. When progressive artists did arrive he spoke approvingly of their 'Honourable exertions', to the rest he showed exasperation at their slowness. And, generally speaking, right through the middle of the century, artists like Botticelli, who did not contribute directly to the understanding of the Renaissance gods were ignored at the expense of those who did: Signorelli and Domenico Ghirlandaio, for instance, for their influence on Michelangelo, Perugino for his on Raphael.

Against this division between seekers and finders, against the continuing use of the scathing term 'childhood of art', the sentimental fallacy was a useful corrective.

It is worth emphasizing how recent was an historical approach to art. An occasional writer spoke up in favour of it, but the general public was not helped even by the chronological arrangement of pictures in schools until the last third of the century. The motive for mixing them up was explained in the Louvre catalogue of 1793 as developing in the best possible manner the genius and taste of students of art. Thus Italians, Flemish, French were all jumbled together. But Denon, when he became General Director of Art Affairs, altered this, and from 1802 the superb Napoleonic Exhibitions were hung in schools. Berlin followed, perhaps because its director, Waagen, had seen the Louvre loot as a soldier, but England held to the earlier principle. The first concession was made at the Manchester Exhibition in 1857 when pictures were hung chronologically, but not by schools, and the next great exhibition, at Leeds in 1868, retained a good deal of promiscuity in the interest of keeping the collection attractive. It was only when controversy about the role of the National Gallery produced the argument that it should teach as well as cater for browsers, that a change came, and it was arranged after the best Continental models for the millions who benefited from the Education Act of 1870.

From the end of the 'forties the pace quickened. In 1848 Lindsay, Ruskin and the collectors Layard and Samuel Rogers were among the founders of the Arundel Society, which published chromolithographs of primitives with written descriptions usually by Ruskin or Layard. The Vatican Fra Angelicos came first, then the Giottos of the Arena Chapel and the Perugino frescoes at Panicale. Ruskin was dogmatizing from Italy, Layard pontificating in the *Quarterly*, Browning buying Giottesque fragments from a Florentine corn shop, when in 1849 the Society of Arts organized their

Mediæval Exhibition. The effect on interest in early art was reflected in the rising prices of the Bernal Sale of 1856, the breaking up of the first large collection of mediæval and renaissance *objets d'art*. The label 'Gothic' still kept down the prices of the Trecentisti, but the masters of the late fifteenth century were moving gently towards a boom.

The attention of the public was focused on them by the Manchester Exhibition of 1857, when many people saw an Italian early master for the first time in their lives. The exhibition was largely due to the encouragement of the Prince Consort, whose fame is muted in the pages of the historians of politics but gaining more respect from those of art. He had a decided taste for primitives, and bought the collection of early German and Flemish paintings that had belonged to his relative, Prince Ludwig-Kraft-Ernst of Oettingen-Wallerstein. It had been offered publicly for sale in London in 1848, but no one wanted it.

They joined a collection which already contained some notable early Italian pictures, still in the Royal Collection; the Duccio triptych, for instance, and the Gentile da Fabriano altar-piece. The Prince lent largely to the new exhibition and we learn from the catalogue the names of the other collectors of pre-Raphaelite works. Some of Roscoe's pictures came from Liverpool, some of the Fox-Strangeways gift from Christ Church, and others were lent by Fuller-Maitland, Fuller Russell and Davenport Bromley. A full third of the paintings in this Art Treasures Exhibition, to give it its proper title, were by artists between Cimabue and Raphael. And by this time the growing taste was echoed by the calculating flattery of copyists. Bellini, Mantegna, Perugino, Fra Angelico, Ghirlandaio, Luini and even Taddeo Gaddi were all popular enough to be forged.

These middle years were also notable for the efforts of Sir Charles Eastlake to get early Italian pictures for the National Gallery. He was ably seconded by his wife, who, as Elizabeth

Rigby, had already written several articles on art and translated Passavant's *Art Collections of England*. Her *Letters and Journals* (1895) describe her taste with the liveliness to be expected from an author whose first published work was entitled: 'My Aunt in a Salt Mine'.

From Florence, in 1855, she wrote 'the Caracci and all their tribe are not calculated to interest the English of the present day, when affectation and mere mechanical facility are out of fashion. I am fairly bitten with all the true pre-Raphaelites.' And to a friend who asked what she should look at in visiting Florence she wrote: 'Try and fill your heart especially with the grandeur and earnestness of the great four – Sandro Botticelli, Dom. Ghirlandaio, Fra Filippo Lippi, and his son, Filippino Lippi, who constitute the *core* of Florentine art.'

And at last someone looked affectionately at the walls of the Sistine Chapel, especially the Botticellis, 'one of which we pronounced to contain every element of art'.

There was, it is true, a rather disturbing feeling that she knew she was doing the smart thing. The Ghirlandaio frescoes in Sta. Maria Novella, she wrote, 'are the right things to study and like more and more'. And to say of Melozzo da Forli that 'for grandeur and beauty he seems the greatest master in the world' is excessive.

The National Gallery, before Sir Charles became Director, had only four pre-Raphaelite Italian paintings. A parliamentary commission had urged in 1836 that early Italians should be bought, but there was an effective check in Sir Robert Peel's 'I think we should not collect curiosities'.

The Gallery was the centre of violent controversy. Should it instruct or only please the public? Should the aim be completeness or superlative quality? It was seldom suggested that both schools of thought could be satisfied at once, that works which illustrated the fifteenth century could also be great themselves.

A boiling point came in 1844 when the Gallery lost the

Michelangelo Madonna and Child with Angels (which they
finally got for £2,000 in 1870) because they would not pay
more than £250, and then, in the same and the following year,
bought two Guido's at sixteen hundred and twelve hundred
guineas respectively. And yet, as Ruskin pointed out, there
were already two good Guidos, but no Perugino, no Fra
Angelico, no Verrocchio – 'what shall I more say, for the
time would fail me?'

His point was taken up by the 1853 Report of the Select
Committee which was set up in response to public outcry at
the Gallery's cleaning policy – even then the cry was familiar:
'Old Masters in danger!' It showed that while some of the
trustees objected to buying 'antiquarian and mediæval pictures', others favoured them, and the Report agreed. 'What
Chaucer and Spenser are to Shakespeare and Milton, Giotto
and Masaccio are to the great masters of the Florentine
School.' And the Treasury Minute of 1855 reconstituting the
Gallery under Eastlake as Director asked especially for the
purchase of 'good specimens of the Italian Schools, including
those of the early masters'.

In that very year the Eastlakes brought back from Italy
works by Botticelli, Mantegna, Bellini and Gozzoli. The next
year brought the windfall of the Lombardi–Baldi Collection
which contained works from Margaritone and Cimabue, and
included some of the most popular pictures in the Gallery:
Gozzoli's Rape of Helen, for instance, and Uccello's Rout of
San Romano. That the Gallery was now ahead of current
collectors' tastes is shown by the small price – £7,035 for
twenty-two pictures. After this, Eastlake's yearly spoils seem
less impressive, though a typical year, 1862, included an
Andrea del Sarto and a Moroni, a Crivelli, Piero di Cosimo's
Death of Procris, and the Bellinesque St Jerome in his Study.
Almost the last purchase made before his death in 1865 was
the Raphael Garvagh Madonna on which he persuaded the
trustees to spend £9,000.

His influence through these purchases was considerable, and the policy was warmly approved by an Edinburgh reviewer who, in 1853, pointed out how absurd it was for the Gallery to go on paying high prices for Guido Reni's when it possessed:

        8 Rubenses, but no Dürers
        9 Rembrandts, without a Holbein
        8 Nicholas Poussins, and one Bellini
        6 Gaspare Poussins and one doubtful del Sarto
        9 Claudes and one questionable Giorgione
       12 Caraccis and three Raphaels
        8 Guidos but no Fra Bartolomeo.

The writer who gave these figures was James Dennistoun, and he provided, in Chapter XXVI of his *Memoirs of the Dukes of Urbino* (1851), the best contemporary résumé of the controversy over the merits of early Italian art.

He wrote as a collector of it himself.

'You are the possessor', he was asked by the Select Committee on the National Gallery of 1853, 'of a small and, I may say, very choice collection of Italian pictures, are you not?'

'Of the early Italian masters,' he corrected.

It included works by Fra Angelico, Giottino, Taddeo Gaddi, Memmi, Gentile da Fabriano, Lorenzo Monaco, Duccio, Sano di Pietro, Cima and others less famous or less definitely attributed. And he was eloquent in the praise of such masters, defending the religious character of their work from the two charges of sameness and papistry. Granted that the range of forms was limited; this did not imply poverty of invention, nor was simplicity inconsistent with the sublime. In these works there was grandeur, strength and reflection, though it was against the current of critical belief to say so, a belief that paid more attention to naturalism and technical merit than subtleties of feeling and expression, a belief that without signposts in the form of unimportant details was unable to find its way into the heart of a picture. And mocking the suspicion of Italian art as papist, he quotes Hogarth's definition of a cherub as typifying the English scorn of religious art; 'an infant's head with a pair of duck's wings under its chin, supposed always to be flying about and singing psalms.' If you could make people see past this prejudice, and demand exalted feeling from a painting rather than a literal copying of nature, the way would be open for the appreciation of early art.

Yet even these excellent sentiments did not sustain him when looking at paintings of a still earlier period than his Duccio. He shared his contemporaries' distaste for Byzantine art; it was a degraded art of 'rigid forms, harsh outlines, soulless faces', and he never gave it a chance after the 'long examination and elevated thought' he applied to fourteenth century painters, to communicate its noble feeling.

For though fourteenth-century art was fine, that of the fifteenth was finer and that of the sixteenth finest of all, with Raphael at the crown. 'The zenith of Italian art, especially of Italian painting, was obtained between 1490 and 1520.' And the idea of progress is clear in his division of Italian painting into four periods: the first, the Byzantine, being 'stationary'; the second, the early middle ages, 'the age of sentiment'; the next, 'the epoch of effort'; the last, 1490–1520, the 'age of mastery'. So he is not claiming that the work of a master of an earlier period is as good as that of a later; his concern is for them to be recognized.

Here, he was encouraged by his historical work, which, for completeness, demanded an interest in the school of the Marches. His concern for Urbino had something to do with his admiration for Raphael and certainly explains his placing Piero della Francesca higher in the scale of excellence than any preceding writer. And again it was the works actually in

Urbino, like the Flagellation, or which he himself discovered, like the fresco of Sigismondo Malatesta in the Cathedral at Rimini, that pleased him most, receiving higher praise than the frescoes at Arezzo. Dennistoun's view was personal and parochial, his taste not so wide as the theory behind it, but he was one of the heralds of the cult of the early masters.

Thanks to the Report of the Select Committee of 1853, we can hear his point of view in his own words, followed by those of Eastlake. The Committee was interested in many points, the administration of the Gallery, the methods of cleaning the pictures, the principles on which the purchase of paintings was to be based. On this latter point, discussion proceeded as follows:

Dennistoun. My wish would be to see for a time the funds of the trustees expended chiefly in purchasing works of the best age. I apprehend the best age of art to have been the period between 1450 and 1540, which period has been hitherto exceedingly inadequately represented.

Lord W. Graham. But if the public taste is not prepared for these pictures, might it not be possible that the public would call them trash?

Dennistoun. I should hope that a very brief acquaintance with those pictures would correct the public taste.

Mr Vernon. Perhaps it is within your experience, as it is within that of a preceding witness [Lord Aberdeen], that of late years the public taste has gone very much in the direction of that severe and earlier school of art?

Dennistoun. It certainly has; within my experience, a very great change has taken place in that direction.

Mr Vernon. Is it not very desirable, both for artists and the public generally, that when we talk of pre-Raphaelites, we should really know what the word means?

Dennistoun. I think it is certainly desirable, although not necessary in the first instance, that the National Gallery of pictures should contain specimens of what ought to be avoided, as well as what ought to be followed, in so far as regards the gradual progress of art. But true pre-Raphaelite pictures, when good, show much to be admired.

Mr Charteris. Do you think that a love of art generally is much more widely spread now than it was some few years ago?

Eastlake. Certainly.

Mr Charteris. Do you think that greater spread of the love of art, and appreciation of the beautiful, is, to a certain degree, owing to the National Gallery, and to the other open exhibitions of pictures to the public?

Eastlake. Undoubtedly; but the improvement of the public taste, I think, is mainly owing to the National Gallery.

Chairman (Colonel Mure). Do you not think that the fact of the National Gallery containing principally specimens of the inferior schools of art, might, in one sense, be more likely to deteriorate the public taste than to advance it?

Eastlake. I think there may be some misapprehension on that subject; there is at present what may be called a rage for very early works of art, because the study is connected with a certain sort of erudition, and is addressed to the understanding rather than to the imagination, and I should say of such persons, that they may cultivate that predilection without having any taste whatever.

Mr Vernon. We have now acquired a much more accurate knowledge of the works, say, of the early Italian masters, and know their beauties more accurately than we did before, and consequently we feel more the want of them in our own gallery, do we not?

Eastlake. Yes; but there was no lack of opportunities for obtaining such knowledge, if English travellers had been disposed to look for it any time within the last forty years.

Mr Vernon. Was not the number of travellers twenty years ago to foreign countries greatly less than it is now?

Eastlake. I am not prepared to say: but there were always fine works by the early Florentines not only in galleries, but in churches and in public buildings in Italy, which were passed over; the taste is a modern one; how it has arisen would be, perhaps, a difficult inquiry; but I venture to predict that, as it at present exists, it will not endure. I think there is a great deal of fashion in it; a large proportion of those early pictures are full of affectation and grimace; and many persons who have, or fancy they have, a taste for those pictures, are insensible to the essential elements of painting, such as beauty of arrangement, harmony of colouring, and natural action and expression.

And, in fact, even sympathizers like Layard soon found the pace too hot. In 1859 he wrote, 'a violent reaction has now taken place, leading taste and artists to an opposite extreme, equally vicious and hurtful. German archaism, English pre-Raphaelitism and the extravagant price now paid for the vilest daubs of what is called early or Gothic art, are symptoms of it.' In the year of Eastlake's death another cautionary note was added in Tom Taylor's *Life of Reynolds*: 'these works, shunned by the educated natives as the evidence of a past tyranny . . . are lauded to the skies by foreigners, we English in particular, who have none but dilettante associations with them'.

Ruskin and Layard again were on the Committee which chose paintings and drawings for the next great provincial exhibition of Old Masters. This was held in 1868 at Leeds, and, by its large mediæval section, showed early painting to the north as Manchester had done to the Midlands and London to the south.

We have now seen Ruskin's name in connection with all three places and as a founder of the Arundel Society. 'It would be scarcely possible to value too highly', a contemporary wrote, 'the services which Mr Ruskin has rendered in aiding, as he has done, the appreciation in England of the greatest Mediæval artists.'

He began a long series of visits to Italy with eyes not radically different from those of Edward Wright. The Cathedral at Florence was 'barbarous', he joined the crowd in exalting Michelangelo and ignoring Fra Angelico and Botticelli. In the Vatican he did not ask to see the Peruginos or Angelicos, and made nothing of the Sistine walls. In Raphael's Stanze he looked at the frescoes as carefully as Reynolds; unlike him, however, 'ascertaining that they could not give me the least pleasure, and contained a mixture of Paganism and Papacy wholly inconsistent with the religious instruction I received at Walworth'.

Returning to Italy five years later, his taste had begun to change. He studied the Angelicos in San Marco and spent undisturbed hours in the chancel of Sta. Maria Novella looking at the Ghirlandaios.

In Venice it was the same. First came the enthusiasm for the vigour and rush of Tintoretto, the sensuous splendour of Veronese. Rich, luxuriant and daring; bright, calm and painstaking; Tintoretto and Angelico are an odd pair, but they are the heroes of the second volume of '*Modern Painters*'.

The charm of the simple grew on him in Venice, too. 'There's nothing here like Carpaccio!' he wrote in 1869. 'There's a little bit of humble pie for you.

'Well, the fact was, I had never once looked at him – having classed him in glance and thought with Gentile Bellini, and other men of the more or less incipient and hard schools – and Tintoret went better with clouds and hills. I don't give up my Tintoret, but his dissolution of expression into drapery and shadow is too licentious for me now. But this Carpaccio is a new world to me.'

As he worked on, with personal catastrophe nursing the love of solitude, a delight in nature, and adding a deep distrust of sensual passion which he expressed as loathing when he could apply it to canvas and stone, the dark ages came to be the bright ones and his own the dark. What came to man from nature or from God was good; what came from man was bad. The artist must use man's knowledge to express himself, but with the utmost caution. His own devoted exposition of stones, trees and clouds was not primarily to help men describe nature but to understand her. Description could come later, but 'Art is valuable only as it expresses the personality, activity, and living perception of a good and great human soul,' and 'it may express and contain this with little help from execution, and less from science'. The great soul was one who looked at nature with calm and devoted attention like Ruskin as a child in the garden at Herne Hill, but to whom, unlike Ruskin, God spoke continually. Beauty was not the same as truth. Upon beauty there was a curse that whoever pursued it for its own sake should become blind to it. The middle ages sought truth and found beauty as well; the Renaissance sought beauty with the cunning of thieves, grappled it with the eagerness of fools, and destroyed it with the lust of Satyrs.

Whereas to others the Renaissance warmed the middle ages to life, to Ruskin it was the cold that blighted them. The delicate tree of Gothic was nipped. 'The Renaissance frosts came, and all perished,' he said, and repeated again. Where others saw life, he saw death. The Renaissance gave man comfortable houses but it deafened him to the voice of God. He quotes the passage of Bede where the god-sent sparrow flies through King Edwin's hall, and comments, with devastating humourlessness:

'That could not have happened in a Renaissance building. The bird could not have dashed in from the cold into the heat, and from the heat back again into the storm. It would have had to come up a flight of marble stairs, and through seven or eight antechambers –'

His definition of the Renaissance, the evil results of which, at least on architecture, 'I have not grasp enough of thought to embrace', was a personal one. It did *not* represent the emergence of the Individual, its hall–mark rather was system. Grammar killed literature, technique killed art. It did represent faithlessness. Man became separated more and more from God, and pride, sensuality and sloth succeeded.

This was not due simply to pagan learning, for the Church was already corrupt and would have foundered anyway. But the study of antiquity taught disastrous lessons. Form was to be respected more than content. Instead of artists using their skill to exalt God, they used divine figures to exalt their skill. Anatomy became 'the science of the sepulchre . . . Foreshorten your Christ, and paint him, if you can, half putrid; that is the scientific art of the Renaissance.' A symptom of coming spiritual degradation was the growing passion for personification instead of symbolism; the one being the recreation of an effete mind, the other a serious stage in the grasping of a great truth. But no amount of trouncing pagan learning as a 'pestilent study', a 'root of the Renaissance poison tree', can obscure the fact that behind these phrases is a settled melancholy. a pessimistic vision of man once free, devout, innocent and beautiful, slipping and tumbling. For men even came to look beautiful in this climactic time. But Latin or no Latin, corruption would have come. Why? Because man wanted perfection, he wanted heaven and the flesh as well. And that, Ruskin knew – though he was deceived for a while by the Venetians – man could not have.

Flesh: its apotheosis went on until at last 'it became really of small consequence to the artists of the Renaissance incarnadine, whether a man had his head on or not, so only that his legs were handsome'. One turned in disgust to the cool trunk of the Gothic column or to the trees themselves.

In 1842 Ruskin had a profoundly remembered aesthetic experience. He was drawing an aspen tree at Fontainebleau when he suddenly for the first time realized that this tree, that every tree was beautiful, 'more than Gothic tracery, more than Greek vase-imagery, more than the daintiest embroiderers of the East could embroider, or the artfullest painters of the West could limn – this was indeed an end to all former thoughts with me, an insight into a new sylvan world'.

And, when the glamour of colour, science and energy had worn off, this feeling came flooding back, helped by a refound religious belief. In this mood he wrote two versions of a periodization of Italian art and history, in *Verona, and its Rivers*, in 1870, and in *St Mark's Rest*, in 1877–9.

The formula is 'the acceptance of Christianity – the practice of it – the abandonment of it – and moral ruin'.

The first period runs to A.D. 1200. During it tribes are bound together and savage faith is gradually softened by Christianity. He called it the Lombard period.

The second, or Gothic period, runs to 1400, during which Christianity is established and unchallenged. Socially, however, all is not well, especially in Venice, since 1297, the date of the Serrata, after which high rank, not necessarily depending any more on military prowess, was corrupted by the growing mercantile luxuriousness of the place.

After an unexplained gap of fifty years we come to the third period which he calls, simply, the Age of the Masters, from 1450 to 1500. Here everything contributed to produce great art. Generations of apprenticeship were now crowned with just enough technical instruction to use, and not be mastered by. Generations of adversity had perfected the physical type which provided the artists with models. They were perfected in imagination by a 'transcendental philosophy', in intellect by civic watchfulness, in industry by fine craftsmanship. 'And now, therefore, you get out of all the world's long history since it was peopled by men till now – you get just fifty years of perfect work. Perfect.'

He names the greatest of the masters it produced: Luini, Leonardo, Giovanni Bellini, Carpaccio, Mantegna, Verrocchio, Cima, Perugino and the early Raphael. The name 'Age of the Masters' was a compromise. If the correspondence between religious and great art had been as great as he had believed, this ought to have been simply the Christian period, not one in which some signs of paganism were appearing, as he admits they did.

But quieter beliefs came with age. The process can be traced by comparing the text of the *Stones of Venice*, written in 1851–2, with the notes he added in the edition of 1881. He had written, for instance: 'the human mind is not capable of more than a certain amount of admiration or reverence, and that which was given to Horace was withdrawn from David.' But thirty years later he commented: 'True, but a good deal *ought* to be given to Horace, nevertheless.' And again, in 1851, he said: 'This double creed, of Christianity confessed and Paganism beloved, was worse than Paganism itself, inasmuch as it refused effective and practical belief altogether.' The later note was: 'True, again, in general; yet the Parnassus is the greatest of the Vatican Raphael frescoes.'

The last period was from 1500 onwards, when the arts, by becoming devoted to the pursuit of pleasure, perished, unless they were saved by 'a healthy naturalism, or domesticity'.

Thus the scheme, stripped of its moral tone, is not unconventional in the light of what his contemporaries were thinking. Like them, he started with a prejudice against and indifference towards the early Italians and came, it does not matter for what reason, to change his mind. If his enthusiasm for the *quattrocento* was uniquely intense, he cut a deeper trench between it and succeeding centuries. If he understood more clearly the use of decorative and symbolic motifs among the Byzantines, he was still capable of a relapse into the old heresy of the miraculous birth, when 'in the thirteenth century, men make as if they heard an alarum through the whole vault of heaven, and true human life begins again'.

The main difference between him and his fellow lovers of the primitives is in the extent of his writings and the audience he aimed at.

He wrote six works entirely devoted to pre-Raphaelite art, and the subject occurs lavishly in many more. He wrote so much, so wildly and so urgently, he lectured so willingly to undergraduates and workmen's institutions, because he thought this sort of art could save civilization. The separation of form from content had happened to society as well as art; through one the other could be regenerated. We want a true Renaissance, not the '(so called) Renaissance', but a 'Restoration of courage and pure hope to Christian men in their homes and industries'.

One of the evils of that old, bad Renaissance had been that it made it impossible for any but great men to produce good work. The cult of learning made it obligatory. Only great men could sustain the load, and craftsmen became mere copyists. The Renaissance not only destroyed art, it destroyed man's right to feel an essential part of his world. The art historian saw the answer in the *quattrocento*, and he came back to crusade against spiritual, social and economic ills, and only incidentally to write a new chapter of art history and to influence taste.

CHAPTER EIGHT

John Addington Symonds

Symonds was not primarily an historian. He made frequent use of historical material, but almost always as a means of self-expression. By nature, and by urgent desire, he was a poet. But a temperament incapable of spontaneity in verse found an easier relief in prose, and in the description of sites and persons belonging to the past he found, obliquely, much of the release he craved.

This did not prevent him from writing volume upon volume of poems. They came fluently and were corrected carefully and he was much concerned about their effect on reviewers. From a child in the nursery, shouting out lines from *Marmion* on a rocking horse, he had longed to be accepted as a poet. 'Oh, how deeply, fervently I wish it,' he wrote in his diary in 1866, 'then I might speak out somewhat of that which is within me.' But as a poet he did not have the gift of nakedness. Self-analysis and embarrassment put the experience at one remove from directness, consciousness of the importance of what he was saying and the desire to give it a form in which it would find a wide response, removed it further, and what should have been lyric remained descriptive.

Even frank descriptions were more exact and harmonious in prose. He watched a sunset from his gondola in Venice:

'The sky was one vast dome of delicately graduated greys, dove-breasted, ashen, violet, blurred blue, rose-tinted, tawny, all drenched and drowned in the prevailing tone of sea-lavender. The water, heaving, undulating, swirling, at no point stationary, yet without a ripple on its vitreous pavement, threw back those blended hues, making them here and there more flaky and distinct in vivid patches, of azure or of crimson. Not very far away, waiting for a breeze to carry them towards Torcello, lay half a dozen fishing boats with sails like butterflies atremble on an open flower: red, orange, lemon, set by some ineffable tact of Nature just in the right place to heighten and accentuate the symphony of tender tints.' Even in the course of utilitarian historical narrative, moments occur when a prose never very firm turns to poetry and the reader sinks in patches of nerveless prolixity, or pauses dazzled by a vague but splendid light.

These encroachments of poetry were not a bar to his success. The *Athenæum* paid a tribute to them in 1881 by complimenting Symonds on using in his *Italian Literature* a style worthy of the subject. But he knew how unsafe was the balance between poetry and prose. 'Like many better men than myself,' he wrote towards the end of his life, 'I suppose that I have fallen between two stools in art.' He knew that this was due to lack of concentration and lack of self-criticism. He complained that he had never been trained to think. Neither at Clifton, where he first went to school, nor at Harrow, nor afterwards at Oxford, was there the sort of mental training he needed to keep him from a perennial amateurishness. Dispirited, he decided that he could aim no higher than at being a good *vulgariseur*. 'I shall end with being what the French call a *polygraphe fécond* – jack-of-all-trades, æsthetical, and a humbug who has gorged and disgorged Hegel.' A *polygraphe* he became – Professor Babington's bibliography contains 457 items – but not because of a faulty education. This helpless fecundity was not so easily to be explained.

Symonds never wrote more sympathetically than when he was describing some writer born for poetry but turned aside, like Jonson, by too much study, or like Boccaccio because of parental disapproval, to become a writer of prose. He quoted Boccaccio's regretful words: 'I doubt not that if my father had been indulgent to my wishes while my mind was pliable in younger years, I should have turned out one of the world's famous poets,' and on his own father's death confessed that though 'it seems unfilial, almost impious, to say so, yet it is true that the independence I now acquired added a decided stimulus to my mental growth. My father had been so revered and so implicitly obeyed by me that his strong personal influence kept me in something like childish subjection.' This was in 1871 when Symonds was thirty-one.

Dr Symonds was a man of physical and mental strength disturbing to a somewhat sickly and nervous child. A busy and fashionable doctor, his interests seemed to his son to embrace everything worth knowing. He published articles on medical matters but he dabbled also in Greek and Italian art, and Egyptian antiquities. He made a mathematical study of the laws of musical proportion and published the *Principles of Beauty* which contained diagrams of the perfect female form, based on smooth sweeps for the eye muscles. No moment was allowed to pass without profit. There was always a Greek or Latin author open on his table and each day a few pages would be read, the more striking passages translated. Ethnology he mastered as he grew older, and then the topography of ancient Greece. Nor was history neglected: he was perfectly familiar with the details of the Parliamentary War, and could discuss the campaigns of Wellington to the admiration of his military friends. Wherever his son looked, the father seemed to have been before him – always with confidence, impassive confidence of success.

They toured the Continent together in a series of what Symonds doggedly called pleasure trips. One took them from Brussels to Cologne, Berlin, Dresden, the Saxon Switzerland, Prague, Vienna, Salzburg, Munich and the Rhine, all in less than three weeks. Nothing of interest was omitted. Picture galleries and palaces were studied, battlefields inspected, they rode out in search of fine scenery, toured hospitals, went to the opera, called on distinguished foreigners, and mastered the topographical, geological and antiquarian features of each district. To secure time for sight-seeing, most of the travelling was done by night, in a swaying, jolting carriage. Even here, while the exhausted son tried to sleep, the father would produce Mills's *Political Economy* and read a chapter, and waiting at railway stations was treated as an opportunity for the reading aloud of Milton or Tennyson.

From such a trip Symonds would return excited by what he had seen but nervous and depressed by what he had felt. The rational capaciousness of his father was something he admired without resentment but he was baffled by its remoteness from his own talents. His mother had died when he was four. The relatives who helped to care for the Symonds family were dour and puritanical. Their disapproval, or Dr Symonds's measured and tolerant persuasion, repelled, one by one, the excesses and enthusiasms of the child. The sense of being alien and inferior spread from one centre of dismay to another. He was conscious of mental ineffectiveness and at the same time ashamed of his physical appearance. Convinced that he was repulsive he dreamed of the ideal beauty of Greek youth, and when his father pointed out, kindly, the morbid element in this, the picture books were shut and the images transferred to daydreams. He became ashamed of his name, of the social status of his family. The daydreams became more frequent, more intense; at times he became confused as to their reality. Yet if his admiration for his father had caused much of this, it also prevented him from retreating altogether into dreams. His father's habits of inquiry, of patient, thorough analysis, had affected him deeply. The challenge was awful, but the duty of accepting it was clear: 'I

vowed to rouse myself, somehow or other, to eminence of
some sort.' However confused and depressed he might be he
'thirsted with intolerable thirst for eminence, for recognition
as a personality'.

This vague ambition, adopted as a shield, became a mania
which had greater scope when he left home for Harrow.
There in a highly competitive life dominated by games at
which he was not adept, his external self, as he wrote in his
autobiography, was 'perpetually snubbed, and crushed,
and mortified. Yet the inner self hardened after a dumb,
blind fashion. I kept repeating: "Wait, wait. I will, I shall, I
must."'

In particular he was saved by his father's doctrine of work;
work as an anodyne; not an ambition in itself, but something
that made possible the fulfilment of ambition. The misfortune
was that his work was writing. The habits formed when he
used writing as a cure were too strong to throw off when
he wished to produce a piece of writing as an end in itself.
Accustomed to finding refuge in headlong fluency, he could
not go slowly, critically, without admitting the doubt and
mistrust from which he had sought escape in writing. Of this
he was fully aware, and recognized that out of many books
he had written few good paragraphs, and no great line. But
the knowledge was of no avail; the confirmed dram-taker
could no longer sip and savour.

He found another advocate of work at Balliol in Jowett,
and was soon forced, again, and finally, to take refuge in it.
For a while, however, his introspection found other channels.
'I went philandering around music, heraldry, the fine arts,
and literary studies ruled by sentiment. I wrote weak poetry,
I dreamed in ante-chapels. I mooned in canoes along the
banks of the Cherwell, or among yellow water lilies at God-
stow.' But the issue of ambition was not to be put aside for
long. On a reading party in the Lake District he overheard
two of his companions discussing him. They spoke of the

languor of his temperament and declared that there was no chance of getting a First. 'I then and there resolved,' he noted, 'that I would win the best First of my year.'

This he did; and for the rest of his life, in spite of a comfortable private income, he worked and wrote, pausing only when uncertain of what to write next. And these periods were always periods of misery. 'It often occurs to me to think with horror: what would happen if literature failed me? If I did not care to write?' he observed in 1880. He had by this time a family of three girls and a large house and had identified himself with the fortunes of Davos Platz, then in its infancy as a *Kurort*. But the pace was to increase. He noted with satisfaction the number of works he had in hand at the same time; he pointed out the speed with which he produced them. Cellini's Autobiography he translated in four months, Gozzi's bulky Memoirs in five weeks. In one year, 1886, he saw the sixth and seventh volumes of *Renaissance in Italy* through the press, wrote *Sidney* for one series, *Ben Jonson* for another, brought out a volume of *Selections from Jonson*, edited Sir Thomas Browne, wrote an article on Tasso for the *Encyclopædia Britannica* and translated Cellini. The task-master of his Oxford days found this as it should be: 'I congratulate you on having finished your *magnum opus*,' he wrote when Symonds had finished the *Renaissance*. 'Your life, notwithstanding its drawbacks, certainly seems to me a fortunate one. For the happiness of life is work, and you are able to do more than anyone else.'

The remark was not a happy one. It was not simply a feeling of social inferiority or physical repugnance that lay behind Symonds's pathological productivity; these were only temporary worries. Nor was it merely a conviction of mental inferiority to his father, though this lasted longer. A more crucial obstacle to his happiness was the homosexual element in his nature. Though the issue could be evaded by fashionable discussions about ideal friendship at Oxford it was forced into the open by four things: scandalous misrepresentation; his wish to marry; a religious temperament that, though unorthodox, insisted on categories of right and wrong; the habit not only of introspection, but of serious self-analysis. These factors did not all operate at once. For some years the old daydreams flowed on in his poems, many of which were altered between the first private publication and the subsequent public editions. The sex of the beloved was frequently changed from male to female, passages were excised which, like the following from the original version of 'The Lotus Garland of Antinous', reveal an emotion which had become inhibited at the stage of sentimental *Schwärmerei*:

                                        the boy
Gazed on his master, and new depths of joy
Unsensual from his limpid eyes brimmed over
Flooding the full soul of his royal lover;
Who seized the cup and bade the bearer bend
As though his breathing mouth new scent might lend
To the ripe vine juice: as he lightly bent
His lilied lips beneath the thyrsus leant,
Their lips met.

And the tragedy of men who love both men and women was expressed in a legend in heroic couplets, later suppressed, of a painter who tired of his mistress and fell in love with a boy; he took him to a feast dressed as a girl, and there the boy met and was murdered by the discarded mistress.

Such a dilemma required a solution. With the aid particularly of Whitman's poems, and later through correspondence with their author, he found one not in rejection but acceptance. For Whitman, the lover of both man and woman was not a freak or an exception, but an ideal.

Fast-anchored eternal O love! O woman I love!
O bride! O wife! more resistless than I can tell,
                          the thought of you!
Then separate, as disembodied or another born,
Ethereal, the last athletic reality, my consolation,
I ascend, I float in the regions of your love, O man,
O sharer of my roving life.

The fervour of Symonds's discipleship touchingly revealed
the gravity of this sexual problem. To an aesthete, a fastidious
dilettante, as he was at Oxford where he first read *Leaves of
Grass*, a delicate scholar with aristocratic learnings, Whitman's personality and style presented formidable obstacles.
But the reassurance he offered was enough to remove them.
Whitman became for Symonds the greatest teacher of the
age: he taught him to accept his own nature, and Symonds
revered him as a Master, thrilled and sustained by his physical
strength, spiritual vitality and courage. 'He is Behemoth,' he
cried, 'wallowing in primeval jungles, bathing at fountain
heads of mighty rivers, crushing the bamboos and the cane-
brakes under him, bellowing and exulting in the torrid air.
He is a gigantic elk or buffalo, trampling the grasses of the
wilderness, tracking his mate with irresistible energy . . .
He is all nations, cities, languages, religions, arts, creeds,
thoughts, emotions. He is the beginning and grit of these
things, not their endings, lees and dregs. Then he comes to
us as lover, consoler, physician, nurse; most tender, fatherly,
sustaining those about to die, lifting the children, and stretch-
ing out his arms to the young men.'

With Whitman's help he came to a working solution. He
could marry, and to woman, as wife and mother and physical
complement, all his sexual activity would be confined. To
man he could extend an ideal love, a *camaraderie*, pure and
intense because it was not forced by duty. In such a life a
deep affection for his wife could be combined with a glowing

admiration for male beauty. Symonds found a wife who understood the dilemma and approved the solution. Indefatigably patient, she helped him to feel secure in it. Balanced between her and a family on the one hand, and the Swiss peasants of Davos on the other, with whom he tobogganed and drank and sang, and whose athletic prowess he so much admired, he found in work a cure for the depressions that still came. The arrangement could not be quite perfect: the 'amative' and 'adhesive' sides of his personality (in Whitman's words) could not mature equally. Poems written out of sentimental attachments for men, even late in his life, reflect the vague yearning of the years in which he fixed their bounds. In the poems of *In the Key of Blue* (1893) evoked by his gondolier and personal servant Angelo, there is a sickliness which his self-criticism would have noticed in any other connection. This was the strain that was found distasteful, that provoked Swinburne's reference to 'such renascent blossoms of the Italian renascence as the Platonic amorist of blue-breeched gondoliers'. The imperfect balance in his nature had a positive effect in his desire to analyse his problem, and to help others who shared it, he did important pioneer work on the nature of sexual inversion and on the ways in which the laws respecting it should be reformed. He wrote two works, privately printed, on the subject, one in 1873 (printed in 1883), *A Problem in Greek Ethics*, the other printed before 1891, as *A Problem in Modern Ethics*. The latter had a somewhat mysterious opening: 'It confronts us on the steppes of Asia, where hordes of nomads drink the milk of mares; in the bivouac of Keltish warriors, lying wrapped in wolves' skins round their camp-fires; upon the sands of Arabia, where the Bedaween raise desert dust in flying squadrons. We discern it among the palm-groves of the South Sea Islands, in the card-houses and temple-gardens of Japan, under Esquimaux show-huts.' etc.; but the tone of both is calm and dispassionate. In none of Symonds's other writings does he argue with such cogency. He had corresponded with Havelock Ellis since 1885 and contributed a great quantity of the material in *Sexual Inversion* published under their joint names in 1897, but thereafter under Ellis's alone.

In this way the distress that Whitman's teaching and a singularly fortunate marriage had not entirely eased was helped by work. In 1863 a scandalous attack had been made on Symonds which caused him so much suffering that he had to give up his recently won fellowship at Magdalen. Writing five years later to console a friend who had suffered a great blow, he said: 'It almost cost me my life; for the nervous troubles which have wasted my last five years, intellectually speaking, date from a sort of brain fever produced by the pressure of one horrible haunting pain.' But there was a cure: 'Time, I believe,' he went on, 'and Work must be the great healers.' And again: 'The only way out to avoid being mad or bad, instead of only sad, is work.'

If work was the palliative for two afflictions, a sense of mental inferiority and sexual ambiguity, the craving for it was the symptom of a third, consumption. Most of his life was spent as an invalid, much of it on the move, searching for a climate that would ease his lung complaint. For this reason he settled permanently at Davos, building a house, Am Hof, and living the active life which his children have described: they refer to the exciting effect of the atmosphere of the Alps, the effect it had in tensing lowland nerves. There was also the consumptive's race against time, the need to emphasize the moments of living by actual achievement. As he wrote: 'I live really as one who holds his lease of life from week to week; and this is one cause of my feverish energy in writing.' And the effort had to be ratified by print. Most of what Symonds wrote he kept. If a manuscript were not published it went into a 'desolation box' from which it would emerge when times were more favourable – not necessarily revised. Poems, essays, whole books, came out of this desolation box, to appear many years after they were set aside. Literary quality was sometimes less important than the building of landmarks to remind posterity that he had achieved more than most men, and to enable his father's ghost to trace the course of an active career such as he would have admired. When his father died, Symonds wrote, in 1879: 'I had, so to speak, done nothing; and the sort of thing he liked, has come to me in plenty since, so that if my health does not revive and I am to have no further career, I may still think (and he would have thought) that *pro virile parte*, with the strength and parts allotted to me, I have lived.'

The temperament that resulted from these conflicts was not an ideal one for a historian. Symonds realized this, and in his autobiography gave an account of his qualities as a writer which make one regret that his habit of analysis was only strong when applied to himself. 'From nature,' he wrote, 'I derived a considerable love of books, an active brain, a fairly extended curiosity, receptivity to ideas above the average, an aptitude for expression, sensibility to external objects in the world of things, and intense emotional susceptibility of a limited and rather superficial kind.' His memory, he regretted, was weak. He could only retain facts with an effort, and when that effort was relaxed, they went. He forgot as speedily as he learned. 'I saturate my mind with rapid reading, devour multitudes of books, and make voluminous notes, feeling sure that I shall obtain a general conception of the subject under consideration. Then I return again and again to the leading documents, check every impression of fact by reiterated comparison of my notes with their sources, verify dates and quotations, force myself to attain accuracy by drudgery.' Worse than this, 'My brain was always impenetrable to abstractions. When I attacked them, I felt a dull resistance, a sense of benumbed and benumbing stupor stealing like a fog over my intellect.' As a result, Symonds's historical works contain few ideas. Inevitably, his treatment of the Renaissance, which is itself an idea, suffered. From his first treatment of it, in a University Prize Essay in 1863, to his last in an article in the *Fortnightly Review* in 1893, there is no significant modification. What he revised was the presentation of facts, not ideas or opinions. His method was to fill simple patterns – such as The Four Periods of Humanism – with a wealth of attractively presented detail. It was not enough, 'But literature is a go-cart for the individual, and I am thankful to get along in it.'

This very comment expresses clear self-knowledge, but an inability to use it. When *Renaissance in Italy* was all over he wrote: 'the odd thing is that one has so little to say upon subjects which have occupied a life-time. I often find that what I wrote between twenty and twenty-five is no shallower than what I can arrive at now.'

In all his life of self-questioning and alternating moods of exhilaration and depression, Symonds only recognized one major crisis. At Cannes, in 1868, all his doubts came to a head. The question posed was a religious one. How could the individual be sure of himself until he knew what was expected of him by the nature of God? The only conformity Symonds respected was with God's intentions as he understood them. He accepted the code of no church nor of society. His own nature must be tested solely against God's. As long as he believed that this knowledge, or a conviction akin to it, could be found, he lived in uncertainty. His longing to know, and his irrepressible scepticism, preserved a constant agitation. The crisis at Cannes brought something like calm. Not because of an illumination that made him see God, but a conviction that he could not be known. Man's duty was to seek him on earth. As his great friend and biographer, Horatio Brown, expressed it: 'for him all *erscheinungen*, all phenomena, are to be studied, none neglected, humanity is to be sounded to its depths, life to be "drunk to the lees".' Symonds's own phrase was 'self-merging into the whole'.

That Whitman stood ready as guide on this new trail was a great consolation. With him, and with the help of Marcus Aurelius and Goethe, he would strive to 'live resolutely in the Whole, the Good, the Beautiful',

> To perfect self, and in that self embrace
> The tri-une essence of truth, beauty, good;
> This is fulfilment, this beautitude
> Throned high above base fears and hopes more base.

For those who denied constant activity, whose sympathy did not lavishly embrace all creeds and extremes, who had not felt love for all, both man and woman, Limbo waited, full of the wailing ghosts of the unfulfilled:

> We lived not, for we loved not! Dreams are we!
> Death shuns us, who shunned life! What hell shall rouse
> Blank souls from blurred insensibility?

Symonds threw himself into the problems of his literary friends and those of the peasants of Davos. On his travels he tried to mingle with all classes. He upheld conventional marriage but sympathized with the experiment of Noyes's Oneida community of having their women, like their goods, in common. But this was not enough. To an invalid, isolated during a great part of every year in a remote Alpine valley, the Whole of the present was out of reach. That of the past was not, however. Through study it could be regained. And the period in which men lived most wholly, and for the first time began to live by the creed of truth, beauty and goodness was that of the Renaissance in Italy. The middle ages denied beauty and had not been shown the truth. Symonds revolted from 'those medieval lies regarding sexual sinfulness, those foolish panegyrics of chaste abstinence, those base insinuations of base-minded priests'. Blank souls in limbo! The

Renaissance brought release, 'we may say with simple accuracy that the Renaissance wrought for humanity a real resurrection of the body, which since the destruction of the Pagan world had lain swathed up in hairshirts and cerements within the tomb of the medieval cloister'.

The mood which sent Symonds to the Renaissance was exactly that in which he had set his children to tearing up his family papers. Morning after morning they sat in a circle and ripped up the letters and records of seven generations of non-conformist physicians. 'I could not bear to think,' Symonds noted, 'that my own kith and kin, the men and women who had made me, lived in this haunted chamber, from which "eternity's sunrise", the flooding radiance of Nature's light, seemed ruthlessly excluded.' They seemed much less recognizably Symonds's own ancestors than the men of the first generations of emancipation, when 'what seems every day more unattainable in modern life, was enjoyed by the Italians'.

Their life, if it were Whole and strove towards the Beautiful, was not necessarily Good. But violent contrasts of good and evil were characteristic of all growth; self-reliance must come first, and it can come, as Symonds knew, only from stress.

> Whoso framed good, framed evil too; and He
> > Knows what the earth's huge heart-throbs need for life,
> > He counterpoised tranquillity to strife,
> > Systolë weighed against diastolë.

Contrast, too, was one of his literary patterns. In mediæval Italy from a 'hurricane of disaster rises the clear idea of national genius'. Time and again the formula recurs, the literary effectiveness supported philosophically by Hegel's thesis, antithesis, synthesis.

The Renaissance drew him too because he saw it as a period

of 'highly perfected individuality', of men who were whole. Symonds revolted against the undistinguished. He had loathed the mean architecture of Bristol, he disliked Richardson because he was 'essentially a bourgeois', for a time he had been ashamed of his own middle-class origin; a race of natural aristocrats, unbound by convention, free to become whatever they willed, indifferent to the herd – these were his heroes, and he found the material for them in Renaissance Italy. His interest in history was above all personal; he had identified the middle ages with the negation of personality – his interest in the *Divine Comedy* waned when allegory and symbolism replaced personality – and he wrote freely only when history could be written in terms of great men. His adviser Jowett supported him: 'the true interest of history begins with remarkable men and their actions.' And from the remarkable Italians of the present Symonds felt cut off. He loved them, sought out all degrees, made of a Venetian gondolier an intimate friend. Yet there was a barrier. He wrote from Italy in 1873: 'I am like a statue walking among men,' and as late as 1889 concluded regretfully that: 'It is difficult to *know* Italians.' Life was the barrier. It was easier to know the dead.

Those of the dead with whom he felt most at home were the men of the Renaissance. They were the first free men of Europe – 'What the word Renaissance really means is new birth to Liberty,' he wrote in *The Age of Despots* – and they achieved at a bound a degree of personal liberty scarcely obtained since. They lived at a time when man's prison had been left unguarded owing to the assault of antiquity on his mediæval gaolers, and he walked at liberty until the struggle was decided. As far as Italy was concerned, Symonds felt, the prison of the late sixteenth century was ranker than that of the thirteenth, so much did he hate Spanish domination, but the impulse had come, the check would be momentary:

> Onward for ever flows the tide of Life,
>   Still broadening, gathering to itself the rills
>   That made dim music in the primal hills,
> And tossing crested waves of joy and strife.

Symonds was not really interested in current affairs. When he thought of them it was as a conservative. But philosophically he believed in the perfectibility of man, in some sort of egalitarian Utopia. He preferred to think of the first stages in this course, when a high degree of free personal development was consistent with aristocratic control.

He did not find Italian studies sympathetic simply because it was in Italy, he felt, that cultural and intellectual freedom had been born. He loved the country for itself; its warmth, the relaxed freedom of many of its social customs, its people and towns. He had no real affection for Spain or France, none for 'the beastly Germans', his affection for Switzerland was tempered by the knowledge that it was also his sanatorium. But he wrote of Italy without reservation, and his travel sketches led tourists to places usually ignored before because of their remoteness, the bad state of their inns, or their predominantly mediæval interest. These sketches, indeed, by drawing attention to towns like Assisi and Orvieto which had been most notable in the thirteenth and fourteenth centuries, helped to balance his Renaissance period, which in *Renaissance in Italy* leaned heavily towards the personalities of the sixteenth.

The Renaissance, then, was a period in which Symonds, detaching himself from the present as best he could, found the whole lives, the vivid contrasts, the self-reliant individuals he admired, the greatest promise given modern man enacted in the country he most loved. And what finally enabled him to write about it was the fact that as the historian of its culture he would be dealing with the sort of history he found easiest, literary history. The standards of cultural history were not yet demanding. He assumed that a literary subject could be treated in a literary way, and without the discipline, which he admitted he lacked, necessary to a technical historian. In talking of the evolving spirit of a people, feeling rather than logic or close control over balanced narrative could be the guide.

Since he wrote the Chancellor's Prize Essay of 1863 he had kept the Renaissance in view as the work that was to occupy and steady his mind. In 1865, when he was reading *Romola*, Villari's *Savonarola*, and Grimm's *Life of Michael Angelo*, he wrote: 'I want to keep my mind on that period of European history.' For a while he wavered between three exclusively literary subjects: Greek poetry, Italian poetry and the Elizabethan drama, but in 1870 finally decided on a general cultural history of the Renaissance in Italy. 'My heart bleeds,' he wrote, 'to think of my own incapacity for a great work. I must not think of it; for the very thought paralyses.' Two years later there is the same note: 'it is so dreadfully difficult', he told his sister. 1875, when the first part was finished, was a year of extremes. At one moment he proposed to his publisher a grand project for following the as yet uncompleted *Renaissance in Italy* with two other works, one on *Italy and the Counter-Reformation*, and another on *Italy in the Middle Ages*, and then condensing the whole series into one *Kulturgeschichte* of the Italian people. At another he was crying that in an attempt to be accurate 'I have ended in dullness; seeking to be comprehensive, I have become diffuse.'

The Age of the Despots (1875) was followed, nevertheless, by *The Revival of Learning* and *The Fine Arts*, in 1877. Again he wrote despondently to his sister: 'It is a task probably beyond my intellectual grasp, as it is certainly beyond my strength of body.' He felt too that permanent residence at Davos, where he settled in 1880, put an end to any hopes of exact scholarship: 'The forces which, since my boyhood, had been directly and indirectly moulding me for a particular kind of writing, were once more operative. I had to remain a man of letters.' Nevertheless two more volumes, *Italian Literature*, appeared in the following year, and two more, *The Catholic Reaction*, in 1886, which concluded the work.

Renaissance in Italy took eleven years to complete. It consisted of four volumes containing a detailed history of Latin and Italian literature from the fourteenth to the early sixteenth century and a shorter account of art in the same period. (*The Revival of Learning* and *The Fine Arts*, 1877; and *Italian Literature*, 2 vols., 1881.) They were introduced by *The Age of Depots* (1875), designed, in Symonds's words, 'to lay a solid foundation for aesthetical criticism in a study of the social and moral and political condition of the people'. The work was closed by *The Catholic Reaction* (2 vols., 1886), describing how the culture of the Renaissance foundered under Spanish and inquisitorial rule in the second half of the sixteenth century.

Eleven years was too long for the work to succeed as a whole. The first volume, though too slight and general to give the literary volumes the support they needed, was stimulating, while the last, done when Symonds had become bored with the subject, were strained, repetitious and extravagant. The unity of individual volumes was imperilled by their construction. Symonds called the chapters essays, and some of them had been published separately in the *Westminster*, the *Contemporary* and the *Cornhill*; the narrative stream was dammed into a series of articles. *The Age of the Despots* was based on lectures given at Clifton School, and Symonds realized that he had failed to revise all the rhetoric out of them. And he worked, in any case, too emotionally to be able to subordinate the parts to the whole; the topic of the moment seemed all important. In spite of an initial warning that no causes of the Renaissance must be looked for other than in a 'spontaneous outburst of intelligence', when writing of the despots he could not forbear attributing a great part of this to them, or, when dealing with the humanists, saying that thanks to them 'the proper starting-point was given to the modern intellect'.

While the length of the work led to contradictions within it, it was unrefreshed at any state by new ideas: the seven volumes were from this aspect scarcely more than an inflation of the prize essay of 1863. The conception of the Renaissance he had gained at Oxford by reading Gibbon, Roscoe, Hallam and Michelet remained the basis of his thought on the subject for the remaining thirty years of his life; in the Sunday Lecture Society paper, *The Renaissance of Modern Europe*, of 1872, the *Renaissance in Italy*, the long *Encyclopædia Britannica* article 'Renaissance' that he wrote in 1885, in the article which appeared in the year of his death in the *Fortnightly Review* on 'The New Spirit, An Analysis of the Emancipation of the Intellect in the Fourteenth, Fifteenth and Sixteenth Centuries', progress was not forward, but upward, in the form of mounting piles of information and literary criticism.

As Symonds described himself as an historian of culture, it is worth considering his indebtedness to Burckhardt. This has been taken to be great. A parallel has been drawn between *Renaissance in Italy* and *Die Kultur die Renaissance in Italien* in which *The Age of the Despots* is said to balance Burckhardt's section on 'The State as a Work of Art'; chapter one of *The Revival of Learning*, on 'The Men of the Renaissance', Burckhardt's section, 'The Development of the Individual', and *The Fine Arts* and *Italian Literature*, Burckhardt's 'The Discovery of the World and of Man'.

Symonds himself said of the *Kultur der Renaissance* in the preface to *The Age of the Despots*: 'It fell under my notice when I had planned, and in a great measure finished my own work. But it would be difficult for me to exaggerate the profit I have derived from the comparison of my opinions with those of a writer so thorough in his learning and so delicate in his perceptions', and in the second edition (1880), when two more volumes had been written, he added: 'or the amount I owe to his acute and philosophical handling of the whole subject.' There is no reason to doubt Symonds's statement that *The Age of the Despots* owed little to Burckhardt. The original publication of *Die Kultur der Renaissance* passed unnoticed in England, and the reviews of Middlemore's translation of 1878 gave no hint that the book would become famous. The *Westminster* admitted briefly that it was a 'most valuable treatise' but otherwise it was ignored or noticed slightingly. The *Athenæum* found it hard to read: 'study should not be so severe as to become wearisome', it remarked before coming to the softer conclusion that it would be quite useful as a reference book to supplement Sismondi and Hallam – 'if an index be added'. Symonds's ideas about the period, besides, were largely formed and the method of their treatment decided on by 1863, before he had read the *Kultur der Renaissance*, and nowhere in his published letters does Burckhardt's name appear as a guide and inspiration – significant in a man so ready to praise those who influenced him. The actual plan for the *Renaissance in Italy* was decided on, and not merely for the first volume, before he had seen Burckhardt's book.

Nor did the alterations in the second edition of *The Age of the Despots* reflect his influence. The only important change was the insertion of a chapter: 'Italian History', giving a political sketch of progress from communes to depotisms which owes nothing to Burckhardt, and the intention of the chapter, to show that during 'this hurricane of disorder rises the clear ideal of the national genius', was directly counter to the other's anti-Hegelian bias. In the following volume of Symonds's work, *The Revival of Learning*, he again acknowledges his indebtedness, though: 'At the same time I have made it my invariable practice . . . to found my own opinions on the study of original sources.' And, in fact, Symonds, although echoing Burckhardt's warning against the exaggeration of the classical element in Italian culture, was unable to take advantage of it. His subject is the revival of classical literature, and nothing shall be more important: 'the culture of the classics had to be reappropriated before the movement of the modern mind could begin'. In *The Fine Arts* he noted his debt to Burckhardt's *Cicerone*, but whereas Burckhardt had insisted that the development of painting in the fifteenth century, its growing realism, its delight in the human figure, the accurate illusion of space, was due to artists following not antiquity but nature, Symonds insisted on a more dramatic view. 'The old world and the new shook hands; Christianity and Hellenism kissed each other.' Symonds, in fact, was incapable of following Burckhardt, even if he had wished to. The Swiss writer had a far better grounding in the political and economic history of the period, even if little of this appeared in his book, and could see development on several levels, while Symonds could only see it clearly on the literary one. He exaggerated the nature of his own debt to the other; the parallels between their work that he was flattered to see were not really parallels at all, except where both men were responding to the suggestion of Michelet that the period should be seen as that of the discovery of the world and of man. Symonds, too, saw the Renaissance far more in terms of the sixteenth century than Burckhardt. Of the six names to whom he allotted a chapter each – Savonarola, Machiavelli, Cellini, Aretino, Michelangelo and Ariosto – only the first was, and was only just, a *quattrocento* figure.

The approach of the two men to history was quite different. Symonds was interested in literature and individuals and therefore he wrote *Kulturgeschichte*. Burckhardt wrote it because he was interested in the educative value of finding out the character of a period, and this could only be done through cultural history which gave *primum gradum certitudinis*. Symonds's purpose was to entertain ('you will find the chapters on "The Prince", the Popes, and Savonarola most lively'), Burckhardt's was to help his readers to understand themselves through the effort they made to get in touch with the spirit of another age. Symonds was fascinated by the exceptional, Burckhardt was not looking for the unique but the recurrent, he believed 'das Wiederholende wichtiger als das Einmalige!' Symonds wrote to forget himself, Burckhardt believed that simply burying oneself in the past was worthless; an uncertain personality would see the past uncertainly. The disadvantages of the necessarily subjective *Kulturhistoriker* were grave, and he recognized them, even going so far as to warn the audience of his first lecture on *Griechische Kulturgeschichte* that he could not be certain that his was the right view; they might by the end of the course come to quite different conclusions. These limitations Symonds never saw. It was because he lacked the deep seriousness of Burckhardt's approach to his subject, his certainty about the object of history and his philosophically justified use of *Kulturgeschichte* that Symonds's use of his material was shallow and that his grasp on the work as a whole was infirm.

This lack of control left him free to shape the work with but slight interference from his judgment. He said firmly at the start of the work, for instance, that 'it must not be imagined that the Renaissance burst suddenly upon the world in the fifteenth century without premonitory symptoms. Far from that; within the middle age itself, over and over again, the reason strove to break loose from its fetters', but his temperamental dislike of the middle ages soon asserted itself, and the Renaissance emerged as he wrote, as the reverse of all that epoch implied of ignorance, sexual narrowness, and priestly superstition. This dislike of the middle ages was in part a dislike of the Catholic Church whose interference with morals he loathed. Forgetting the narrowness of his father's church, he concentrated all his hatred of clerical authority on Rome, especially once man had gained the chance of freedom by breaking with her. Of Spain and priests in sixteenth-century Italy he wrote with special emphasis. 'Dukes and marquises fell down and worshipped the golden image of the Spanish Belial-Moloch – that hideous idol whose face was blackened with soot from burning flesh.' Man had for a time obeyed his own conscience, but now 'over the Dead Sea of social putrefaction floated the sickening oil of Jesuit hypocrisy'. The longer the work went on, the more temperament was left unrestrained. The imagery became at the last almost humorously lurid: Italy 'lay trampled on and dying'. Spain 'reared her dragon's head of menacing ambition', Germany 'heaved like a huge ocean in the grip of a tumultuous gyrating cyclone'. Reality had quite gone when the historian could write of music at this crisis that it 'put forth lusty shoots and flourished, yielding a new paradise of harmless joy, which even priests could grudge not to the world, and which lulled tyranny to sleep with silvery numbers'.

It is unfair to judge *Renaissance in Italy* by its last two volumes. The tendency to extravagance in prose reflects a love of exaggeration in action noticeable in the whole work. Symonds was neither timid nor particularly frail, but he was fascinated by violence – witness his appendix on 'Blood-madness' to *The Age of the Despots*, and he relished striking contrasts. And because he saw these from the point of view of a strict notion of right or wrong, the contrasts appeared more lurid than they would to a matter-of-fact observer. The attitude of the amoral man, who killed his enemy and returned to paint an angel, or slept with his daughter and descended to administer the sacrament without a sense of disturbance was one he did not choose to comprehend. He wrote as if they were conscious of their wickedness, turned from good to evil, normal to abnormal with a sense of grinding contrast. Burckhardt described violence without becoming involved in it: Symonds entered the arena. 'Under the thin mask of human refinement', he reported in the *Revival of Learning*, 'leered the untamed savage'. In *The Fine Arts* he pointed to the contrast of Perugino painting his bland pure saints and paying a bravo to assassinate a rival; when he came to the story of Signorelli, confronted by the slain body of his son, he broke into verse to supplement the prose description of how the impassive artist stripped the body and painted it; in a whole chapter on Cellini's contrasted and violent career he permitted himself the self-contradictory observation that his life was 'the most singular and characteristic episode in the private history of the Italian Renaissance' – the exceptional was the rule. Italian life, he wrote in *Italian Literature*, Vol. 2, 'furnishes a complete justification for even Tourneur's plots', and 'who can say that Webster has exaggerated the bare truth?' This is far from the milder travel sketch 'Vittoria Accoramboni', where he refers to 'the laboured portrait of Flamineo' and admits that Webster's Italian tragedies are true 'not so much to the actual conditions of Italy, as to the moral impression made by those conditions on a Northern imagination'. It was sad that the historian of the *Renaissance in Italy* should have been debarred by his nature from describing the actual conditions of his subject in the same way.

Symonds was mainly interested in individuals. He published lives of Dante, Shelley, Sidney, Jonson, Michelangelo, Whitman and Boccaccio. Of history he wrote: 'We have learned to look upon it as the biography of man,' and true to this attitude he found that 'the Italian history of the Renaissance resumes itself in the biography of men greater than their race'. Rootless and independent himself, consciously exceptional, he found it natural not to relate his protagonists to a background which would, while it explained, absorb them. While Burckhardt emphasized the individual to understand the mass, Symonds laboured to detach him from the mass. 'The work achieved by Italy for the world in that age was less the work of a nation than that of men of power.' It was as true of artists as of despots and humanists: 'the old custom of speaking about schools and places, instead of signalizing great masters, has led to misconception, by making it appear that local circumstances were more important than the facts justify'. Yet as a result of this preoccupation with the individual there emerged much less than a fully representative portrait gallery. In 1863 he had urged that to understand the Renaissance science and exploration must be considered as well as art, philosophy, religion. But as it was only the last subjects that were relevant to his own nature, the great men of science and exploration were barely mentioned. Columbus and Vespucci are passed over. Galileo is noticed in a few words, while Bruno, his contemporary, receives the full treatment appropriate to one whose philosophy had been an inspiration to Symonds. This personal approach increased the disadvantages of concentrating on great men. Though he believed, for instance, that Raphael was a greater artist than Signorelli, he devoted more space to the latter because of his influence on his special hero, Michelangelo.

This was one of the disadvantages of Symonds's real originality. He knew probably more about the period than anyone living. He had read the works he wrote about and never put down a second-hand opinion. If he subscribed to certain earlier views it was from conviction, not from habit. It remained a period of picturesque and dreadful personages. Alexander VI still provoked titillating censure ('the universal conscience of Christianity is revolted by those unnameable delights, orgies of blood and festivals of lust'), liberty was still the cry. But here Symonds differed from earlier views. He did not praise the republican age, Italy's glory and man's freedom depended on the despotisms, on the unrivalled development of character they fostered: 'the facts of the case seem to show that culture and republican independence were not so closely united in Italy as some historians would seek to make us believe'. But neither did he follow his old source of 1863, Roscoe, admiring the Medici. To Symonds they were tyrants, who, so far from promoting the good, progressive elements in the culture of Florence, encouraged the bad; with his strong belief in the self-sufficient individual, Symonds was not much concerned with patronage.

The amount of information in *Renaissance in Italy* makes it still useful, especially the *Italian Literature* volumes, which remain the fullest literary history of the period obtainable in English. Nor is there any substitute in English for *The Revival of Learning*. Symonds remains a useful authority on the central part of his work; it was when he tried to relate this information to a general conception of the Renaissance that he failed.

His use of the term was deceptive. With regard to the arts, there were firm limits. For architecture he followed the divisions of Burckhardt's *Cicerone*: 1420–1500, the age of experiment; 1500–40, of achievement; 1540–80, of decline. For painting, likewise three divisions: from Cimabue to 1400; from 1400 to 1470, from 1470 to 1550, during which the Renaissance 'may be said to have culminated'. For literature, again three periods: from Dante's vision in 1300 to Boccaccio's death in 1375; from 1375 to Cosimo dei Medici's death in 1448; from 1448–1530, which Symonds called alternatively the 'Golden age of the Renaissance' or 'the true Renaissance'. The crucial dates are, then: 1500–40, in architecture; 1470–1550, in painting; 1448–1530, in literature. From his choice of representative individuals and of the *Orlando Furioso* as the representative poem of the Renaissance we can see that as far as the arts were concerned, the first generation of the sixteenth century was the key one, and this definition of the close of the period at least was aided by the generally waning admiration for late sixteenth-century painters. In what he expressly said, then, Symonds was entirely conventional. But because his work, which called itself *Renaissance*, covered the fourteenth and fifteenth centuries, artists of these centuries, particularly the *quattrocento* (the effect of Burckhardt's work was the same) were associated with the term. And Symonds fostered this association by the use of phrases like 'the dawn of the Renaissance', which could cast the terminological net as far back as the small fry of the thirteenth century.

His limits of the period as a whole were less rigid than those he gave the arts. In the preface to *The Age of the Despots* he wrote: 'Two dates, 1453 and 1527, marking respectively the fall of Constantinople and the sack of Rome, are convenient for fixing in the mind that narrow space of time during which the Renaissance culminated.' But to set limits to a culmination reflects Symonds's need to pin down and deal with the complex and abstract by analysis. So we have three ages of this and four of that, neatly dated; moments of caution – 'we have to be on our guard against the tyranny of a metaphor', moments of irresolution – 'the so-called Renaissance', alternating with precise dates. He knew that it was an age of transition but could not avoid cutting it into segments. He reserved the full sense of the term for the late fifteenth-early sixteenth centuries, but under cover of the title of the book, and images of dawns, beginnings and first glimmerings, the men and the manners of the previous two centuries came in.

His unease when dealing with the theoretical part of his subject caused him to hazard some very shaky theories. The Renaissance Italians were responsive to beauty because in some districts 'circumstances and climate had been singularly favourable to the production of such glorious human beings as the world had rarely seen'. Rapt in a vision of the country and the time 'when lads with long dark hair and liquid eyes left their loves to listen to a pedant's lectures', Symonds allowed himself to suggest an explanation: 'Surely the physical qualities of a race change with the changes in their thought and feeling'.

Similarly uncritical was the use of Hegelian ideas. He often referred to 'the spirit of the times', 'the half-unconscious striving of the national genius', the *Zeitgeist*, without realizing what nonsense this made of his insistence on the dominant role of the individual. He was capable of remarks that reduced the importance of personality to zero. 'The *Zeit-geist* needed Petrarch. He, or someone like him, was demanded to effect a necessary transition.' The creative talents of the humanists which are lauded in one volume, become less independent when in another he states that humanism 'was imperatively demanded not only by the needs of Europe at large, but more particularly and urgently by the Italians themselves'. His faith in progress clashed with his faith in the individual. From one point of view Italy passed on to the rest of Europe the achievements of her great men, from the other she was simply used for a while by the current of the world spirit which was leading Europe to her goal of freedom. Symonds's judgment slept, too, through another clash – that between his prejudices and his optimism. The former caused him to denounce abuses, the latter persuaded him that everything that happened was for the best. The middle ages had been superstitious and ignorant; during them man was degraded and enslaved – but all was for the best, for they kept man fresh, full of illusion for the blessing of the Renaissance: 'Ennui,' said Symonds feelingly, 'and the fatigue that springs from scepticism, the despair of thwarted effort, were unknown.' Classicism led to the neglect of vernacular literature – but this was for the best, for how otherwise could the European nations have become conscious of their bonds with the classic past? The levelling down of the component parts of Italy under a common despotism in the sixteenth century meant the destruction of her most valued characteristic, but it was for the best, for it was a prelude to her becoming a nation. Symonds did not see that when everything, however veiled, is for the best, because the present is as yet the best, the historian is left with little scope for censure of the past.

As early as 1878 the *Quarterly Review* noticed this weakness: 'We find throughout his work a constant conflict between his moral instinct and his philosophical principles, the result of which is a double point of view that produces an impression of infirmity of judgment.' However conscious of this, Symonds could not escape. Dealing with subjects that stimulated his imagination made it hard to be cool and critical. 'Long after work is over,' he noted in the autobiography, 'the little ocean of the soul is agitated by a ground-swell; the pulses beat, the nerves thrill and tingle.' He knew that 'changes of style and purple patches deformed the unity and gravity of a serious historical work. Relief from thoughts which had become intolerable had to be sought in brain-labour. That being so, I did not sufficiently count the cost, or approach my theme in a calm artistic spirit.'

This warning did not reach the public, nor perhaps would they have heeded it. Admiration for Italy, once more a free nation, was intense. Travel was cheap and easy. There were guide books and guided tours. From industrialized England lovers of quiet and beauty came, many of them to settle permanently in Italy, where life had such grace and was so inexpensive. And it was not antiquity that appealed, but the Renaissance, with its morality so different from that of the Victorians, its great men they knew so well how to appreciate. With Pater and Ruskin they studied the art of the *quattrocento*, exercising on painters like Botticelli what Symonds called 'our delight in delicately poised psychological problems of the middle Renaissance'. Socially secure, and delighting in the sun, a host of intelligent Englishmen and women dipped their pens in a haze of aesthetic goodwill, and began, with scant historical equipment, so chronicle the towns, the men and the manners of the Renaissance.

The mood even penetrated a tart article on Campanella in the *Edinburgh Review* in 1879. During the Renaissance 'A strange glamour was over men's eyes. As of old, the earth seemed dædal with many-coloured delights. Sorrow and death were hardly perceived as a jar in the universal spring-song of the intellect and the senses.' There was much tearful gratitude for what Italy had done for modern man. She created him and then herself was slain; 'this nation', said Symonds gravely, 'had to suffer for the general good.' He emphasized that the story he told in *Renaissance in Italy* was a tragedy. He showed Italy at the height of her joy and creative power – then her pathetic ruin 'while the races who had trampled her to death went on rejoicing in the light and culture she had won by centuries of toil'. The Italians accepted the task of re-appropriating the classics which were to free mankind, a task which cost them their own literary independence and political liberty. This was false, but no matter how far from the truth sentiment took him, its appeal disarmed criticism.

The effects of his attitude can be seen nowhere more clearly than in the work of Vernon Lee (Violet Paget). In her *Euphorion* (1884) she paid a tribute to Symonds, praising the specially adapted gifts, his infinite patience and ingenuity 'occasionally amounting almost to genius'. She, too, lauded Italy for sacrificing herself for posterity, and went further than her master. She set herself to judge the period, to be shocked, tolerant, understanding and forgiving, as though its tumultuous generations stood before her like an erring but repentant choirboy: 'Our first feeling is perplexity; our second feeling, anger' – but as evil is a necessary part of the mechanism for producing good, we must forgive. How can we help it 'in looking down from our calm, safe scientific position, on the murder of the Italian Renaissance; great and noble at heart, cut off pitilessly at its prime; denied even an hour to repent and amend; hurried off before the tribunal of posterity, suddenly, unexpectedly, and still bearing its weight of unexpiated, unrecognized guilt'?

Her other master was Pater. She aped the purposeful delicacy of his style, she took her title from a passage in his *The Renaissance*. *Euphorion* was named after the child of the mystic marriage of Goethe's Faust and Helen – the worn-out middle ages joined with age-old but divinely young antiquity to produce the Renaissance. But this technical description is soon set aside. Renaissance is used to describe anything vague but splendid that happened in Italy between Dante and Michelangelo, and anything that resembled it in the north where 'the Renaissance is dotted about amidst the stagnant Middle Ages'.

The term that had grown up to supplement the Revival of Learning and that Burckhardt had tried to restrain to Italy, was washed free of restrictions by a flood of subjective writing. Rebirth was a fatally attractive image to an age confident of progress. The objections were few and they were brushed aside. Men wished to see the Renaissance by the light in which Symonds had painted it. They accepted the tyranny of a metaphor that he had served but feared.

NOTES

CHAPTER ONE

p.   l.

2   12   The *Lucubratinculae Tiburtinae* of Robert Flemmyng, *v.* R. Weiss, *Humanism in England During the Fifteenth Century*, 1941, 97–105.

     15   For Thomas, *v.* E. A. Adair, in *Tudor Studies*, ed. Seton Watson, 1924, 133–60.

     26   in *The Works of William Thomas* . . . ed. A. D'Aubant, 1774.

3   7   *The fyrst boke of the Introduction of Knowledge* n.d., n.p., but *v.* ed. by F. T. Furnivall, 1869–70.

5   9   in Strype, *Ecclesiastical Memorials*, ed. 1822, II, ii, 59–78, and *Works*.

     30   *Principal Rules of English Grammar, with a Dictionarie* . . . 1550.

6   32   *v.* F. A. Yates, *John Florio*, Cambridge, 1934: and 'Italian teachers in Elizabethan England,' *Journal of the Warburg and Courtauld Institutes*, v. 1, 103–17.

7   23   *Florio His first Fruites: which yeelde familiar speech, merie Proverbes, wittie Sentences, and golden sayings. Also a perfect Induction to the Italian, and English tongues, as in the Table appeareth. The like heretofore, never by any man published*, 1578, chaps. 13, 2 and Grammar.

8   8   John Florio, *A Worlde of Wordes, or most copious, and exact Dictionary in Italian and English*, 1598.

     23   *Il Passaggiere: The Passenger, English and Italian on opposite pages*, 1612, 485.

     29   *The Italian Tutor Or A New And Most Compleat Italian Grammar*, and *A Display Of Monosyllable Particles Of The Italian Tongue* . . . *Also, certaine Dialogues* . . .

9   10   *The Italian Reviv'd: or, The Introduction To The Italian Tongue* . . . , *v.* end of last dialogue.

9 20   *v.* M. A. Scott, *Elizabethan Translations from the Italian*,
        N.Y., 1916. Supplemented by C. R. Baskerville, *Modern
        Philology*, 1919, 213–18; and J. de Perott, *Romantic Review*,
        1918, 304–8; and H. S. Bennett, *English Books and Readers
        1475–1557*, Cambridge, 1952.

   27   G. C. Moore Smith, *Gabriel Harvey's Marginalia*,
        Stratford, 1913, 162.

10 22 Eleanor Rosenberg, 'Giacopo Castelvetro Italian
        Publisher in Elizabethan London and his Patrons',
        Huntingdon Library Quarterly, 1943, 119–45.

11 12 *The Unfortunate Traveller*, 1594, ed. R. V. McKerrow,
        1910, 301.

12   9 Unpub. M.A. Thesis University of London by Jeanette
        Fellheimer, *The Englishman's Conception of the Italian in the
        Age of Shakespeare*, 1935, 68.

   20   William Lithgow, *A Most Delectable, and True
        Discourse . . .* , 1614.

   32   *v.* below, 58.

13 12 *The English Romayne Life Discovering The lives of the
        Englishmen at Roome*, 1582.

   16   *A Booke of the Travaile and Lief of Me Thomas Hoby*, ed.
        Edgar Powell, Camden Misc. x, 1902.

   32   V. J. Flynn, 'Englishmen in Rome during the
        Renaissance', *Modern Philology*, 1938, 121 ff.

15   4 *An Itinerary Written by Fynes Moryson Gent . . .* 1617.

   13   *The Rare and most vvonderful things vvhich Edvv. VVebbe
        hath seene and passed in his troublesome trauailes . . .* 1590.
        Though probably true in outline, the details of Webbe's
        book are unlikely to be exactly true; he was seeking
        preferment from the Queen for whom he had suffered so
        much.

   30   Mary F. S. Hervey, *The Life Correspondence & Collections
        of Thomas Howard Earl of Arundel*, Cambridge, 1921,
        83.

16 28 *A True Description and Direction of what is most worthy to
        be seen in all Italy . . .* Anon, Harleian Misc., v. 1810.

17   6 *An Itinerary contayning a Voyage made through Italy in the
        Yeere 1646–7 . . .* 1648, 69.

    7   Among the most useful books on travel are:
        E. S. Bates, *Touring in 1600. A study in the Development
        of Travel as a Means of Education*, 1911.

E. G. Cox, *A Reference Guide to the Literature of Travel*, i, Seattle, 1935.

L. Einstein, *The Italian Renaissance in England*, New York, 1902.

Clare Howard, *English Travellers of the Renaissance*, 1914.

M. Lettes, Bibl. to ed. of *Francis Mortoft: His Book, Being his Travels through France and Italy, 1658–1659*, Hakluyt Soc., 1925.

Lewes Roberts, *The Marchants Mapp of Commerce . . .* , 1638.

J. W. Stoye, *English Travellers Abroad 1604–1667*, 1952.

A. d'Ancona, ed. of Montaigne's *Journal du Voyage*. 1895, bibl.

19	22	*Diary, s.a.* 1646.
	28	Raymond, 40.
21	26	*The Oldest Diary of English Travel*, ed. W. J. Loftie, 1884, 12.
23	1	*v.* Richard H. Perkins, 'Volpone and the reputation of Venetian justice', *Modern Language Review*, 1940, 11–18.
24	18	*The Parly of Beasts; or, Morphandra Queen of the Inchanted Island . . .* , 1660, 199.
26	31	*Travaile . . .* , 25.
27	32	II, i. Quo. P. Rebora, *L'Italia nel dramma inglese (1558–1642)*, Milan, 1925, 219.

CHAPTER TWO

This chapter owes much, including its title, to the work of Professor Herbert Weisinger, particularly to the following articles:

'English attitudes towards the relationship between the Renaissance and the Reformation', *Church History*, 1945, 167–87.

'The study of the Revival of Learning in England from Bacon to Hallam', *Philological Quarterly*, 1946, 221–47.

'The Idea of the Renaissance and the Rise of Science', *Lynchos, Annual of the Swedish History of Science Society*, 1946–7, 11–35.

'The English origins of the sociological interpretation of the Renaissance', *Journal of the History of Ideas*, 1950, 321–38.

'English treatment of the relationship between the rise of science and the Renaissance', *Annals of Science*, 1951, 248–74.

This is perhaps the place to record two other works that helped stimulate my interest in this subject:

Roderick Marshall, *Italy in English Literature 1755–1815. Origins of the Romantic Interest in Italy*, Columbia Univ. Press, 1934.

C. von Klenze, *The Interpretation of Italy during the last Two Centuries. A contribution to the Study of Goethe's 'Italienische Reise'*, Univ. of Chicago, 1907.

33   7   *The History of the House of Esté, from the Time of Forrestus until the death of Alphonsus the last Duke of Ferrara . . . ,* 1681.

      25   Anon, *Conspiracy of John Lewis . . . de Fieschi . . . ,* 1693; and F. Midon, *The History of the Rise and Fall of Masaniello, the Fisherman of Naples . . . ,* 1729.

34   11   *v.* Z. S. Fink, *The Classical Republicans*, Northwestern Univ. Press, 1945, *passim*.

      24   *Weekly Miscellany*, 21st October 1738; *v.* Boswell, ed. G. B. Hill, i, 135. *Critical Revue*, 1761, 169.

37   28   *Works*, 1720, i, 164.

38   18   *Remarks on Several Parts of Europe, relating chiefly to their Antiquities and History. Collected on the Spot: In several Tours since 1723*, 2v., 1728, Preface, x.

40   4   i, 202.

41   14   Paris, 1761–70.

      26   *The Modern Part of an Universal History, from the Earliest Account of Time. Compiled from Original Writers. By the Authors of the Antient Part*, 1759–66. The relevant vols. are: xxv, xxvi (xxv mostly taken up with last part of history of France), 1761, *The History of Italy* (largely Rome and the Papacy), xxvii, 1761, *The History of Venice*; xxviii, 1761, *The History of Naples* and *The History of Genoa*; xxxvi, 1762, *The History of Florence*; xxxvii, 1762, *The History of Bologna, Parma and Placentia, Milan, Modena and Ferrara, Mantua*.

42   1   *v. D.N.B.* Archibald Bower and George Psalmanazar.

45   14   *A Catalogue of Books relating to the History and Topography of Italy, collected during the years 1786, 1787, 1788, 1789, 1790* (twelve copies printed), 1812.

45   30   4v., 1749.

46   3   op. cit. i, 50, footnote.

      28   1766, 406.

47   13   Humphrey Hody, *De Graecis illustribus linguae Graecae literarumque humaniorum instauratoribus . . . ,* 1742.

47   28   1770, 353.

48   3   Henry Home (Lord Kames), *Sketches of the History of Man*, 2v., Edin., 1774; and Adam Ferguson, *Essay on the History*

		of Civil Society, Edin., 1767.
50	34	*History of England*, 1770. I quote ed. 1796, iv, 35, 37.
51	14	Herbert Weisinger, 'English Attitudes towards the Relationship between the Renaissance and the Reformation', *Church History*, 1945, referring, 178, to *The Works*, 1885, v, 308.
	33	I quote from 1st complete ed. *The Divina Commedia of Dante Alighieri . . . Translated . . . By the Rev. Henry Boyd, A.M.*, 3v, 1802, 58.
52	12	Preface, xii, xiv, xxiv.
	33	Joseph Priestly, *Lectures on History*, Birmingham, 1788. I quote ed. 1826, 289.
54	6	Alexander Tytler, *Plan and Outline of a Course of Lectures on Universal History, Ancient and Modern, delivered in the University of Edinburgh*, Edin., 1782, 146.
	18	op. cit., 259.

CHAPTER THREE

Works of general interest for Chapters III and V:

T. Borenius, 'The rediscovery of the Primitives', *Quarterly Review*, 1923, 258–71.

J. W. Draper, *Eighteenth Century English Aesthetics. A Bibliography*, Heidelberg, 1931.

C. von Klenze, 'The growth of interest in the Italian Masters', *Modern Philology*, 1906, 207–74.

H. V. S. Ogden and M. S. Ogden, 'A bibliography of seventeenth-century writings on the pictorial arts in English', *The Art Bulletin*, 1947, 196–201.

Luigi Salerno, 'Seventeenth-century English literature on painting', *Journal of the Warburg and Courtauld Institutes*, 1951, 234–58.

And for Chapter VII:

John Steegman, *The Consort of Taste*, 1830–70, 1950.

55	3	By Mrs J. Foster, 1st Italian eds., 1550 and 1568.
57	15	Foster, i, 31.
58	5	ibid.
	14	Pungileoni's *Life of Correggio*, v. *Quarterly*, June 1840, 1.
59	19	Of 1655, given in Mary F. S. Harvey, op. cit.
	25	For private collectors in the seventeenth century v. E. K. Waterhouse, 'Paintings from Venice for seventeenth-

century England: Some records of a forgotten transaction', *Italian Studies*, 1952, 1–23.

33 Harvey, 453.

60 6 ibid, 394.

    31 *An Idea of the Perfection of Painting . . . Written in French by Roland Freart, Sieur de Cambray, and rendred English by J. E. Esquire*, 1668, 'To The Reader'.

62 15 *The Painter's Voyage of Italy*, by [William] L[odge].

65 30 *A Tracte containing the Artes of curious Paintinge, Carving & Buildinge written first in Italian by Jo: Paul Lomatius painter of Milan and englished by R.H. student in Physik*, Oxford, 1598.

66 19 *De Arte Graphica. The Art of Painting by C. A. Du Fresnoy with Remarks. Translated into English, together with an original Preface containing a Parallel betwixt Painting and Poetry. By Mr Dryden. As also a short account of the most eminent painters, both ancient and modern . . . by another hand* [Richard Graham], 2 pts., 1695.

68 12 in *A Miscellany of the Wits*, ed. K. N. Colville, 1920, 32.

69 5 J[ohn] E[lsum], *Epigrams upon the Paintings of the Most Eminent Masters, Antient and Modern, With Reflexions upon the several Schools of Painting*, 1700, 131, 132.

    19 ibid., *The Art of Painting after the Italian Manner . . .*, 1703, 128.

70 15 *Idler*, No. 76, 29th September 1759.

    22 *Literary Works of Sir Joshua Reynolds*, ed. H. W. Beechy, 3v., 1883, iii, 428 ff.

71 15 quo. E. W. Manwaring, *Italian Landscape . . .*, 1925, 31.

    16 *Travels through France and Italy Containing Observations on Characters, Customs, Religion, Government, Police, Commerce, Arts and Antiquities*, 2v., 1766.

    35 *Some Observations made in Travelling through France, Italy, &c. In the years 1720, 1721, and 1722*, 2v., 1730; and *Catalogue of the entire collection of Pictures . . . of Edward Wright, Esq: (deceased) Late of Stratton in Cheshire*, n.p., 1st February 1754.

72 34 Gilbert Burnet, *Bishop Burnet's Travels through France, Italy, Germany, and Switzerland, etc.*, Rotterdam, 1685.

74 3 *Two Discourses. I. An Essay on the whole Art of Criticism as it relates to Paintings . . . II. An argument in behalf of the Science of a Connoisseur . . .*, 1719, 77 (second discourse).

22   *An Account . . .* , Preface.

34   ibid., 270.

75   13   ibid., 79.

24   ibid., 43–4.

76   7   *A Catalogue of the Geniune and Entire Collection of Italian and other Drawings, Prints, Models, and Casts, Of the late Eminent Mr. Jonathan Richardson, Painter, Deceas'd . . . Sold . . . 22d of January, 1746–7 and the Seventeen following Nights (Sundays excepted)*, n.p., n.d.

77   8   *v.* note, p44 30, ibid., i, 170, 205, 213 and 130.

24   *The Letters of Horace Walpole*, ed. P. Toynbee, Oxford, 1903–5, i, 339–40. Ap. 4, 1743.

78   7   *v.* his Memoirs in *Walpole Society*, v. 32, 1946–8, 54.

18   *Second Characters.* I use ed. 1914, 129. There is more about painting here than in *Characteristicks*, 1711.

30   *v. Walpole Society*, v. 28, 1939–40.

79   10   J. Northcote, *Life of Reynolds*, 1814, 391–2.

27   *The Life of Masaccio*, n.p. (1770), ii. This date is from Introduction. In B.M. copy *The Life of Fra Bartolommeo della Porta, a Tuscan painter*, n.p., 1772, is bound with it.

81   9   *Vita di Anton Domenico Gabbiani Pittore Fiorentino descritta da Ignazio Enrico Hugford suo discepola*, Firenze, 1762.

CHAPTER FOUR

82   15   *Miscellaneous Works*, 1796–1815, i, 140.

19   *Antiquities of the House of Brunswick*, 1814, 120.

83   11   *Decline and Fall of the Roman Empire*, cap. lxvi.

22   ibid.

84   10   *Sketch Book*, 1849, 22.

22   The *Balia* of Luigi Tansillo.

85   23   *The Life of William Roscoe by his son Henry Roscoe*, 2 v., 1833, i, 29.

85   35   ibid., 44.

86   25   ibid., 61.

87   4   Printed in *Life*, 67.

88   22   *The Letters of Horace Walpole*, ed. P. Toynbee, Oxford, 1903–5, xv, 342, letter dated 4th April 1795.

35   T. J. Mathias, *Pursuits of Literature*, 'Dialogue the Third', 1796, 47. In a note to this passage he says: 'It is pleasant to consider a gentleman, not under the auspices of an

university or beneath the shelter of academic bowers, but in the practice of the law and business of great extent (resident in a remote commercial town, and where nothing is heard of but Guinea-ships, slaves, blacks and merchandise, *in the town of Liverpool*), investigating and describing the rise and progress of every polite art in Italy at the revival of learning with acuteness, depth, and precision . . .'

89	7	*Life*, i, 313.
96	16	*v*. J. Mayer, *Roscoe, and the Influence of his Writings on the Fine Arts*, Liverpool, 1853, 24.
97	11	*Life*, ii, 94.
99	5	p. 274.
	30	*Leo*, Preface.
100	21	*Memoirs of the Illustrious House of Medici*, 1797, 453.
	34	*On the Origin and Vicissitudes of Literature, Science and Art*.
101	2	*Life*, Appendix I.
	6	W. Buchanan, *Memoirs of Painting* . . . , 1824.
	12	*Leo*, Preface.
	17	*On the Origin and Vicissitudes of Literature* . . . , quo. *Life*, ii, 157.
102	14	ii, 384.
	32	ii, 517.
103	3	i, 106.
	11	i, 287.
	22	April 1803, 45, 43.
	30	*Edinburgh Review*, April 1808, 185.
105	9	ii, 1.
	28	Quo. H. Weisinger, 'English Attitudes towards the Relationship between the Renaissance and Reformation', *Church History*, 1945, 184.
106	21	*Memoirs of Lorenzo da Ponte*, trans. and ed. L. A. Sheppard, 282.

CHAPTER FIVE

109	11	p. 61.
	20	*Aedes Walpolianae: or, a Description of the Collection of Pictures at Houghton-Hall in Norfolk* . . . (1743) in v. ii of *The Works* . . . , 1798, 230.
110	15	Quo. Borenius, *Quarterly Review*, 1923, 263.

ENGLAND AND THE ITALIAN RENAISSANCE

26   *The Italian School of Design*, 1823; and *A Series of Plates
. . . Intended to illustrate the history of the restoration of the
arts of design in Italy*, 1826.

111   13   W. Buchanan, *Memoirs of Painting with a Chronological
History of the Importations of Pictures into England since the
French Revolution*, 2 v., 1824.

112   2   Henry Roscoe, *The Life of William Roscoe*, 2v., 1833, ii,
139.

8   *Edinburgh Review*, August 1810, 303.

11   ibid., September 1814, 281.

15   1891, 90.

114   3   pp. v–vi, xxiv. *The Dream of a Painter* was originally
published in *The Artist*, 1807, and republished among
'Varieties on Art' at the end of Northcote's *Memoirs of Sir
Joshua Reynolds, Knt.*, 1813. I quote from this.

115   8   [Richard] C[olt] H[oare].

116   4   Buchanan, op, cit., i, 100.

117   8   *Quarterly Review*, January 1865, 313, in an article on
several works bearing on the history of the Louvre
during the Napoleonic Wars and treaty-making, e.g.
Wellington's *Supplementary Dispatches*, xi.

17   Quo. F. H. Taylor, *The Taste of Angels*, 1948, 586.

119   3   *The Life and Writings of Henry Fuseli*, ed. John Knowles,
3v., 1831, iii, 182.

120   7   *Praeterita*, 3 v., 1886–1900, ii, 213.

14   And discretion. *The Athenæum*, 4th August 1860, reported
Layard telling a meeting about the Filippino frescoes in the
chapel of S. M. Novella. 'A scaffold was erected in front
of it, on which, when he was there, were three gentlemen
with pails and brushes almost of the proportions of mops.
He inquired what they were about to do, and they
replied, "We are engaged to *rinfrescare* (or refresh)
Filippino Lippi." ' p. 165a.

122   19   I quote from 1815 ed. of her *Letters from Italy*, 1800, i,
173. The work was several times revised and the 'guide'
parts expanded under different titles, et.g. *Travels on the
Continent: written for the Use and Particular Information of
Travellers*, 1820; *Information and Directions for Travellers on
the Continent*, 1828; *Travels in Europe, for the use of
Travellers on the Continent, and likewise in the Island of Sicily*,
1833. The last eds. were handy in size, double column,

listed paintings in collections, described churches,
antiquities, etc., gave doctors, hotels, routes. Murray
published all but the first ed.

123 16 MS. April 2nd.

124 2 v. 'Preliminary Observations' to the Handbook.

125 18 MS. June 25th.

26 MS. n.d.

126 34 MSS. letters Ruskin to Murray.

127 17 *Quarterly Review*, 1840, 'The Fine Arts in Florence', 350.

19 ibid., 324.

CHAPTER SIX

130 14 *Quarterly Review*, 'The Fine Arts in Florence', 318.

22 ibid. June 1812.

132 29 ibid., 358.

133 6 June 1818, 154.

19 July 1832, 367.

32 ii, 613.

134 27 Anne Manning.

136 26 The Rev. J. C. Eustace, *Tour through Italy*, 1813.

138 7 ii, 48.

139 8 *European Review*, October 1824, 142.

16 Ed. 1830, note on p. 244. The first version of *Italy* was
published in two parts, the first, anonymously, in 1822,
the second, in 1828. They were based on his experiences
during a tour in 1814.

140 30 p. 110.

141 2 *Quarterly Review*, November 1809, 311.

4 *Edinburgh Review*, October 1835, 134, of Waddington's
History of the Church.

5 G. D. Whittington, *An Historical Survey of the Ecclesiastical
Antiquities of France* . . .

13 *Edinburgh Review*, October 1829, 86.

143 12 1816, ii, 53–4.

144 17 v. Anon., *A Memoir of the Life and Writings of Charles Mills*,
1828, 77.

35 i, viii.

145 7 In ii, pt. i, 27.

22 No. 554.

148 34 iii, 1.

150	16	*Memoirs of Early Italian Painters*, 1845. 'Ghiberti', opening paragraph.
	25	John Leland, *Collectanea*, 2nd ed., Vol. v., Oxford, 1774, 137. I owe this reference to Professor Weiss.
	30	For terms *v.* W. K. Ferguson, *The Renaissance in Historical Thought*, Cambridge, Mass., 1948, *passim*, but n.b. the quotation from Paolo Giovio, *Elogio Virorum literis illustrium*, is at p. 9 of the Basel, 1577, ed.
	33	*The Italian Schools of Painting.*
	35	*The Italian School of Design*, and *A Series of Plates* . . .
151	26	*Memoirs of the Dukes of Urbino*, Preface.
	35	*Culture and Anarchy*, 159.
152	1	Diary, quo. Horatio Brown, *John Addington Symonds. A Biography*, 2 v., 1895, i, 354.
	2	Essay on Voltaire quo. N.E.D. n.b., N.E.D. gives a usage 'Renaissance' from Lowell, essay on Keats in *Keats Prose Works*, 1896, with date 1854: 'in him we have an example of the *renaissance* going on almost under our eyes.' This passage is not in the 1854 ed. but is interpolated into that of 1896. I owe this information to Mr O. W. Neighbour of the British Museum.
152	8	N.E.D., *Athenæum*, December 25th.
	16	iii, 434.
	26	January, 372.

CHAPTER SEVEN

153	13	Berlin, 1797.
154	15	*Praeterita*, 1887, ii, 186.
	25	T. Borenius, *Quarterly Review*, 1923, 267.
155	9	*Quarterly Review*, June 1840, 48.
158	11	iii, 420.
	21	June 1847, 56.
	32	Francis Sylvester Mahony, *Facts and Figures from Italy. By Don Jeremy Savonarola, Benedictine Monk. Addressed during the Last Two Winters to Charles Dickens, being an Appendix to his 'Pictures'*, 1847, 75.
159	20	*Quarterly Review*, January 1863, 190.
160	35	*v.* Pearl Hogreve, 'Browning and Italian Art and Artists', *Bull. of the University of Kansas Humanistic Studies*, i (1914), No. 3.

162 14 *Letters and Journals of Lady Eastlake*, ed. C. E. Smith, 2 v., 1895, ii, 76, 89.

21 ibid., ii, 89, 108.

28 Quo. Sir Charles Holmes and C. H. Collins Baker, *The Making of the National Gallery 1824–1924*, 1924, 8.

163 8 ibid., 19.

164 12 p. 406, April.

22 *Report From the Select Committee on the National Galley*, 4th August 1853, 3356.

26 The Catalogue of the Sale, 14th June 1855, is printed in v. i of the 1909 ed. of *Memoirs of the Dukes of Urbino* . . .

168 17 Questions 5830, 5836–8, 6463, 6465–6, 6471–2.

24 *Quarterly Review*, April 1859, 353 quo, Steegman, *Consort of Taste*, 240.

29 1865, i, 469.

169 8 *Westminster Review*, October 1863, 469.

19 *Praeterita ed. cit*, ii, 57–8.

170 3 *Letters on Art and Literature by John Ruskin*, ed. Thomas J. Wise, 1894, 41.

17 *Stones of Venice*, Collected Ed., xi, 301. First pub. 1851.

26 cf. *The Laws of Fiesole*, Coll. Ed., xv, 344. Issued in parts, 1877–9. And *Modern Painters*, Coll. Ed., iii, 324.

30 *Stones of Venice*, Coll. Ed., x, 278, and xi, 22.

171 5 ibid., . . . iii, 77.

8 *Lectures on Architecture and Painting*, Coll. Ed., xii, 97. Delivered 1853.

20 *Ariadne Fiorentina* (Appendix), Coll. Ed., xxii, 483. Lectures delivered 1872.

26 *Stones of Venice*, Coll. Ed., x, 370.

172 2 *On the Old Road*, essay on 'The Three Colours of pre-Raphaelitism', Coll. Ed., xxxiv, 160. Written 1878.

11 *Praeterita, ed. cit.*, ii, 136–7.

173 25 Coll. Ed., xi, 128, 129 for both quotations.

174 5 *Ariadne Fiorentina*, Coll. Ed., xxii, 343.

174 9 *Giotto and His Works in Padua*, 1860.

Val D'Arno. Ten Lectures on the Tuscan Art directly antecedent to the Florentine year of Grace (1250). Delivered 1873, printed 1874.

The Aesthetic and Mathematic Schools of Art in Florence. Delivered 1874, printed 1906.

Mornings in Florence, 1875–7.

St Mark's Rest, 1884.

The Bible of Amiens, 1884. (The only completed part of Our Fathers Have Told Us.)

18   The Eagle's Nest, Coll. Ed., xxii, 284. Delivered 1872.

CHAPTER EIGHT

175 15   Horatio Brown, *John Addington Symonds. A Biography*, 2 v., 1895, i, 9.

176 10   *Fortnightly Review*, 'Venetian Melancholy', February 1893, 258.

     15   p. 332.

     20   *Letters and Papers of John Addington Symonds*, ed. Horatio Brown, 1923, 259.

     30   *Biog.*, ii, 28.

     30   Percy L. Babington, *Bibliography of the Writings of John Addington Symonds*, 1925.

177   6   *Giovanni Boccacio*, 1895, 18.

     12   *Biog.*, ii, 71.

     32   ibid., i, 63.

179 12   ibid., i, 74.

     33   ibid., i, 221.

180   3   ibid., i, 120.

      9   *Letters and Papers*, 110.

     27   Margaret Symonds, *Out of the Past*, 1925, 216.

181 22   Babington, 22.

182   8   *Walt Whitman, A Study*, 1893, 155.

183 19   Quo. Van Wyck Brooks, *John Addington Symonds*, 1914, 93.

184 16   *Out of the Past*, 43.

     17   ibid., 260.

     31   *Letters and Papers*, 102.

185 11   ibid., 21.

     34   *Biog.*, ii, 61–2.

186   9   *Out of the Past*, 264.

     15   *Letters and Papers*, 203.

     34   *Biog.*, ii, 25.

187   8   *Animi Figura*, 1882, 19.

     15   ibid.

     35   *Whitman*, 58.

188   5   *The Renaissance of Modern Europe . . . Being a lecture*

*delivered before the Sunday Lecture Society the 24th
November, 1872, 20.*

	14	*Biog.*, i, 25.
	18	*Age of the Despots*, 2nd ed., 1880, 383.
	29	*Animi Figura*, 22.
	32	*Despots*, 2nd ed., 30.
189	15	*Out of the Past*, 214.
	19	*Letters and Papers*, 62.
	21	ibid., 220.
190	4	*Animi Figura*, 107.
191	17	*Biog.*, ii, 58.
	28	*Out of the Past*, 266.
	33	ibid., 267.
192	3	*Biog.*, ii, 169.
193	22	By W. K. Ferguson, *The Renaissance in Historical Thought*, NY., 1948, 202.
194	10	January 1879, 179.
	15	August 1878, 171.
196	2	*Letters and Papers*, 73.
	7	*Griechische Kulturgeschichte*, 1898, 4.
198	25	*Italian Literature*, 1881, ii, 529.
	28	*The Revival of Learning*, ed. 1900, 3.
	34	ibid.
199	4	*The Fine Arts*, ed. 1906, 133.
	34	*Despots*, ed. 1880, 62.
202	7	*Boccaccio*, 12.
	11	*Italian Literature*, i, 123.
203	10	*Biog.*, ii, 339.
	15	ibid., ii, 99.
	28	*The Fine Arts*, ed. 1906, 181, note.
204	3	January, p. 140.
	11	*The Revival of Learning*, ed. 1900, 398.
	34	i, 54, in chap. called 'The Sacrifice'.

BIBLIOGRAPHICAL NOTE

BOOKS PUBLISHED SINCE 1954

G. B. Parks, *The English Traveller to Italy*, Vol. i, *The Middle Ages (to 1525)*, Rome, 1954.

A. L. Sells, *The Italian Influence in English Poetry*, 1955.

G. A. Treves, *The Golden Ring. The Anglo-Florentines, 1847–1862*, 1956.

J. R. Hale, *The Italian Journal of Samuel Rogers, with an account of Rogers' life and of travel in Italy in 1814–1821*, 1956.

C. P. Brand, *Italy and the English Romantics*, 1957 (this contains a most important bibliography).

M. Praz, *The Flaming Heart*, 1958.

Van Wyck Brooks, *The Dream of Arcadia*, 1959. Deals with American attitudes to Italy from the mid-eighteenth to the early-twentieth century.

INDEX

The Civilization of Europe in the Renaissance

John Hale

Winner of 1993 *Time-Life* Silver Pen Award

The Civilization of Europe in the Renaissance is the most ambitious achievement of Britain's leading Renaissance historian. John Hale has painted on a grand canvas an enthralling portrait of Europe and its civilization at a moment when 'Europe' first became an entity in the minds of its inhabitants. The book does not simply survey 'high' culture but with an astonishing range and subtlety of learning builds up a gigantic picture of the age, enlivened by a multiplicity of themes, people and ideas. It contains memorable descriptions of painting, sculpture, poetry, architecture and music; but Hale is not simply concerned with the arts: he examines the dramatic changes during the period in religion, politics, economics and global discoveries. At a time when we are thinking more and more about what 'Europe' and European culture mean, this is a book which shows us more than any other where we can find the roots of both of them, and how much the present and future can be illuminated by the past.

'A superb evocation of the Europe of "the long sixteenth century", wonderfully fresh and rich in its copious illustrative detail, full of innumerable incidental delights. [The book] takes its place as the summation of John Hale's career as a historian, and as the crowning achievement of a master-designer whose richly fabricated works have given so much pleasure.'
                                                        J. H. Elliott

'This study deserves to stand alongside Braudel's classic account of the Mediterranean in the time of Philip II. Hale is as generous as he is knowledgeable; his life's work has culminated in a meticulous masterpiece.'
                                        Frederic Raphael, *Sunday Times*

'This is a magnificent book which fills a long-standing gap. It is the product of a lifetime's scholarship by someone with a quite irrepressible curiosity and prodigious breadth of reading . . . together with the enviable gift of writing clearly and beautifully.'
                        A. V. Antonvics, *Times Educational Supplement*

ISBN 0 00 686175 X

Landscape & Memory

Simon Schama

'This is one of the most intelligent, original, stimulating, self-indulgent, perverse and irresistibly enjoyable books that I have ever had the delight of reviewing...'   PHILIP ZIEGLER, *Daily Telegraph*

Landscape & Memory is a history book unlike any other. In a series of exhilarating journeys through space and time, it examines our relationship with the landscape around us – rivers, mountains, forests – the impact each of them has had on our culture and imaginations, and the way in which we, in turn, have shaped them to answer our needs. Schama does not make his argument by any conventional historical method. Instead he builds it up by a series of almost poetic stories and impressions, which cumulatively have the effect of a great novel. The forest primeval, the river of life, the sacred mount – at the end of *Landscape & Memory* we understand where these ideas have come from, why they are so compelling, what they meant to our forebears, and how they still lie all around us if only we know how to look.

'Schama long ago established himself as one of the most learned, original and provocative historians in the English-speaking world... *Landscape & Memory* is that rarest of commodities in our cultural marketplace, a work of genuine originality.'

ANTHONY GRAFTON, *New Republic*

This is a *tour de force* of vivid historical writing... It is astoundingly learned, and yet the learning is offered with verve, humour and an unflagging sense of delight.'

MICHAEL IGNATIEFF, *Independent on Sunday*

'Schama's intensely visual prose is the product of a historical imagination which is not restrained by conventional academic inhibitions...It is his ability (and willingness) to write this sort of narrative prose that makes Simon Schama the obvious modern successor to Macaulay'   KEITH THOMAS, *New York Review of Books*

ISBN: 0 00 686348 5
Price: £16.99

Anthony Storr

Music and the Mind

'Anyone who feels like reflecting about the origins, the impact and the significance of music will find Dr Storr's book helpful and stimulating.'
Alfred Brendel

In this challenging book, Anthony Storr, one of Britain's leading psychiatrists, explores why music, the most mysterious and intangible of all forms of art, has such a powerful effect on our minds and bodies. He believes that music today is a deeply significant experience for a greater number of people than ever before, and argues that the patterns of music give structure and coherence to our feelings and emotions. It is because music possesses this capacity to restore our sense of personal wholeness – in a culture which requires us to separate rational thought from feelings – that many people find it so life-enhancing that it justifies existence.

'This beautifully written book, humane, intelligent and thoughtful, is a significant contribution to our understanding of those mysterious movements of the mind.' Adam Lively, *Times Educational Supplement*

'It is a stimulating inquiry aimed at discovering what it is about music that so profoundly moves so many people, in the course of which he describes the physical effects of mescaline, considers the relation of bird-song, the burbling of babies and the language of literature to music, and touches on many other fascinating topics, concluding that its most significant aspect for us is its power to create order out of chaos.'
Frances Partridge, *Spectator*

'Reading Storr's work is always like being taken on a journey through a foreign country by a great enthusiast. It doesn't matter if you don't know the language because he teaches you what you need to know along the way. His knowledge is vast and his enthusiasm infectious . . . Storr is an extraordinarily gifted communicator.'
Mary Loudon, *New Statesman & Society*

ISBN 0 00 686186 5

The Interpretation of Cultures

Clifford Geertz

'One of the most original and stimulating anthropologists of his generation.'
                                                    Contemporary Sociology

Clifford Geertz is arguably the most distinguished anthropologist of our time. First published in 1973, *The Interpretation of Cultures* has become an established classic. Through a discussion of subjects ranging from ritual and sacred symbol to nationalism and revolution, Geertz consistently attempts to clarify the meaning of 'culture' and to relate that concept to the actual behaviour of individuals and groups. Not only do these essays embody his view of what culture is, they also put forward a particular view of the role culture plays in social life, and how it ought properly to be studied.

Geertz's elegance of thought and style, his gift for startling and illuminating juxtaposition, his easy movement between the most exotic and the most commonplace cultures, have made this collection of essays one of the most widely read and influential works in modern social science. *The Interpretation of Cultures* is essential reading for students of anthropology, sociology and history.

'Geertz's "reading" of the cockfight is a composite pageant of erudition and insight, and is deservedly famous as an example of what skilled "interpretative anthropology" can be.'
                                                    New York Review of Books

'One could celebrate the range of subjects on which he knowledgeably touches . . . the toughness of [his] mind, as well as the acerbity with which he exercises that toughness . . . It's invigorating to stretch one's mind on the Nautilus machine of his prose.'
                                                    New York Times

ISBN 0 00 686260 8